INGMAR BERGMAN, WERNER HERZOG, STANLEY KUBRICK, FRANCIS FORD COPPOLA, RIDLEY SCOTT, ANDREI TARKOVSKY, FEDERICO FELLINI, AKIRA KUROSAWA, WILLIAM SHAKESPEARE, FYODOR DOSTOYEVSKY, FRANZ KAFKA, HEINRICH BOLL, HERMANN HESSE, ALBERT EINSTEIN, FRIEDRICH NIETZSCHE, MARTIN HEIDEGGER, LUDWIG WITTGENSTEIN, ANTON WEBERN AND MIHAJLO BUGARINOVIC

MIHAJLO BUGARINOVIC

Gotham Books

30 N Gould St.
Ste. 20820, Sheridan, WY 82801
https://gothambooksinc.com/

Phone: 1 (307) 464-7800

© 2022 Mihajlo Bugarinovic. All rights reserved.

No part of this book may be reproduced, stored in a retrieval system, or transmitted by any means without the written permission of the author.

Published by Gotham Books (November 09, 2022)

ISBN: 979-8-88775-138-2 (sc)

ISBN: 979-8-88775-139-9 (e)

Because of the dynamic nature of the Internet, any web addresses or links contained in this book may have changed since publication and may no longer be valid.

The views expressed in this work are solely those of the author and do not necessarily reflect the views of the publisher, and the publisher hereby disclaims any responsibility for them.

I always write a preface, first! (The-fake...) Which is the usual "self-conscious"/post-structural as the illusion of my philosophy's language... The philosophy and language being same of each other/modernist... My attempt being to rationalize the bibliography of my philosophy... (Think of it as a sequel to my *Deconstructing Dostoyevsky IV,* with the lie intact...) The appearance being itself/that-I-try-to-break-off-from-those-four-philosophies-thatintended/pretended-to-aspire-to-a-deconstruction-of-Dostoyevsky... I now attempt a full bibliography, as to what this philosophical-essay does intend... And the pseudonyms being the name of the book... (A two-difference...) So as to think a "clarification," now as asymmetry of a name to a sequel... *That I was always very good at asymmetries too,* Nietzsche being the best great philosopher of my philosophy! (To represent the irrational as a-symmetry...) (That my philosophy always aspired to rationalism never matched...) What is the symmetry of my philosophy? Rationalism and IQ, probably... It is an Einstein-smart Nietzsche rational-philosophy that I always wrote! (The symmetry, as asymmetry, meant a combined-possible/writing-a-philosophy-Einstein-intelligent-while-retaining philosophy philosophically-inclusion...) Has to do with why my philosophy exists... *All my philosophy...* Writing a philosophy and-Einstein genius of philosophy that is Einstein's IQ...

So as to create what I "hybrid" out of a total-bibliography... *I was always to change my name instead!* As by combining everything my philosophy is in a major way... (The best possible genius of my philosophy...) Probably costs too much... And that that being an idea as is/a-relative-bibliography-on-relative... (That my philosophy writes the self-evidence-of-bibliography as the reader-freedom relativized the limit-of-bibliography and how that relativizes anyhow...) *It is a left-wing-irony*/as-the-apolitical-left-wing-of-liberal... Which was a mystery like anything in the sense of combining polarity and a mystery-as-is... (I mean measure as the prioritized-bibliography, as the billions of bibliographies writing my philosophy relative of the billions of bibliographies I do list to name this philosophy...) Bergman as the best film-director, Herzog as the second-/third-best, Kubrick, Francis Ford Coppola and Ridley Scott as the best from Hollywood/at-some-similar-level-as-Herzog, Tarkovsky as the second-best film ever made, Fellini of the third-best film ever made and Kurosawa as the fourth-best film ever made... *Persona will always be the best film ever made to my philosophy!* And that Bergman be the first-best with or without that film above every made... So as to list all those writers (Shakespeare, Dostoyevsky, Kafka, Boll and Hesse) as the best writers of my philosophy as the art-difference of my philosophy... *I don't have a favorite writer,* and I always have a favorite film director... (That was a close one/either-Dostoyevsky-or-Shakespeare...) (Why?) I must be making that attempt to generalize art as is, seeing as my philosophy being Nietzsche a contradiction as the best great philosopher: mathematics, physics and logic will always be why my philosophy exists... *What do I have to do with art?* At Einstein always reaches that limit of science in my philosophy/the-only-scientist-my-philosophy-likes... Relative of Nietzsche, Heidegger and Wittgenstein: the first-, second- and third-best great philosopher, consecutively/respectively... (Nietzsche will always be the first-best place, strangely...) Or, had Heidegger not joined Hitler... (The best great philosophy of my philosophy being *Being and Time...*) Why do I include Webern in my bibliography? Does it have to do with the three IQs/mathematics, physics and logic/three-crowning-achievementsof-IQ-on-the-planet-that-I-combined-so-as-to-retain-all-three? Probably (an-absurd) ... The two art-forms of my philosophy being the film-director and the writer... (As the absurd question...) All three art-forms combined, seeing as no art-form got to that stage of "combinatoric" as is... Bugarinovic naturally included: one must realize that the greatest bibliography of my philosophy will always be me... (What transcends every combination of my philosophy's bibliography will always be me...) Meaning, I include, so as to exclude... I am above the rest included in my bibliography... And that that bibliography had that vicious... (I didn't mention that I am one of the four geniuses of IQ of my philosophy/me, Einstein, Bergman and Wittgenstein, as the smartest people in history...) Generally, ... (It is symmetrical or imperfect-on-imperfect...) The rational-philosophy being on rational-bibliography... A combined-possible, as an Einstein-combinatoric/the-IQ-child, Einstein-smart and a genius of philosophy inclusive of philosophy as the Einstein IQ *included...* (*It is all my philosophy!*) What I claim I can achieve... Combining philosophy and an Einstein-IQ in a philosophy... (The completely-original of my philosophy...) That philosophy, to my philosophy, ended at Derrida's death... Which is when I start to write philosophy for the first time... (Why do I devise a completely original way to think philosophy?) That I probably see me for way-too-genius... (Or something...) And that I am a Serb/usually-have-nothing-to-do-with-philosophy... The-extreme: historically, and as a world-region, *Germany* as the only country, history and part of the world to write philosophy to my philosophy... (Does that magnify or diminish that I be a self-hating-Serb?) And that it is true/I-write-the-ultra-German philosophy-as-is... That it is an Einstein-smart philosophy will always be as something like French-left, to retain the principal idea of the never-ending Germany while writing Einstein's IQ as that Germany... (Why my philosophy exists...)

What does it have to do with? Chaos? Arranging a bibliography from Bergman to me, as an "order," is absurd and chaotic... (Did I mean the relative/same of the bibliography?) That I didn't start at philosophy, so as to advance to IQ as from philosophy, as to how the priority of every bibliography of my philosophy always progresses... Which is absurd/must-be-that-that-being-the-reason-why-I-side-with-chaos... (Do I love IQ above philosophy?) That philosophy and IQ always being a same-competition of my philosophy... I wanted to be something like a physicist/an-IQ-profession/discipline... (I like my philosophy...) That I compensated the whole thing, as by writing a philosophy at the level of an Einstein-IQ... Which always shrank the talent-part... *That I be philosophy and IQ...* And that I be a self-loving/German philosophy... (I can't be a self-hating-philosophy....) The French-left, of my philosophy, has a specific-purpose/equilibrates-philosophy-and-IQ... It is a self-loving-philosophy, that is Einstein smart... (I did have to start a bibliography at one of the two/philosophy-or-IQ...) Or, the bibliography did have to begin someplace at philosophy... (According to me...) Wittgenstein, as the first-best genius of IQ, to my philosophy, as the third-best genius of great philosophy, to my philosophy, was always the natural-challenge/potential... (Such a shame...) That he is always the ideal-potential of my philosophy, seeing as I am the first-best genius of philosophy and first-best genius of IQ, as to how my philosophy always thinks me and my philosophy... That I always, strongly, dislike my name... (The name needed to be something German, Jewish and French, in the same even-measure of same...) That I don't change my name because of the mystery/the-unknown... (The three races did combine...) That I mean German and Jewish, seeing as the French-part of my philosophy usually serves to combine both impossible races... (That I am the smartest man that ever existed always had to augment as the level of philosophical-genius...) Or, what is always so great about the IQ-part of my philosophy: my philosophy doesn't believe in the idea of the smartest man in history... To me/my-philosophy I, Einstein, Wittgenstein and Bergman scored the same genius-IQ level relative of the rest included in the bibliography to relative that genius-IQ I am... (That all four Einsteins be Einstein and that philosophy and IQ never became the only bibliography I am to base on as the philosophy-part of my philosophy...) The four Einsteins, film, the-writer, classical music, etc... (The problem of the IQ of my philosophy solved racially and bibliographically/doubly-made-sure...) The skepticism, of the whole thing, of a way to include philosophy and Einstein's IQ in a genius philosophy... (The concept of a great-mind always had to participate, so as to differentiate the greatest possible IQ and greatest possible great mind as the greatest possible great mind of both...) Does something like the greatest possible great thinker/something-like-Nietzsche help too? (It is a *three*-difference...) IQ, a great mind and a great thinker: the mathematics shrank, while "retaining" ... *Logic, mathematics and physics* combined too... So as to utilize all that solves that IQ-problem of my philosophy... (The three crowning achievements of IQ/greatest-IQs-in-history/mathematics, physics and logic...) (So as to invent an artform...) Must be that equilibrating IQ and art solved the uneven-measure of IQ and philosophy of my philosophy... (I always devise a system to a philosophy that is philosophy and IQ in a philosophy...) Or, that my philosophy would be a system of philosophy...

More of a combinatoric than Einstein physics... Which was always the strange conundrum... (The Einstein IQ, that is imagination, as the child playing with a combination, that is to assume the role of mathematical combinatorics while retaining Einstein as the principal idea of the Einstein IQ...) The French-left-part always helped, as to how I view the three-race of my philosophy... (*Why French-left instead of anything else?*) (Could have been anything noncontextually...) *Must be that I mean anything to help make possible the impossible...* Or French-left, as the postmodern problem, that French-left got to both left-wing differences, and that both meant of-same-difference anyhow/prior-to French-left... (A Continental first-order logic...)

My infinite love for mathematics always delimits... (It is Einstein, not mathematics...) What is the difference... Or, that my Einstein-smart-philosophy be mathematics as the idea of a crowning-achievement/the-greatest-possible magnitude-of-IQ... Me siding with Einstein because of the imagination/"creative-part" ... (To my philosophy IQ always has the psychological-prerequisite of imagination, idea and tabula rasa...) Einstein is ideal... (Mathematics is my IQ without the imagination of my IQ/imagination-of-every-great IQ, so to speak...) As to how I always compared the greatest IQ in history, Einstein, and the greatest IQ in history, mathematics... (Mathematics will never be as-smart...) Not to my philosophy... And that the idea of Einstein already four-extended/meant me, Einstein, Wittgenstein and Bergman, as four Einsteins... (My philosophy never thought it possible to conceptualize the smartest man that ever existed...) The shared first-best-place/all-four-Einsteins... It is literally four Einsteins as Einstein... (That I don't assume anything, in the same way Einstein would assume that he is a child/above mathematics-as-mathematics, will always be a four-value...) The abstract-Einstein, who always applied to himself and the other three Einsteins... (I would be a never-ending mathematician...) That I am a never-ending Einstein always rested on that one simple-fact of imagination/that-IQ-to-my-philosophy-never-existed-without-imagination... Combinatorics, as Einstein, as mathematics, as Einstein... And that I mean science, mathematics and logic combining... (I was never science, because of the rationalism-of-my-philosophy, never mathematics, because of the IQ-prerequisite/imagination, and never logic, because of the implying mixed-logic as that logic have so many kinds to think as my philosophical and mathematical logic/that-my-logic-tends-as-one-of-the-major-philosophicalbranches-of-my-philosophy/logic-and-that-something-mathematical-with-always-appeared-logical-as-is...) It is a physics-paper as idea... (Does the three-race make it possible?) What Einstein do I mean? His special relativity... Which is untrue/all-that-is-great-by-him-made-it-to-my-philosophy... The strange/controversial/last period (the theory-of-everything...) was always either/or... And that what he was to ahead of, by "half," already never all that assimilated with me... (I probably side with those other opinions/that-something-like-the-string-theory-alwaysbecomes-too-abstract/mathematical-to-be-the-IQ-of-Einstein...) (That I can like Ed Witten in the sense of *idea*...) Which will never base on anything... *Have I ever read a physics paper?* I never have... Einstein is idea prior to the idea of Witten... (Naturally/intentionally...) I mean Einstein as idea... Which was natural/already-became-idea-on idea (four Einsteins and four literal Einsteins...) It is the basic conundrum... (How can I be writing an Einstein philosophy-and-philosophy genius of philosophy without ever learning how to read Einstein?) That it will, probably, always, be Einstein and idea-of-Einstein... (I mean idea...) And that something like Wittgenstein already has no intellectual-comparison... I mean the most famous IQ-genius...

So as to degenerate the speech-part of my brain... (I always aspired to the autistic IQ-geniuses of this world...) Which will always be just-as-strange/I-am-a-philosopher... And that that based on the doubly-impossible... (What do I have to do with a genius of IQ and what does a philosopher have to do with autism/genius-of-IQ?) That I have everything to do with the greatest possible genius of IQ... The infinitely-complex relation of my philosophy... (A genius of IQ, philosophy, autism, Einstein as idea, whether Kant had autism, all that "autistic-writing" I do in philosophy, that my philosophy has very little relation to a writer, etc...) It is "infinite-regress-wise" ... And that I aspire to that Einstein-autism of IQ... That my IQ being Einstein never meant searching for a way to shrink that IQ... (The exact point of all my philosophy being that IQ relative of philosophy in a philosophy...) Why my philosophy exists is proving that Einstein's IQ and philosophy can find co-existence in a genius of philosophy... Which is the double-digit/I-write-an-Einstein-smart-philosophy-since-my-every-original-aspiration-had-to-do-with-becomingsomething-like-a-physicist/mathematician... It is not like I am a self-loving-philosopher... (I love IQ, not philosophy...) That I can appreciate philosophy as the unknown of art and science in-one... Which was never "Sufficient-enough"/something-like-science-always-had-to-augment-over-art-as-IQ, and was always mixed/the augmented-always-shrank-as-my-hate-of-everything-empirical... (I like philosophy as an appearing-reminder/same appearance-of-definition...) Isn't philosophy and mathematics the only two "professions" that will never have the "clear-definition?" (So as to complicate...) I *don't* like the reminder/what-is-to-prove-my-Einstein-IQ-isphysics/what-has-imagination-relative-of-IQ... So as to complicate... (I combined all three greatest-achievements-of IQ...) Didn't mathematics include as physics and logic? (I *do* like the reminder...) (Isn't that always the basic challenge of my philosophy too?) How to combine all three groups of the smartest people that ever existed while retaining all three while combining all three... Mathematics, logic and physics combine! And that that be Einstein, me, Bergman and Wittgenstein/the-strange as Einstein... (Art has nothing to do with a genius of IQ or greatest possible genius of IQ, philosophy being the limit of a genius of IQ without the greatest possible genius of IQ...) Bergman being the only Einstein-smart artist, in history, so as for me and Wittgenstein to become the only Einstein smart philosophers, in history... (A hermeneutical/meaning Einstein-smart-philosophy, that is metaphysics, aesthetics and logic as metaphysics...) And that my philosophy always go with such primordial definitions of philosophy-and-philosophy... *Philosophy is metaphysics...* which is to me always the God-definition of philosophy with or without that philosophy have no definition at all... (That there are no unsolved-problems of philosophy will always be that metaphysics is the only in-itself-branch of philosophy...)

How is my autistic-writing to compare with my philosophy? As autistic-philosophy/every-next-form-of-same... That it is the Jewish philosophy as IQ/a-Jewish-IQ-philosophy will always be the Hitler/ideal Wagnerian problem of appearance... *I as appearance write all those billions of Wagner-Hegel philosophies...* That something becomes as ideal as the same tie/dependence of billions-of-philosophies... I write the one philosophy, that comprises billions-of philosophies... (What shrinks something like Wagner, infinitely, will always be what writes him...) The philosophies, to synthesize as the one philosophy, of the billions-philosophies, are all same/*minimalism*... That I write the Einstein-smart-philosophy had to do with infinite monotony of my philosophy/a-literal-*every-next-form-of-same literally*... It is the one-philosophy, that is an infinite number of philosophies as appearance/as-illusion... How the fact of my German Einstein-smart French-left-philosophy always solved... (The mathematics of my philosophy make me Einstein-smart...) And that I be so typical of Einstein as the imagination-IQ that is Einstein-smart... (I was to locate a profession matching of my IQ...) That I write an Einstein-smart philosophy was-sufficient... As long as I prove my Einstein-IQ in some way... The rest being compensating the naturally-untalented-philosophy... (As with the help of something like the French-left...) I infinitely always become so ideal of me... (Proving my IQ, while writing a genius of philosophy that proves that I am Einstein-smart...) Nothing more ideal of me... And that the whole-thing always grew as the thesis on philosophy-and-a-Serb... (Has that challenge of a Serb writing a genius philosophy and greatest possible genius of IQ...) That a Serb has nothing to do with philosophy or IQ... (I am infinitely ideal of me...) (That I would always be the "proud-Serb"/engineering-to-me-never-compared-tosomething-like-physics...) Tesla never creates that "half" of potential... Or, mathematics, science and logic... (I combined all three crowns-of-greatest-IQ-possible...) Tesla never made it possible for me to stop being the "self hating-Serb" ... The four Einsteins of my philosophy being the four Einsteins of my philosophy as the only science I ever like/Einstein... (Again/as-the-imagination-prerequisite-of-all-great-IQ-to-my-philosophy...) (What does engineering have to do with imagination?) And that Einstein always got to astrophysics/an-augmented-imagination: idea, imagination and tabula rasa/the-three-basic-prerequisites-to-Einstein... (I so emphasize my never-ending-IQ as Einstein mainly as due to all three prerequisites I do share with Einstein...)

So as to share my philosophy with two people... (I never minded being more private than the infinite-regress itself...) The famous "fascist-potential" of my philosophy, always liberalized as the century I am in... (My private philosophy being liberal, seeing as the century I am in has nothing to do with philosophy/is-a-fascist...) That I am a left-wing philosopher was always "same" ... To my philosophy, itself, being the liberal/"left-wing" profession regardless of the polarity... That I am the liberal apolitical-left-wing-philosophy will always be just as right-wing... Which is vicious/Isn't-my-left-wing-right-wing-in-nature? ... (It is a chaos-way to name my philosophy...) Something to go with the order of the order of my philosophy's bibliography... (Why do I begin listing with Bergman?) Must be an absurd... Or, must be that primitive-fact of all my philosophy: that my philosophy always relativizes its bibliography and that my philosophy doesn't build on a bibliography without a self-evidence-of-bibliography... (It is same where I start to mention something concretely to relate to my philosophy...) The main idea being philosophy and IQ in a philosophy... (The rest being relative...) Which was always relative too... The absolute list of great philosophers never solidified what the Einstein *Einstein* is... (It is not like I ever read one of Einstein's papers to the end...) Einstein always being the idea of the greatest possible IQs of my philosophy/Bergman, me and Wittgenstein/what-I-have-read/do-know...

That all three are to be represented by Einstein, as idea, as the idea of the greatest possible IQ possible, will always whether Einstein included or excluded as Einstein in-Einstein... (It is *Einstein/Einstein* and *idea/idea*...) What I know is that I, Bergman and Wittgenstein score two-hundred on the IQ test... (Will I ever know whether I do agree that Einstein is Einstein?) (So as to engineer a truth...) And that it is not like I did get to that stage/finally-did-find-the-two-professional-philosophers... (My philosophy is, thus far, the two-assumption/whether-I-am-a-philosopher-and-whether-I-prove-my-two-hundredIQ-as-by-writing-a-philosophy...) *What is so great is that there is nothing in the century I am in/no-philosophy-in the-century-I-am-in...* (I am not in the prior-century, so as to collect all that money, so as to enroll at the highest possible education in Germany at the best university in Germany highest with philosophy...) All that "cardio," in the twenty-first-century simply infinitely-cardio... (What is the never-ending extreme-measure of the self-taught-man of my philosophy?)

I emphasize *idea*... Which was always some-realism of my philosophy and Germany, philosophy and Germany! The rest being the fascist-potential/infinitely-insular, and that I would mean as a fascist problem of Germany/idea... (My philosophy infinitely being-natural-of-everything-ideal-as-potential...) That all those billions of philosophies, that I write, that are the one-philosophy, are a one-philosophy will always be a Wagnerian-appearance as Hegel, to something Jewish-in-form... The billions of pages of philosophy being the first thing I wrote in philosophy/always shrink... And that being the basic-care, to go with, as a German-philosophy that is always Jewish as IQ... (Had to be a liberal-Germany, so as for Einstein to correlate with philosophy as the impossible made possible...) That it is a strange "half" of IQ (two Jewish Einsteins and a Swedish and a Serbian Einstein) probably helps too... An absolute definition, of something Jewish, in my philosophy, will always be Judaism as the best religion of my philosophy, not

IQ... (Relative of liberal-religion, that is my philosophy, and my philosophy's Christ to comprise all those liberal Christian-churches/every-liberal-Christian-church, relative of the inferior religion of my philosophy that is Christ...) Did the Jewish-absolute of my philosophy relativize too! (How does liberal-religion relate as Judaism as the best religion?) And that my philosophy love Judaism as the absolute/"non-prostitute" religion, as to why my philosophy thinks Judaism a superior-religion to begin with... (Something doubly relativized Judaism of my philosophy/in-my philosophy...) (Both Jewish definitions (IQ and Judaism) become vicious...) And that both were vicious of each other... (The highest man on the planet will always be me...) In history/ever! (That I so love Einstein's IQ will always be that I never read him...) And that I am a philosopher... (The IQ-part means to be a genius-of-IQ-limit/one fifty, not a greatest possible IQ in history...) However, that I did become a philosopher because of my greatest possible IQ... (I was to match my Einstein-IQ with a profession...) That I am a philosopher always has to be the strange Einstein-smart philosophy, that I write, that challenges itself as philosophy/constantly-has-to-equilibrate-thephilosophy-and-Einstein-IQ-in-a-philosophy... Which turns out very great... (I philosophy become a genius as much as the greatest possible genius of IQ...) As long as I did match my IQ anyhow/became-a-relative-Wittgenstein... And that I am a first-best genius of philosophy... (I am infinitely self-loving...) (And the self-taught-man of the whole thing was always in the century I am in...) There is nothing to change in the fact of the greatest self-loving-man that ever existed... I am in the twenty-first-century... (The philosophy absurd of philosophy and IQ...)

(Why do I aspire in IQ?) Two people find out that I am Einstein-smart... (Probably so as to match my IQ with "something" ...) And that it is a philosophy... (Why do I aspire in philosophy?) Two people find out that I am a philosopher... (*That is why!*) Or, it isn't zero-people! (It is two people "out-of-pity" ...) That I, one day, get to be in Wikipedia, as the two paragraphs to mention, as a main article on me, maybe, will always be "proportion" ... (It is two or zero paragraphs!) I'll be just as famous as Einstein... (It is in the twenty-first-century the same magnitude...) (Factually as-so...) (To make a change, in the way I view my success, is highly unnecessary...) That I am to me the only absolute man on the planet in the century I am in... (That I am the most self-loving man that ever existed will always be zero paragraphs instead of billions of paragraphs!) (Each-to-his-own being so infinitely natural...) I exist for the sake of independence/it-is-the-most-private-man-that-ever-existed... That the freedom, of my philosophy, be independence, as the liberal, of left-wing, naturalized! *What is the principle behind my freedom?* Which was always absurd/it-isn't-like-I-ever-become-something-authentically-left-wing... (It is right-wing...) That I mean of-infinitefreedom will always be the private-freedom/my-freedom... That used to be the infinite-slave in the prior century... Meaning, my infinite-freedom naturalizes in the twenty-first century naturally and naturally... Or, I am infinitelyfree... Which is what the freedom of my philosophy is... (I am infinitely-free in the century I am in...) I fight for my freedom... Which was never a freedom... The effect being so simple... (I become the freest man that ever existed...)

(I mean a fascist-problem as the century I am in, not freedom in the sense of freedom...) So as to make a probability-theory out of my philosophy... (My unfinished-creation/left-wing as a "probability" instead...) That it is not like I start deconstructing something... And this philosophy being the next-sequel, as the total-continuity of a strange appearance I begin writing ten years ago... Billions of "illusions," on that I would break away from my second period/deconstruction as an illusion and that illusion be why I write those illusions past my deconstruction as my deconstruction... (The most famous illusion my philosophy hears of is always film/the-best-dream/the-absolute-illusion...) Meaning, my mathematically logically-scientific philosophy, that never got to art, that always categorizes the writers and film for the best art-form "of" my philosophy... (That that be by half and as excluded/not-as-my-favorite-art-form...) So as to write an illusion as the three-IQ relation/mathematics, science and logic... I haven't selected the deconstructed of the deconstructing... And *Ingmar Bergman, Werner Herzog, Stanley Kubrick, Francis Ford Coppola, Ridley Scott, Andrei Tarkovsky, Federico Fellini, Akira Kurosawa, William Shakespeare, Fyodor Dostoyevsky, Franz Kafka, Heinrich Boll, Hermann Hesse, Albert Einstein, Friedrich Nietzsche, Martin Heidegger, Ludwig Wittgenstein, Anton Webern and Mihajlo Bugarinovic* being of the prior recent-correlate/a-sequel... Meaning, I resume doing the retarded-free-association as appearance/as-an-illusion... Free-association usually did include in my philosophy anyhow... Now as some irrational-*prioritized,* as irony and my favorite Jews/Einstein, Wittgenstein and Kafka... *(Freud has nothing to do with me...)* I always love a theory! (As long as it be theoretical...) A probability theory, as my usual theories of my philosophy... (That Dostoevsky's *The Idiot* is always the next thing to deconstruct...) Except, I haven't finished reading his masterpiece to the end... (It is a "liberal-Dostoyevsky" ...) "People" never appealed, seeing as I mean a metaphysical/philosophical Dostoyevsky as the German-interpretation/Nietzsche, as *The Notes from Underground* and *The Idiot*... So as to naturalize something-Dostoyevsky with my abstract-IQ/greatest-possible-magnitude-of-an-Einstein-IQ... (Why do I like Dostoyevsky?) I am a philosopher... Meaning, I am, purely, very much German as value...

And that I mean IQ/*Einstein* as Germany/within-my-Germany... Dostoyevsky is one of my favorite writers and that I don't have a favorite writer, as to why... (That he be one of the greatest great minds of my philosophy, not IQ...) That is... And Russia to me exceeded in mysticism... That Russia be very-unrelated to philosophy... And that I be infinitely unrelated to mysticism... And so on... The sense being very-clear... (I coincidentally get to Russia coincidentally...) As it is theory! (There is nothing I like more...) Which is natural/IQ... (That I become a philosopher will always be that something/anything needed to match/prove my Einstein-IQ...) It is not like I will ever be an actually self-loving-philosopher... That I always mock something like the Analytic-traditions in philosophy will always be relative/that-such-people-already-exceeded-in-IQ-as-the-logical-part... I so emphasize Germany due to talent/because-I-did-become-a-philosopher... (I don't want to be untalented...) Or something... The proof-to-IQ always had to be fixing-the-un-talent... Always... (IQ and talent had to equilibrate...) Or, that Analytic philosophy to me be dumber than the infinite-regress... (Philosophically...) Itself... (Which is great...) One more reason to become a philosopher... (A philosophical-challenge/original-philosophy was set prior to me doing so...) An Einstein smart German-philosophy will always be impossible to think, seeing as it is an Einstein German-philosophy... (What the basic challenge of the whole thing is...) And that it is the self-taught-man... (What proves that I am philosophy or Einstein?) With me, all those low "self-esteems" always ascended to the most self-loving man in history... (The general basic-coincidence of all my philosophy I write...) I, last night, finish watching *The Serpent's Egg* to the end, with my mother... (The tiny-genius film to my philosophy...) That I was always alone with that film... Or, I am the only man to name that film a tiny-genius... (Or something...) Can't mind it as re-watched... (An okay-thing to do...) A film with me the Freud, of Hitler, as the Jewish question of Jewish identity, as Kafka... (I always loved the combinatoric of the film...) Bergman's IQ never shrank/I-love-Einstein... As is the rest, to me, up to his usual standard/Sven-Nykvist... And that I never mind a film on "difference" ... (A film *different,* as on difference, of indifference, as difference and difference...) On how to contextualize something like Derrida's *difference*... And that the goal contextualized as me instead... (I always love competing with Germany, so as to outdo Germany...) To me something similar to take place with Bergman and his exile... The generally-German-period, to me... How genius does that part, of his exile, get to be to me? *Sweden, North-Germany, South-Germany, Germany...* (The only objection being that he is dealing with something from Sweden...) Bergman never aspired in philosophy... (Why I shrink the genius to a tiny-proportion-potential...) It is art, IQ, film, second-best genius of psychology, etc., not philosophy... (I probably love the film "subjectively," seeing as I will always be trying to better Germany, because of philosophy/since-I-am-a-philosopher...) Something "appears"/reminds... The European, who is a Serb, who has nothing to do with philosophy since he is a Serb, to mean as Europe without West, so as to, always, structure Germany without Europe or West... (Etc...) *It was already vicious!* Or, it was already linear! (I am a Serb since a man German without the European or Western difference...) Which is untrue... (I am not a Serb since a man German without the European/Western-difference...) What always lowered the potential of the stupidity of the whole thing? That it is the three crowning achievements of IQ... (Or, how do I expect to match Germany, so as to outdo Germany's philosophical genius?) As by writing a mathematical scientifically-logical philosophy and writing an infinite mathematical-scientifically-logical philosophy...

So as to combine all the inferior races on the planet... Which is that I remain the inferior-one as the total combination of them... And that all the races be inferior in the century I am... (And so on...) Some vicious-issue, as with defining my racial self-hate... And that that will always complicate even-further... (What is a Jewish German, of the French origin, relative of a Serb?) And so on... (Something is all three races or all three races "separately" ...) What do I mean by the *German-Jewish-French?* That I outdo all three races as the German-difference... (The goal being that I end the whole thing on Germany...) Seeing as I am a philosopher... However, that the IQ-part retained... (It is German-Jewish...) Which is *What am I to do with the German-Jewish?* Which is that I complicate... (I mean Jewish as IQ...) So as to complicate... (Einstein, me, Wittgenstein and Bergman...) Which simplified... (The idea of all four greatest possible IQs will always be Einstein/idea...) (Einstein has the doubled-effect...) (*Unknown* by Jaume Collet-Serra...) I love watching all that un-talent past the year/end-of-everything... (Where the twenty-first-century begins...) Everything finished being possible... (The film's name is of appeal...) Reminds of Star Trek... (Or something...) Always a positive concept... (Not that I can ever be the actual Trekkie or any Trekkie...) I like Star Trek instead of Star Wars... Which was always relative... (The best film ever made will always be Persona...) What do I have to do with Star Trek? (Making a film, on the unknown, in the twenty-first-century, as the theme and paranoia, is probably some thought-out thing anyhow...) Left-wing, film, paranoia and the twenty-first century... (Or something...) Probably an okay-cinema to see anyhow... (I never know how to think the "infinite-mathematics" of my philosophy...) As long as I mean a Jewish-IQ, generally, in a German philosophy... (As long as I did omit Jewish-philosophy from my philosophy all-in-all...) And that something like Judaism always be the best religion of my philosophy... Or something... (That-solved-it!) The mixed IQ-part of my philosophy always had an issue with purely-defined German-philosophy that thinks Germany as the only philosophy there ever was as Europe, West and any world-region... (Etc...) On the other hand, that that mixing-never-ending-genius-IQ mix as should be/relate-in-a German-philosophy... (The symmetries had to be ideal/perfect, so as for philosophy and IQ to correlate for the first time and correlate at all/to-begin-with...) I can discard with the "French-left-part!" (Einstein as idea and literal idea, as to how I see the actual-solution to the whole IQ-problem of my total-philosophy...) Why is my philosophy French-left? Due to irony/the-general-irony-of-my-philosophy... (Or, as realism, to a philosophy just as left-wing as right-wing, as the liberal concept of my liberal philosophy...) Or, realism... (My philosophy always thought all philosophy as liberal-anyhow...) Philosophy will, to my philosophy, always be just as left-wing as right-wing/leftwing... (It is a "left-wing-profession" ...) Where the liberals meet... (It is psychology...) Except, nothing relates psychologically in my philosophy... (Not actually...) That I can comprehend something like the greatest genius of psychology/Dostoyevsky... Which will never be that I know how to do psychology myself... (Psychology includes as concept in my philosophy as my philosophy...) Or, the simple psychology/self-conscious... Which is due to other reasons... (I can't be the greatest possible genius of IQ and a greatest possible genius of psychology...) (Bergman did reach a second-best-genius status with psychology as the greatest possible genius of IQ...) (I always lower my psychological-potential...) That the philosophy be "self-conscious" will always where I stop with psychology... (It is as some-irony as left-wing/self-conscious-creation of unfinished-creation as left-wing and Dostoyevsky and Nietzsche, probably...) Or, probably as Nietzsche and left-wing, and that I have to solve the problem/that-I-am-aNietzsche-left-wing-philosophy... (On that my philosophy always had to evolve in the director of liberal left-wing as apolitical...) Left-wing and communism can *appreciate* Nietzsche... Which was always history of philosophy and left-wing and communism to left-wing and communism... (I will always be the first Nietzsche left-wing-philosophy ever devised...) Meaning, something had to base on thought as originality...

A "will-philosophy" means writing a genius of philosophy that is Einstein-smart... (I discard with the idea of becoming something like a mathematician...) So as to evolve a philosophy from an Einstein-smart-philosophy to a genius of philosophy, while retaining the Einstein-IQ of that philosophy... (A "two-will" ...) The care being with talent, not with philosophy... (That I need to write a genius of philosophy will always be talent instead of philosophy/it-is-not-like-I-am-ever-an-actually-self-loving-philosopher...) I love my IQ... Which always subjectifies my love for philosophy... Art and science being the uneven measure/I-love-science-over-art-as-IQ... And that my IQ be all three crowns... (That I am a German philosopher will always be as talent/instead-of-philosophy...) Combining German philosophy and IQ... (Some sort of a realism...) Free-association without deconstruction... (Must be that I am attempting a structure on nothing/atheism...) Or, that I, as the liberal theist-philosopher, never wrote on the opposite... (*It is very paranoid...*) What is the Freud of this essay and why it is him... (I love Einstein, not Freud...) Am I writing some-realism on the relative-Einstein of my philosophy? Perhaps... (That a Jew be the IQ race of my philosophy was always a half...) As is Einstein idea of literal-idea... (Perhaps something on the problem of me and Einstein...) The four geniuses of IQ of my philosophy, that Einstein be one of them, and that Einstein become all four... (I searching for a Jew completely-unrelated...) Or something... (And that Dostoyevsky be one of the greatest great minds of my philosophy with Einstein...) (There is never anything actual about me and Einstein...) The "purely-defined" being that he is so famous with IQ, so as to become the natural idea of me, Bergman and Wittgenstein... (I, Bergman and Wittgenstein are just as smart as Einstein...) That the four IQs evolved out of Einstein is for Einstein to evolve out of all four... (So as for Judaism to complicate too...) The best religion of my philosophy, relative of the IQ-race of my philosophy and that the IQ divided/is-half-Jewish-half-Christian... (And so on...) Judaism can't go with the IQ-race, seeing as the religion is to correlate as the half-IQ-race... (Or something...) That I always love a deconstruction... Which is that I love my/difference-deconstruction, the idea-deconstruction of a positive-negative, as an irony/technology and the century I am in, as idea... Derrida was always the last great philosopher of my philosophy, not one of the great philosophers of my philosophy... (The combinatoric Einstein-IQ German philosophy was always unrelated to Derrida as is, seeing as something like the French-left already meant the strange relation to resolve the impossible of possible...) The attempt being to contextualize my philosophy with something like Derrida, while retaining Nietzsche, Heidegger and Wittgenstein... (Judaism is the interpretation...) Or, that Derrida be so post-structural or postmodern... (Derrida can be Judaic with me...) (What is my Wittgenstein?) The third-best great philosophy as the first-best genius of IQ/Einstein... The structural philosophy, as Derrida... Or, a structural-Derrida... So as to write on paranoia... What is the meaning of a free-association anti-deconstructive essay I would write?

What do I read of the French-left? Derrida and Sartre... And that I haven't read anything by the former... (It is an idea!) Or, some subjective, of idea, as French-left, apparently to solve the problem of my impossible/problem- philosophy... An idea-French-left being a subjective-French-left... (On top of the limit/my-reading-of-French-left...) Something "doubly-subjective," to make possible philosophy and Einstein in a philosophy... (A strange new period of my philosophy...) Which is always an illusion/*I-am-deconstructing-!...* There is no sudden "resolve"/creating-adifference-of-all-my-philosophy-and-a-difference-of-my-two-periods-of-my-philosophy... (My love for a difference deconstruction over deconstruction didn't evolve to that extreme-measure...) *Why?* I will be keeping the free association as short as possible... (It is a philosophical-miniature

I write: deconstruction is always the most natural thing for me to be doing in philosophy/I-deconstruct-as-my-idea-deconstruction...) Or, that all those deconstructions I wrote prior to the illusion/that-I-am-entering-a-new-period-in-my-philosophy (a deconstruction of me, Kafka,

Bergman and Wittgenstein) introduced my deconstruction/are-an-introduction... (I love my "idea-deconstruction" ...) That I mean as a difference-deconstruction... Meaning, I never wrote an actual/postmodern deconstruction that is a deconstruction... (Derrida is to me always the last great philosopher, not one of the best great philosophers of my philosophy...) That I become so infinite with "deconstructing" will always be that I never deconstructed... And that my deconstruction-period always tied to the first period, so as to write billions of similar-things as the shrinking German-nationalism shrunken to my usual/Jewish proportion/measure... (That I become an infinite-Wagner will always be one of the principal illusions of my philosophy...) It is an attempt to be national, relative of my hate of all nationalism on the planet... (Judaism is the best religion...) And that IQ did split in half as Jewish as the total Jewish idea of IQ... The idea of all four greatest geniuses of IQ of my philosophy will always be Einstein with or without the literal-idea of the whole thing/that-I-never-read-one-of-Einstein's-papers...

My deconstruction/Heidegger, Wittgenstein and Derrida... (I mean Heidegger and Wittgenstein...) How did that deconstructive system of mine always go? As an idea-deconstruction, as the two philosophers to inspire Derrida/an idea-deconstruction... (Which is natural...) I never wrote a postmodern-deconstruction... And that the two grounds to-deconstruction always be modernist... (Is it because of the modern-postmodern difference?) Perhaps... (Wittgenstein is already the third-best great philosopher of my philosophy as my IQ/the-greatest-possible-first-best genius-of-IQ...) And that Heidegger delimited/got-to-the-second-best-great-place-of-great-philosophy-of-myphilosophy-coincidentally... (That Heidegger joined Hitler...) Meaning, Being and Time to never goes with the politics of the man who wrote it... (Whether modernism and postmodernism be similar in nature...) I differentiate... (It is impossible to write a postmodern theist-philosophy...) Or something... (Does all my philosophy base on possible?) Not actually/it-is-a-liberal-left-wing-of-apolitical... Something like Einstein/IQ is already a problem with the polarity of my philosophy... Or, the doubly-solving-Einstein-philosophy/impossible... (Why I so love my philosophy will always be that I omitted becoming an IQ profession as by writing Einstein-smart philosophies...) The rest being talent... That I can conceptualize philosophy for talented or untalented... (The self-hate/love-for-IQ never annihilated the basic-belief/that-Germany-be-the-only-philosophy-on-the-planet...) In my case the vicious, not that Germany outdo everything culturally...

I lag Wittgenstein's first period ten years, so as to, to this day, deconstruct *Tractatus Logico-Philosophicus* as potential... The text being ideal of me as IQ... Why do expand on the question of a third-best great philosophy... Is it since Nietzsche won't ever deconstruct as my interpretation of Nietzsche? (Why not deconstruct Heidegger instead of Wittgenstein?) Must be something subjective/my-infinite-love-for-my-infinite-*genius-IQ*... That that never made any sense... (I can't stop with Wittgenstein, so as to finish reading The Idiot, so as to deconstruct that Dostoyevsky of the greatest possible magnitude of genius...) That The Idiot was always the next *deconstructed*... (Wittgenstein's IQ gets in the way ten years...) Or something... (That Dostoyevsky will never be as smart as the four geniuses of IQ of my philosophy...) Must be that Dostoyevsky always became one of the greatest great minds of my philosophy, relative of Shakespeare and that I don't have a favorite writer... Which is always irrational/I-learned-howtocontrol-my-never-ending-genius-IQ-from-the-start/when-I-began-to-write-my-first-philosophy-I-wrote... That Wittgenstein can't end, so as for Dostoyevsky to start being the deconstructed instead, will always be something irrational... (My philosophy always had the French-left-participant...) Or, I did solve the philosophy and IQ of my philosophy... *Maybe deconstruct Heidegger instead...* Or something... (That my Heidegger never became Nietzsche as my interpretation/the-essentially-bound-forms-of-every-next-form-of-same-literally...) My Heidegger does deconstruct... However, as Wittgenstein/my-deconstruction... (A-bore...) I deconstructed Wittgenstein... (Heidegger and Wittgenstein being my idea-deconstruction...) (Meaning and IQ...) Must be something hermeneutical as IQ, as to what so grows on me... (Tractatus Logico-Philosophicus...)

Deconstructing Nietzsche is absurd... (I read him "metaphysically" ...) Or, all those things he wrote, as essentially bound to each other, as the metaphysical-reality to comprise everything he wrote, rationally, as every next extent of the same reality/metaphysics... (I go with Heidegger's conception...) *Nietzsche is the last metaphysician...* I would always deconstruct Heidegger, had I the basic need for "dull" as intention... (IQ and imagination to me being essential of each other...) Something has to be creative, first, so as to get to Einstein's IQ, second... (As to what the basic psychology of Einstein, to my philosophy, will always be...) (Heidegger, as the always-potential of my deconstruction, without much potential relative of my deconstruction...) That he means my deconstruction always annihilated the potential as is, probably... (I resume the deconstruction of the early Wittgenstein...) So as to expand on the issue of my absurd-interpretation of him... (Propositions and proofs, absurdly absurd of each other...) And that that always meant imagination as absurdism... (Or, the IQ always got to my IQ...) Meaning, Einstein, imagination, tabula rasa, etc., all those psychological prerequisites, that matched with me as Einstein/as-Einstein... Wittgenstein always being one of the Einstein-IQs of my philosophy...

The never-ending deconstructed-early-period-Wittgenstein... (When do I finally actually stop to expand him as the deconstruction of him/my-*On-the-Case-of-Italic?*) I know that he always becomes so ideal of my IQ... (Einstein, Wittgenstein, Bergman and me...) However, that his philosophy realistically gets to that third-best great-philosophy place out-of-pity/naturally... (Used to be a last-great-great-philosophy like any Analytic-philosophy-kind...) Why not move on to the rest of the IQ of my philosophy... (Must be since I did deconstruct, me and Einstein...) There is no way to do a deconstruction of Einstein... Or, my strange philosophical-miniature (*Relativity of the Half-being of Representation*), that I always named the-deconstruction anyhow... (Einstein doesn't deconstruct...) Or, that that miniature be the deconstruction of him... Or something... (Science doesn't deconstruct...) Or something...

(Deconstructing Wittgenstein past a deconstruction of him always became just-as-same...)

So as to undo the desire... (The difficulty is the obvious: I became a philosopher to match my Einstein IQ...) It is not like I will ever be an actually self-loving-philosopher... Einstein (the four IQs) to me being above philosophy... (Which relativized...) An okay-thing (I always mock Analytic philosophy in the context of German-philosophy) ... That I am the natural mockery-of-everything/*naturally-mock* will always be that I so respect German philosophy above philosophy... (The German-philosophy, as the only kind to realize that there are no unsolved problems of philosophy (the-vicious of philosophy) and Analytic philosophy as the one science of one real one solution to one real as the one science...) Etc... I infinitely mock the opposite of a

German philosophy... That I always have to shrink my Einstein-IQ will always be that I never needed to do anything... I do care what philosophy is... And that I write a philosophy that is science was always the three-IQ-thing/ all-three-crowning-achievements-of-genius- IQ-as profession-or-discipline/ science, mathematics and logic... (So as to read the Wittgenstein's late period...) The obsessive-compulsive disorder, that <u>On the Case of Italic</u> made out of Tractatus Logico-Philosopicus may find the final way to a cure as the antithetical-period/his-system-philosophy... (Or, that I shouldn't praise a system of philosophy...) Nietzsche is the best great philosopher...

That my quotient always be the same-thing... Philosophy and IQ... Which always aspired to a same-magnitude, so as to be mixed... (I love my IQ...) That my philosophy is to be a genius of philosophy never intended as my Einstein IQ of my philosophy... (What is so great about the philosophy-part being that I am a Serb/great-anyhow...) Or, that the genius-of-philosophy part of my philosophy be great-anyhow/a-Serb-writing-a-genius-of-philosophy... That the comparison never matched... My philosophy, that is always too strong on IQ, as the relatively genius-level of a genius of philosophy... (What always heals the whole thing?) That a Serb to me being unrelated to philosophy or IQ... (Which is a bit too relative...) The Jewish IQ divided in half/is-Swedish-and-Serbian-as-the-two-JewishEinsteins-and-that-all-four-be-Einstein... How think such a thing... And that I always complicated... (Judaism being the best religion of my philosophy...) The basic desire, of my philosophy, being to make philosophy an even philosophy-and-IQ-philosophy, while including both in a genius-philosophy genius-enough... (Nobody likes to be untalented...) Seeing as my IQ had the specific purpose to prove itself as something as-something, and isn't welcome in a philosophy... (How does the IQ of my philosophy function in my philosophy?) As proof of my Einstein-IQ and originality-in-philosophy/a-philosophy-that-is-philosophy-and-IQ-in-a-genius-philosophy-while-retaining-thatgenius-philosophy-as-philosophy-and-IQ... (Everything did work out just fine...) Which is ancient/I-always-writeon-that-I-and-my-philosophy-always-be-infinitely-ideal-of-each-other... I do become the self-loving-philosopher as the infinite-regress-love, seeing as I always became the infinite self-love of my philosophy... (I mean my philosophy...) And that Einstein never annihilated my Continental-German-philosophy... (Generally-too...) What is philosophy to me? German philosophy... (France always being the second-best great philosophy of left-wing/theFrench-left-instead-of-philosophy...) My self-love for philosophy then being that simple combinatoric of the specific and general just-as-much... How I always solved the total-problem of all my philosophy... (Instead of a "self-hating" a philosophy an infinitely self-loving-philosophy *instead...*) (I always become an infinitely self-loving-philosopher in the place of infinite-self-hate that is the original intention of my philosophy...) (The system/cure...) That my philosophy always did think a system-of-philosophy possible as Nietzsche as the extensive-bibliography of my philosophy... (What makes my Nietzsche system-philosophy possible?) That it is always natural for me to assume the role of mockery... Do I mock everything? Maybe... (The easiest thing for me to do/to-mock...) That one part based on the pure value/Nietzsche... In my case subjectively... (My self-love must a form of illness...) Or, what is my mental condition? Not mocking Germany, Jewry and France... (Or something...) The antithetical period being an illusion... (I never stopped to deconstruct...) (Dostoyevsky is always the thing to cure me from all those illusions I write after <u>On the Case of Italic...</u>) Except, that being an illusion... There is nothing to cure/it-is-an-illusion-that-I stop-to-deconstruct... That I am so impossible to read will always the strange in my philosophy... (What does an excessive-Hegel have to do with a genius-of-IQ philosophy?) How is the genius-IQ to relate to Hegel as is/with-or without-making-something-like-Hegel-so-infinite? As by naming it an impossible prior to the infinite-Hegel... (The task is synthesizing philosophy and IQ while retaining philosophy, not combining an infinite-Hegel with a genius IQ...) Something like Hegel was always directed to Spinoza and Heidegger... Or, Hegel is not the only evolutionary dialectic part of my philosophy... (Spinoza and Heidegger became the same logic...) I don't mock Germany, Jewry and France... (In the twenty-first century that I do see everything as below...) (How does my twentieth-century like of the three races always appears vicious?) That Germany always had a clear "divide"/philosophy-without-West-or East... The half-Jewish-IQ and Judaism meant Jewry/Jewish...

What do I like most of all/more-than-anything-on-the-planet? An Einstein-IQ combinatoric... (Philosophy will never be as ideal of me as my Einstein IQ...) That it be natural that it will always be my IQ that is in the way of my philosophy... (I always had to suppress my IQ to-some-extent...) Or, I had to find a way to raise my philosophy's standard to the level of my IQ... That I do, always, think me the most standard man around, on the planet, in history... Which was always an ambivalent-concept/a-genius-philosophy-aspiring-to-Germany... I can equal-Germany without outdoing it... (The "nobody" (zero success and zero higher-education) always being an even-measure/an-absolute somebody-in-the-century-he-is...) That I do think me a German genius-of-philosophy at the same level... (To me...) Germany to my philosophy being the only philosophy there ever was... And that I mean as the completely original way to think philosophy as is... (Philosophy and IQ in a philosophy...) A completely new invention... And that it be German... (I do think me the infinitely-strange-Serb writing an actually genius German philosophy at the same level of German genius-of-philosophy...) To me, that I become a philosopher to match my IQ always had the philosophy part of the philosophy too/became-a-genius-of-German-philosophy-to-go-with-the-Einstein-IQ-of-my-philosophyand-my-Einstein-IQ... (Why I always name my philosophy the most ideal relation in history...) Something originally-to-intend-as-mixed (a content thing as IQ *philosophically mixed-as-potential*), to me always an infinitely ideal-relation... Which never changes... (I can't care too much for the success- and self-taught-man-part of the whole thing...) What is so content about the whole thing will always be that I am in the century I am in... The to-me always moved from a fascist-polarity to the liberal-left-wing of apolitical that is my philosophy... That I am the most self-loving man that ever exist doesn't mean a form of mental-illness... (The vicious relation/a-Jew, of my philosophy...) How to conceptualize the "Jewish-part" ... (The Western race, that is the universal race, relative of my "international-philosophy" ...) That the French-left/France be West as the Jew... (Or something...) The rest, from the racial-question, of my philosophy, won't ever base on clarity-of-thought... (France, as the French-left, of West, as Communism (*Where is Communism?*), and that a Jew be West...) And that I be against Communism... (What is the modern-postmodern difference of French-left?) What is a Jew? Which mixed as the liberal-religion-Judaism of best religion and half-Jewish-IQ of Einstein/that-a-Jew-be-the-IQ-race... (That I and Bergman meant the second-half of the total-IQ of my philosophy doesn't change the Jewish-fact of that IQ...) I and Bergman mean as the greatest possible genius of IQ as Einstein/to-remind-of-Einstein/as-Einstein's-fame... (To me...) Or, all that "mix," of unclarity, as "Continental-philosophy"/the-intentionally-anti-Analytic-philosophy-philosophy, probably did in the end simplify towards-clarity while retaining that I am against clarity-in-philosophy... The genius-IQ and philosophy in a philosophy synthesized *as* French-left... The genius-IQ *is* Jewish... (In effect, what, finally, seeks an equilibrium between philosophical clarity and German philosophy...) That I always search for a cure for my "mixed-philosophy" will always be an illusion... (I mean as philosophy/the-mixed!) To so infinitely exceed in logic, as science and mathematics, will always be absurd/in-the-way... Logic being one of the philosophical branches of my philosophy... And that I so mix every type of logic... Which doubly mixed... Therefore... (A *strange...*) To retain the greatest possible genius-IQ in a philosophy with a philosophy is always improbable... And what does Nietzsche have to do with Einstein? Nothing at all/Wittgenstein-was-the-only-"Einstein-one" ... (As soon as I finish composing this preface...) The actual intention, of the essay, being a deconstruction of The Idiot... Dostoyevsky always being the next thing to deconstruct... (It is my plan...) Something I was going to consider doing ten years ago/after-On-theCase-of-Italic... My "Hegel/psychological" interpretation of The Idiot, that is a Nietzsche approach to the text... (Nothing too spectacular...) It is not like Dostoyevsky will ever be above Germany to me... Or, the three races... The relation of Dostoyevsky, to me, to my philosophy, always being one of the greatest great minds in history and that I don't have a favorite writer...

It is supposed to be as simple as a "simple-itself" ... (Philosophy and Einstein in a philosophy...) Making the impossible possible... Or, what is so great about my philosophy... Instead that I always had to "simplify" ... The three races, that always so "smudged" ... (Does my philosophy simplify anyhow?) So as to undo what does complicate the simple-intention... (That my philosophy always be infinitely-ideal of me...) There is nothing to change in the way I do philosophy... (It is an illusion that I can dislike my philosophy...) At all/at-all... That it will always be "to-me" was implied prior to me becoming a philosopher... (Without success, and that it be billions of self-taught-man-philosophies...) The illusion... (I succeeded in philosophy and I have a Ph.D. in philosophy...) The extreme difference of the century I am in being that-infinite... That I so infinitely-always-become-just-as-standardas-the-measure-of-the-planet-I-am-on-existing-at-all... My never-ending German-standard being matching of success/a-Ph.D... (The two always matched...) All that logical-*science-mathematics,* in the form of a German philosophy... (Always so infinitely ideal of me...) And that I to me achieve both in one while retaining the German philosophy-part... (It is incredible...) Why I always conceptualized me for an infinitely self-loving-man as the racial self-hate of relative... That the IQ-part (Einstein-IQ) be infinitely ideal of me prior to the philosophical inclusion and that it is philosophy... (How ideal, of me, as infinite-regress, do I get to be of me?) Therefore? (It is an-infinite regress...) Ever? (I do consider me the greatest genius in history...) Which was as the greatest possible genius of IQ...

(Becomes a mental-illness every-time...)

(Always...) Must a monotony, as an invention... Or, Nietzsche/recurrence-of-same, as Webern, of "minimalist-art," and Bergman/"minimalism" ... That, too, being a general-illusion... (I don't invent the next period in my philosophy...) Nietzsche (all those things he writes, as the generalized-concept/recurrence-of-same, as some irony/that-concept-be-against-his-philosophy) ... (I undo the desire to deconstruct illusion-wise...) That I be ten years back, to this day, deconstructing Wittgenstein, writing On the Case of Italic... (The incredible/*infinite* illusion being as an illusion...) Wittgenstein *didn't* turn into an obsessive-compulsive disorder... An infinite-regress-illusion... Or, on the concept of infinite-regress-illusion... Or something... A nothing-of-language... (As if I attempt how I would think atheism as possible in my philosophy...) The problem being that I mean the-illusion... Again... And that, to my philosophy, being *art,* in my philosophy Christ... Or, atheism, as Christian-theism...

(There is nothing to deconstruct...)

Deconstruction and I go way back... Which was probably always an illusion too... (I don't create a "period" ...) Isn't all my philosophy essentially-bound/a-literal-Bergman, Nietzsche and Webern... (I create the idea of *nothing* without atheism as representation...) There is no irony... (Deconstruction is a way to progress my philosophy...) The aim, always, being an illusion-Wagner as Hegel/an-illusion and that Hegel do have a relative-relevance as the progressive-dialectic/Spinoza-and-Heidegger to an extent... *Dragged Across Concrete* by S. Craig Zahler is a verypleasant-thing-to-watch... Finally a film to mock the recent action-genres... All that never-ending un-talent, past the end of film/at-the-very-beginning-of-the-century-I-am-in... Must be some two-joke, as irony... (I film intentionally slow, to mock all that hyperreal-action, as the decently-violent-film-against-itself...) (Something self-conscious...) Or something... That it is true/film-becomes-infinitely-untalented-like-anything-in-the-century-I-am-in... (I am a philosopher since I am a Serb...) A Serb has nothing to do with philosophy, that is... (Or, that my philosophy always had that outside-challenge...) How to isolate philosophy from the century I am in is all it is... (I write philosophy since it is a two-professional-philosophers philosophy...) Or, a philosophy literally infinitely private... (I doubly isolated the issue...) There is nothing about my philosophy to self-contradict... (The outside-parallel, that is me and my philosophy...) (Deconstructing Wittgenstein will always be the most natural thing to think...) Except, that being "slightly-mixed" ... My deconstruction being natural of Wittgenstein, relative of the great philosopher third-best in the sense of great philosophy/how-the-great-philosophers-of-my-philosophy-categorize...

How my philosophy can appreciate Hegel... (Isn't it the logic as homage?) I "create" ... So as to imply art, as imagination, as by annihilating all-art, while retaining that imagination be the integral part of the Einstein-IQ nihilist of-art... That I always love something Einstein-smart... However, that Wittgenstein stop with his IQ-seduction of me... (His Einstein IQ will never measure up to my philosophy-talent...) *The deconstruction is Heidegger too...* Philosophy is German-philosophy, not Wittgenstein... That it be philosophical-un-talent, that I know how to pervert into talent...

How my philosophy can appreciate Hegel... (Isn't it the logic as homage?) I "create" ... So as to imply art, as imagination, as by annihilating all-art, while retaining that imagination be the integral part of the Einstein-IQ nihilist-of-art... That I always love something Einstein-smart... However, that Wittgenstein stop with his IQ seduction of me... (His Einstein IQ will never measure up to my philosophy-talent...) *The deconstruction is Heidegger too...* Philosophy is German-philosophy, not Wittgenstein... That it be philosophical-un-talent, that I know how to pervert into talent...

My infinite love for IQ... (When do I finally stop with Wittgenstein?) This time some really-strange-coincidence... I never predicted that <u>On the Case of Italic</u> would cause an obsessive-compulsive disorder... (The great philosopher is to my philosophy a third-best great philosophy...) And that it be one of the four IQ-seductions of my philosophy... (I, Bergman and Einstein went smoothly...) Why especially Wittgenstein? (Wittgenstein is not the only greatest possible-magnitude of genius-IQ of my philosophy...) *Isn't there four of them? A Hegel expanded-concept...* Or something... I mean as German-philosophy... There was never all that obsessive about my Einstein-IQ... It is an inclusion, so as to exclude, so as to prove that an inclusion can be just-as-excluded... (The IQ serves-to-prove...) That there will never be anything essential about the IQ of my philosophy... It is philosophy and IQ... And that I mean in a philosophy... (My philosophy always existed to prove that I am a genius of philosophy at the same level of Germany and the greatest possible genius of IQ...) Doesn't appear all that pure/an-impossible-category... When do I finally deconstruct Dostoyevsky? (Wittgenstein rhymes well with Einstein, not with me and Bergman...) That the deconstruction of Wittgenstein expired ten years ago... The unimaginative ten-years are always too much for me to un-limit... Has to do with my natural infinite-talent... (Why do I so infinitely love IQ?) Is it because of the category/logic, mathematics and science as a combined-possible? Probably... (I love my Einstein-IQ...) The deconstruction being a coincidence... As is the so-called first-period just as coincidental... (Everything synthesized as philosophy and IQ in a philosophy...) Seeing as all my philosophy has the primitive challenge... It will always be an illusion that I build on the idea of "divide" ... (I never deconstructed...) Why I so infinitely love my philosophy... The one-philosophy I-write... Which was great with plagiarism too... *It is impossible to change or steal my philosophy/the-happiest-man-that-ever-existed...* (I never have to infinitely kill me...) To pervert my philosophy into something else is absolutely-impossible... (A literal Bergman, Nietzsche and Webern, as the logical science of mathematics...)

How is Hegel to go with the Einstein-IQ? As by stopping at the idea of logic... It will always be Spinoza and

Heidegger as Hegel... Or, that is how... And that Heidegger doesn't sort with the other two as the second-best great philosophy of my philosophy... (The obsessive-compulsive disorder/intentionally-minimalist/*zero*-language...) What is the meaning of the "un-language" of my third period... That it be an illusion/language-and-the-second-period... (A two-illusion...) That appear to be homaging something like Webern is an illusion/an-illusion-Webern... Webern being one of the possible-bibliographies... And that he is art... (Would always have to be an illusion-one...) What is the greatest possible reference of me? (From the total-bibliography...) The three great philosophers and all that is IQ... (Or, what combines the two categories, while retaining the philosophy-part...) I always try the impossible... (Combining the great philosophers and IQ without annihilating the former without annihilating the latter...) What to name it? That I am a Serb/challenged-philosophy-as-is and that the primary-impossible be philosophy and IQ in a philosophy instead/without-the-Serbian-challenge/a-Serb-writing-genius-German-philosophy... Or, the threechallenge/writing-a-genius-philosophy-past-Derrida's-death... Isn't Derrida where to me philosophy ends prior to my philosophy... (That I write a philosophy intended for a few readers per the century I am in will always be infinite way-too-great...) All that challenge/assumption, that is to base on the idea of assumption... (How I go from clinical depression to the happiest man in history...) Always... That my philosophy always have that major potential defect/the-self-taught-man-to-think, that never got to itself/isn't-the-self-taught-man... All that never-ending category and assumption always shrank as the century I am in/doesn't-even-exist-to-begin-with... How I afford my philosophy... (Everything goes smoothly/as-planned...) That I am a philosopher will always rest on the primitive-fact of the century I am in... (Why I am a philosopher...) All those billions-of-philosophies-I-write... I write the one philosophy... And that that philosophy be the infinite-limit/more-private-than-the-infinite-regress... An-impossible category/my-philosophy becomes natural/something-I-will-always-write... (There is nothing "Wagnerian" or infinitely-public about my philosophy...) A first-best genius of philosophy and IQ/appearing-Wittgenstein will always be possible of me... Me... A really-strange-coincidence... My infinite love for IQ, that has to be discontinued at some point in my life... (I mean to equilibrate mathematics and philosophy in a philosophy...) That I so become the extreme-opposite of me/an-Analytic-philosopher must shrink/equilibrate... (The wrong expanded-concept...)

Isn't Wittgenstein the only Analytic philosophy I can potentially like? Absolutely (the half-Continental-possible) ... The philosophy-part of his philosophy always by-coincidence being so third-best/the-third-best-great-philosophy... (An-impossible-category...) Or, possible as IQ... (Something like Analytic philosophy will always seduce with the logic...) An extreme-infinite that was always an issue with my philosophy... (A philosophy that loves IQ/Analytic philosophy, so as to always prioritize Germany as the only philosophy there ever was on the planet...) And that I always wanted to be a profession matching of my IQ... (Why do I become a philosopher?) It is not like philosophy will ever be my IQ... (Must be something-specific...) On the other hand, that I do so infinitely mock Analytic philosophy as is... (My philosophy proves that I am Einstein-smart and at the same level/German-philosophy...) I never imply that I can be a self-loving-philosopher *generally*... Or, something more specific than the infinite-regress itself... (That I am probably too lazy to get a degree in something my-IQ...) The easier way out...

That it is known that I infinitely have nothing to do with the planet I am on... Which is sixty-three-yearsmore/waiting-to-find-the-two-professional-philosophers... (Theory...) It is theoretical how I succeed... That I turned thirty-seven yesterday... And that I intend on becoming a centenarian... (Is it posthumous-fame, succeeding at my death or finding success at some point in my life?) That the system will always be same/sending-the-philosophy-to professional-philosophy... Finding two of them, out of billions of them, is always infinite... (Basing on the possible...) Does become a bit too ideal... (Two professional philosophers, Einstein-smart, with the infinite amount of time available to comprehend me, as the billions of dependencies, etc...) Always an *infinite-regress* and *coincidence*... (The happiest man that ever existed...) Something had to compensate the self-taught-man, of my philosophy, and the century I am in... Or, the twenty-first-century, that made the self-taught-man-part well... (Why it was possible to become a self-taught-man-philosopher at all...) That there will never be anything essential about the concept, relative of my philosophy... And I never like being self-taught in philosophy... (The self-taught-man will always be very "one-dimensional" with me...) Jewish, in that respect too... (With me everything has to be a class system, school, the known, etc...) That I base on the unknown was a liberal left-wing of apolitical/the-known... Or, the infinite indifference-of-class/education will always be the century I am in as well... (What is the exact polarity of my philosophy?) Left-wing and right-wing, and combining both in one, as a total polarity-indifference as is... (I am in the century I am in...) It is same what is left-wing, right-wing or anything... (Or, I mean as philosophy...) (That I infinitely don't relate to money/right-wing will always be the money I infinitely have nothing to do with...) Never bases on a principle matching of the philosophy that I write... (It is already-anti-capitalist...) There is no philosophy in the century I am in... Right-wing becomes left-wing as philosophy in the twenty-first-century...

It is a coincidence that I create a whole never-ending third-period in my philosophy... Which was, also, always, so great as the illusion of that coincidence... (Illusion and coincidence...) And that I never mean a period in my philosophy as is... (A *three*-negation of the third-period...) So as to make a philosophy out of money in the century I am in... (It is left-wing anyhow...) That the Einstein-combinatoric Einstein-IQ philosophy already be right-wing as left-wing... (With or without that "money" ...) The unknown was always liberal/the-known... It is the planet I am on... Seven-billion infinite slaves of me... I mean liberal in the century I am in... (How, infinitely, does my philosophy get to be potential of an infinite-fascism without that century?) As Jewish or anti-Semitic... (It is a Hitler infinite fascism philosophy as appearance...) That my philosophy always became liberal and Semitic, as should be, is the limit/potential... Something usually infinitely-fascist and anti-Semitic as is...

I do base on potential as idea... Which will always mix... (Something Einstein-IQ can't be communist...) A liberal left-wing of apolitical, that is an Einstein-smart-philosophy... And that I do define the polarity of my philosophy... (The potential will always be potential...) Idea and Germany naturalized... Or, my German-philosophy... The potential/*freedom* were never a natural concept... A German left-wing-philosophy, French-left as potential, so as to actualize what the "actual-race" of my philosophy is... (The actual/Germany, relative of the potential/France...) It is not like I will ever actually-be-French... France is the absurd-race or absurd-category... Anything to think German philosophy and Jewish IQ in a German philosophy possible/actual... (It is an illusion that I mean France actually...) *The liberal apolitical-left-wing philosophy is naturally German since German...* Is that a proposition with a sense? Maybe... (I am German philosophy, not Analytic philosophy...) Which is a lot of extents away... (What proposition with a sense...) I mean Nietzsche instead of Grass, as to what I probably mean... (My Germany won't ever get to the actual left-wing political-polarities...) Grass being so socialist/communist... I base on the usual-belief: a political-Nietzsche is a Hitler-Nietzsche... Or, the correct-Nietzsche... It will always be that my, and every, correct Nietzsche be apolitical... What is Nietzsche now/past-Hitler... That a Hitler-Nietzche never needed-to-be... (Hitler is Nietzsche as politics with or without a Hitler-politics...) What is the *potential* in my philosophy? A mild-potentiality (mild-same-thing) and the concept of unfinished-creation... Something usually thought of as the split-argument/ambivalence, seeing as I mean as postmodernism with the latter/unfinished-creation... (The reader finishes to write what I wrote...) Which was always just as split-potential as the mild potential as unfinished-creation... (I mean as religion as unfinished creation...) Or the modern-postmodern difference as the modernism of the mildly-potential... (And as the obvious relation to my philosophy I write generally...) That I literally write the-one-philosophy did finish that unfinished creation... (How does my *Bergman-Webern-Nietzsche-Bugarinovic* relate as a finished-creation?) The always same rewriting circle, of recurrence of same, as representation, to represent Nietzsche as representation representing his strange/*real* representation, Bergman's Sixties-period in-general and Bergman, Webern's twelve-tone compositions of self-copy *self-copying* and Bugarinovic's Bergman-Webern-Nietzsche-Bugarinovic relation... The Einstein-smart was always a strange obscure-thing of a mathematical logic of science, that is Bergman, Webern, Nietzsche and me, to double the strange/philosophy-and-Einstein-in-a-philosophy... (To complicate/write-Continental-philosophy, so to speak...) And that that never did stop to make a composite-argument out of the whole thing: Is Einstein one of the four infinite geniuses of IQ of my philosophy or all four as himself in my philosophy?

Something always too strong on idea... (I mean as Germany, Jewry and France?) Why is my philosophy excessively German above the rest? Since it is philosophy... Or, France serves to synthesize Germany and Jewry as Germany... A Jew to my philosophy being IQ, not philosophy, as to why... (I lessen that idea-part of my philosophy with the help of the Jewish/IQ...) That the mathematical logic of science be mathematics, logic or science... Or, what is the miracle of nature, of my philosophy? That I write a German-Jewish philosophy that is German and German Jewish... Why my philosophy always existed... A Jew is in the way, so as to synthesize... I make such claims that I can achieve a rock-and-a-hard-place... (It is not between-rock-and-a-hard-place...) Something completely original... A German philosophy/a-genius-of-philosophy, that is German-Jewish, that is German... An even-Wittgenstein: a simultaneous genius of philosophy and genius of IQ in a genius philosophy... (Wittgenstein being the third-best genius of philosophy as the first-best genius of IQ...) While I make such claims that I achieve a same simultaneous genius as between philosophy and IQ... (Wittgenstein would always be the best great philosopher of my philosophy...) Why I always so ideally and infinitely love my philosophy... It is not like there is a natural love for philosophy to begin with... I love my philosophy... I write my philosophy because of IQ... A philosophy that achieves philosophy and IQ, and is in-a-philosophy... (I am a self-loving-philosopher as my philosophy...) It is not like I will ever, purely, like the rest of philosophy from philosophy... (Always had to be three great philosophers, as the best great philosophers of my philosophy, so as to generalize within a total-bibliography and that I am one-extra bibliography/the-in-itself-bibliography...) That is how... It is not like the greatest geniuses of great philosophy of my philosophy will ever be above my philosophy... Or, probably as to how I do achieve that impossible miracle of nature as France and with or without the absurdity of France getting me to my impossible-philosophy... (Is it the French-left-part or the perfectly thought-out bibliography to do the job prior to France?) And that it be the usual: two professional philosophers and the self-hating-self-taught-man... (That compensated too...) It is not like I am in the prior-century... Something "proportional," and without the necessary P.h.D, probably creates the necessary "care" too... It is good that I be infinitely-insular and an assumption of the self-taught-man-kind... (I split the genius-IQs in half/the-pure-value-of-Jewry-of-my-philosophy-will-always-be-Judaism, not IQ...) Or, is it Judaism, that in the long run, solves my philosophy? (My love for a "half" won't be delimiting any time soon...) What does liberal-religion have to do with Judaism... And that I mean four Einsteins as Einstein... (France, a bibliography, the infinite-insular and bad-self-taught-man do solve my philosophy...) My philosophy is possible... So as to write an overlong-preface, that means to introduce in a philosophy towards a deconstruction of Dostoyevsky... (Will I deconstruct him or make a joke out of the whole thing as a self-conscious-preface?) To write a miniature-philosophy wouldn't be anything too-new... (I did write "three-page" philosophical-riddles in the past...) It is a riddle or a philosophy...

That Judaism always be the best religion of my philosophy... Which had to "compensate" as the liberal-religion of my philosophy... Or, probably as two half's... As to what was, always, the only Jewish-relation possible in my philosophy: IQ and Judaism... A contradiction, that was to resolve of two-half's... And as the vicious-IQ... *Is the French-left-part really all that necessary?* The IQ is by-a-half... I probably did lower my two-hundred IQ... (Two Jewish and two Christian geniuses of IQ...) All four would be Einstein... Or, does the liberal-religion, of my philosophy, make my absolute-Judaism vicious? If I find the imagination to find an "imagination/the deconstructed" ... (Do I lower my IQ as by writing this philosophy?) Something very unimaginative, against the basic prerequisite of all great IQ to my philosophy... (Imagination being very-necessary...) Relative of tabula rasa and idea will always be imagination as the necessary psychology... (As long as I mean the illusion of this essay...) I never stopped relating to imagination as my two-hundred-IQ/it-will-always-be-an-illusion-that-I-becomemonotonous, so as to lower my IQ as for a reason... That I write-anything is the absurd-illusion of the essay... And the riddle being as philosophy and mathematics of scientific-logic... A three-split... Or, the illusion, that is the riddle, that is the riddle making that illusion possible... (I will get a Ph.D. in the meantime...) The newest claim of my philosophy... That I can write a riddle as by omitting imagination from my philosophy...

The physics-paper needs more imagination... (Which is the illusion of this essay...) I never stopped deconstructing/I-don't-need-to-up-the-imagination-part... *How does one define that I am doing an illusion?* As by naming it irony instead... Or, metaphysics is one of the major branches of my philosophy... And that I mean the field of philosophy above the rest I do in philosophy... (One of my branches and the only in-itself branch...) Irony, as the prioritizing-field of philosophy of my philosophy... Or, on that metaphysics be philosophy to my philosophy... That metaphysics never existed to begin with, to my philosophy... Not to my philosophy... And that this be the general definition of philosophy and Heidegger and philosophy-itself... (Philosophically, Heidegger will always be the best great philosophy...) That I do a physics paper, of mathematics, as logic, of science, will always be the impossible/metaphysics... The illusion of the essay proposes, directly, on the problem, of all my philosophy, that is that four-IQ-relation and metaphysics/the-impossible... (Am I writing a dream or illusion...) Or, as the problem of illusion in my philosophy and whether I up that illusion to the level of dream/that-the-illusion-to-my-philosophy-beso-extreme/complete-as-film/the-dream... (What is the relation of the best possible art-form of my philosophy to my philosophy?) That it be a four-IQ-metaphysics would presuppose that it is possible to include the best possible artform of my philosophy in my philosophy, seeing as art didn't exclude from my philosophy while "including" ... The ancient vicious-relation of all my philosophy I write more ancient than creating the planet itself... And that art be so essential of metaphysics to my philosophy... Or, my philosophy, that does go with those classic definitions of metaphysics, art and Christ, as to how my philosophy always sides with the generic-definition to all three... (To compensate is the fact of Jewish-art/that-a-Jew-not-make-a-work-of-art...) (I always lower the standard of Jewish art...) Naturally (Judaism is the best religion of my philosophy) ... Or, that a Jew to me so exceed religiously... (There was nothing to compensate...) As the usual definitions of my philosophy/usual-definitions... I will always be going with the fact of an inferior-religion/Christ, that is bad psychology/ideal, caused in the fact of superior art, representation/Christ, already so art prior to making a work of art as the art-religion that is prior to art... There is nothing representation about Judaism, as to why nothing causes in the direction of art to begin with... (The realreligion, that never had to be compensated as art...) As the usual/what-I-always-went-with... Dostoyevsky won't ever be a smart as Wittgenstein... Not to me... That I mean one-of-the-greatest-great-minds-in-history... That my philosophy doesn't have a favorite-writer never prevents from the next-deconstructed/Dostoyevsky within the greatminds-scope-potential/Einstein... A deconstruction to go with my Relativity of the Half-being of Representation... And that I did deconstruct Bergman and Kafka/make-a-general-art-term... (Judaism as the best religion, relative of Dostoyevsky as one of the two of the greatest great minds in history...) Or something... (Which was never all that vicious...) Walter Kaufmann will always be my Dostoyevsky... (Or, the man who becomes Jewish as by converting to Judaism as the percentage Jewish-blood...) Isn't my interpretation of Dostoyevsky always the total Continentalconnective/*ancient*? Surely as so: Nietzsche, Heidegger, Kafka and Dostoyevsky... My Dostoyevsky being the Kaufmann... I am a philosopher... Or, that it be natural that Dostoyevsky can't become all that much with me and is a Continental-German relation... Germany will always be above Russia... (Dostoyevsky is possible at all, as my reading of him and the greatest great mind possible/Einstein...) Why would I like anything Russian at all? That I love IQ (Russia was never a major country to relate to) ... And that I am a philosopher means that I am... (I don't care what my actual self-love/self-hate for philosophy in actual fact is...) *I love philosophy...* I sure that choose to be talented anyhow... The IQ-philosophy is a genius of philosophy...

(Maybe a bad idea...) Who is to intuit that I am doing an illusion... (As long as I insert an indicator...) That my philosophy always based on self-evidence had to be as mathematics, science and logic... (My ancient-problem, of synthesizing the mathematical science of logic with metaphysics as aesthetics and logic...) As long as I write billions of philosophies... I am bound to get to a factual-state of doing that synthesis... And so much assumption always based on affording to write my philosophy at all... (All those categories I always mention, that annihilate the question of assumption of my philosophy...) (Deconstructing Dostoyevsky is such a great potential...) So as to stop doing the ten-year illusion I have been writing ten years/after-On-the-Case-of-Italic... It is going to feel nice... (An experimental period in my philosophy, that I never get to like all that much...) (The illusion is an illusion...) And so on... Something like deconstructing The Idiot... That Christ always include in my philosophy as philosophy and art... As long as the rest (philosophy and a genius-IQ, in a philosophy) never stopped being possible... (The illusion is an experimental stage to an experimental period...) (Needs more language and a deconstructed...)*Wittgenstein is always good to deconstruct because of his IQ matching of my deconstruction/philosophy as the deconstructed...* A good comparison/similarity: a first best genius of philosophy first-best genius of IQ and a third-best genius of philosophy first-best genius of IQ... (He nearly became the best great philosopher of my philosophy...)

To name it an experimental-philosophy/philosophy-and-IQ-in-a-philosophy... I exchanged it with language/acompletely-original-system-of-philosophy-to-think-a-philosophy... Or, Nietzsche as the first-best-great-philosophy limit/ Heidegger-as-the-best-great-philosophy-*philosophically...* The language intuits-why, as the intuitive/visual *language of self-evidence,* in the sense of "correlate"/a-self-evidence-of-language-to-go-with-itsphilosophy/philosophical-self-evidence... I compared me and Wittgenstein throughout... It is all my philosophy, that I write, that is that comparison, as the coincidence-On-the-Case-of-Italic... (On the Case of Italic does become essential...) *Idea* always too-emphasized, with or without the relative-Germany of the three-race-philosophy... (Or, the aim being in the same-even-measure of Germany and Jewry...) That it be German-philosophy will always be the Jewish-IQ/IQ of that philosophy and German-philosophy *absolutely...*

The "intuitive" language is to correlate the two categories of self-evidence *correlating...* And that I mean an intuitive language of visual-language and prerequisite to all great IQ... Intuition always thought tabula rasa, imagination and idea as a three-synthesis... (*As IQ too!*) Which was natural... (Theory is IQ...) Theory, logic and the a priori... (Naturally/all-that-is-IQ...) (Am experimental-philosophy...) The aim being to double the idea of originalphilosophy, seeing as I write philosophy after Derrida/past-philosophy's-demise... There is no philosophy after Derrida... (Why am I a philosopher?) The personally-subjective, of my philosophy/I-like-my-philosophy... Or, since I do write billions of Einstein-smart philosophies that are a genius of philosophy... (That is why...) And that Derrida be the French Jew... Which is probably why too... (How philosophy ended will never be to my liking...) A German didn't end the German profession that is philosophy... (It is like any challenge past something-ending...) That everything ended, in the twenty-first-century, doesn't mean that those infinitely obsolete-potentials/two-readers-per that-century come to an end too... Something is for two professional philosophers per that century that I am in... (Or, *that* is *why...*) I named it *clearly...* I made sure that too much justify me becoming a philosopher after Derrida's death... (Watching Hitchcock's *Vertigo* last night...) My mother's favorite-Hitchcock, to me a great film I never get to like all that much due to the romance-part of the film, probably... (I love *Psycho* and *Topaz...*) That I can love Kim Novak instead of the film... (Or something...) Or, what I do like about the film... (The famous heterosexual philosopher, that I am...) I eat women... Or, my illness, that was always a bit too excessive... (Take it easy with women...) Eating all those beautiful women... (Or something...) To me the homosexual never existed... Which probably justified in the German-fact of my philosophy that was always a fact instead of opinion and that I mean an IQ-philosophy... (The language...) (The rock-and-a-hard-place, of my philosophy, that had to solve the sexuality of the philosopher too...) Had to be something completely-new, as identified as self-conscious... A conscious fact of all my philosophy... (It is a genius of philosophy that is heterosexual...) What to call it? A Serbian writing a genius of philosophy... (Or something...) Or, that a heterosexual-chauvinism never get to the homosexual-chauvinism... Persona is the best film categorically/rationally! All those things, that I love about that film, relative of my heterosexually-chauvinist room... (The rest was never feminist...) That it is professional-philosophy will always be vicious... A German philosophy, without West, East, anything, history, Europe or anything, as the vicious fact of race/German, Jewish and French... I mean a rock-and-a-hard-place... (France is to solve the Jewish-part of my philosophy...) Not a rock-and-a-hard-place... Or, a conscious rock-and-a-hard-place... Self-consciously... (What is the between-rock-and-a-hard-place of my philosophy?) `So as to find one more genius of IQ to go with my philosophy... (Why not five Einsteins instead of four?) It is always becoming very unimaginative/monotonous, with or without the illusion of-it... Must be that I am missing one more Einstein... Or something... Simply what always becomes the essence of my philosophy... (Why my philosophy exists...) German philosophy and a genius-IQ in a German philosophy... (I don't mean that a rock-and-a-hard-place assume a positive value...) That it be an infinite-coincidence... Or, that France solve that never-ending coincidence... Meaning, why France? Why not anything else... (The coincidence based on the doubly infinitely-coincidental...) How is the French-left to make my impossible possible? As the "same-coincidence" of France to me assuming the same value of philosophy as philosophy... (Doesn't something like Jewish philosophy to me always go with the French kind...) Or, the "progressive" ... France would be the second-best genius of philosophy, so as to get to the un-talent in philosophy/Jewry... (That is probably how...) Something philosophically *style, France,* is to make the same stylisticexercise out of Jewish-philosophy/style... Which is progress: France never gets to be as bad as the rest of philosophy that is style... (Isn't France, to my philosophy, philosophically second-best?) That I simply need an extraEinstein/*the-fifth-Einstein...* Or anything as the added same-category... (A fourth-best genius of great philosophy, one more same-favourite-writer, etc...) What to do? (The conscious-choice/free-association-without- deconstruction...) As long as I create an illusion out of the whole thing... That was I don't have to throw out billions of third-period philosophies... (That is a lot of potentially wasted paper...) It is known that I never write what I don't like... Or, that I be the infinite genius, to me... It is an illusion that something changes, as the illusion of the third period and illusion that I switched to a third period...

Where is the switch, to switch my second-period mode on? Where the progressive-philosophy/all-three-periods is...

I "create"... So as to name it a "progressive-philosophy" ... Which always implied *progressive*/the-left-wing... Meaning, must be a form of irony/an-apolitical-progressive-left-wing-party... On the mild of my philosophy... I simply named it infinitely-peaceful... Or, the necessity: something infinitely unrelated to anything... Or, not as any principle on peace... (The infinite privacy always correlated infinite peace...) A switch to a more "dynamic" mode will never be made possible... (Two professional philosophers...) And that I mean an Einstein-smart-philosophy intended for two professional philosophers... (How peaceful is it?) Left-wing was always a coincidence... That I am attempting an Einstein-smart-philosophy, not a left-wing at the same level of IQ as Einstein... (Why make something impossible doubly impossible...) And that philosophy to my philosophy meant the indifference-of-polarity... (In the century I am in...) I am left-wing, since a philosopher, since in the century I am in... To name it a Hegel progressive philosophy... (A strange liberal-left-wing apolitical-Hegel Hegel...) That I always try to be original past Derrida's death... Or something... Which inessential... (Hegel being one of the "three," so as to exclude the third one/Heidegger...) *Does it become essential in any case?* That my philosophy doesn't have much relation to Hegel, and does always think a basic concept of him as possible, is a strange/an-un invented Hegel... Meaning, maybe Hegel does become essential of Nietzsche, Heidegger and Wittgenstein in my philosophy... (The fourth-best great philosopher of my philosophy...) (So many deconstructions I wrote, as Hegel, Spinoza and Heidegger...) And that my deconstruction never "differentiated" ... A strange-relation, of all my philosophy... (All three "evolutions," as by excluding Heidegger, as by including him, relative of what always appeared as a fourth-best-philosopher as Hegel...) So as to invent new-categories of my philosophy... (Lots of add-on things...) On how to annihilate the "dull" ... Which is absurd... What happened to my deconstruction? Nothing at all... (I don't add new bibliographies to my extensive-bibliography/*relative-sixteen*...) As long as I annihilate deconstructing Wittgenstein... (Deconstruction will always be a positive-concept of me...) Or, my deconstruction... That all my philosophy be all my philosophy... (That Derrida never meant more than a last great philosophy/on-how-to-end-philosophy was never an issue...) My deconstruction, as my philosophy, as my philosophy... Writing so many philosophies was always the one philosophy I write... *Doesn't philosophy to me end at Heidegger's death?* Writing so many deconstructions was always the literal-synthesis as a literal Bergman, Webern and Nietzsche... It is a concept-deconstruction, of a *positive* and *negative,* to remind of technology, as irony... Or, something appearance-language... (I combine a − and + of an ideal deconstruction...) Like the rest of my philosophy... It will always be the greatest-possible-of-genius-IQ and-German-philosophy in a German-philosophy... (Nothing changes...) My deconstruction, that is my philosophy... Nietzsche "generalized" ... (That he be the best great philosopher of my philosophy will always be some sixteen bibliographies of relative as relative...) What had to be very-lame, in that respect, seeing as he agrees *philosophically* with my philosophy, seeing as he never agreed *philosophically* with my philosophy... Seeing as he is the best great philosopher... A sure thing/the-usual: that my philosophy is the greatest possible genius of IQ had to mean as the infinitely-thought-out/thought-itself... Or, a philosophy to base on the idea of thought... Infinitely... (The perfectly thought-out and a never-ending-genius-IQ to my philosophy correlated...) The simple of all my philosophy... Thought and IQ are always perfectly-thought-out... Or, that it be a philosophy infinitely-rational is the never-ending genius-IQ of my philosophy... (Nietzsche is vicious...) Or, Nietzsche, as the irrational, as the usual philosophy-IQ of the genius-IQ limit... (That my two-hundred-score IQ-test-score never get to Nietzsche's one-fifty/the-IQ-of-all philosophy as rationalism instead of irrational/Nietzsche/the-irrational...)

I know that Wittgenstein always means the ideal match of my IQ... However, that that never be all that sufficiently philosophy-as-my-philosophy... Why do I protract him so much-expand-on-the issue-of-his-philosophy-past-a deconstruction-of-him... That he be one of the great philosophers of my philosophy one of the principal IQs of my philosophy... (The relation being so mixed...) I emphasize something relatively-mild... The actual IQ genius-of philosophy, that is Einstein-smart, will always be me... And that I did deconstruct me... (The emphasis, past deconstruction, needed to be me...) That I should probably go back to the deconstruction I did of me, so as to compensate all that "excessive" ... *A ten-year lag, of Wittgenstein, past a deconstruction of him...* A fatal blow... So as to overexpand on the issue of the very first thing I write in philosophy... Opening my *On the Theory of Unnatural Unnaturalness Becoming Natural Unnaturalness: An Analysis Through Poetics (That Which Would Prove the Existence of a* Beyond, *if Architecture=Denotation...* (The title was always self-conscious-enough...) Why do I lag a "Secondary-Wittgenstein?" (Must a Nietzsche-irrational, again...) Or, some subjective-thing of a subjective-self-conscious... (Thought never becomes Wittgenstein as philosophy...) That my Wittgenstein always be the three-split difference: a first-best genius of thought, a third-best genius of philosophy, a first-best genius of IQ... (Nietzsche is the best great philosopher...) Or, I don't have to compensate the irrational/lagging-Wittgenstein-ten-years... That I probably mean Nietzsche's irrational as my irrational/comparing-the-two-irrationals... Which is always of interest... That my Nietzsche can't deconstruct (is a metaphysical irony of rational reality of everything he wrote) ... All those things he writes... Or, every next thing he wrote, as every next of the rational/metaphysical reality of dependence... (To devise something general of the best great philosopher of my philosophy is always great...) Without the deconstruction, and that my philosophy departs from writing the one-philosophy... (Something to go with both periods of my philosophy, that aren't both periods of my philosophy...) (I never transcend the first-period...) How I think the irrational ten-year-lagging... (Nietzsche, as the last-metaphysician...) That my Nietzsche was always that early/very-first-correct Nietzsche that is Heidegger... A strange old-fashioned-Nietzsche, with all those last-Hitler correct Nietzsches, of the present-day correct-Nietzsche... (My philosophy always thought Heidegger as the revolutionary in that respect too...) A correct interpretation of Nietzsche prior to Hitler, that is the Judaic/correct Nietzsche... (How Heidegger always got to the second-best great-philosophy place of my philosophy, without being last- or first-best...)

So as to write an "irrational" without the "first" or "second" period... That my philosophy can't write on the best great philosopher of my philosophy... (Something had to invent...) *Or, why not write something transcending of my one-philosophy?* That way I can finally address my favorite great philosopher in my philosophy, without making an indirect value/a-self-evidence or deconstructing him... (Heidegger would always make me feel better...) (Searching for the fifth Einstein...) Something categorically must-expand within my philosophy... Which is absurd... (How many infinite-bibliographies do I require?) My philosophy already being so relative as "bibliography" bibliographically-infinite as relative... (My philosophy grew obsessive-compulsive-like...) Ten years ago... (The "damn-Wittgenstein" ...) It seems some mistake I make, that is very-without-prediction... (That it is meant to be the most ideal thing possible of me as

IQ...) Or, that never happened to me before/I-never-should-have-deconstructedhim-or-began-a-deconstruction-of-him... The ideal-IQ can't be coming to an end, simply put... (An infinite-regress, that doesn't come to an end of its infinite...) Or something... Should have been the three Einsteins out of four being deconstructed... Or something... So as to search for a next Einstein or category... (I do have to get to that deconstruction of Dostoyevsky at some point in my life...) I can't forever delay Dostoyevsky as the deconstructed... (*Ten years...*) So as to throw Wittgenstein out of my room... Or something...

It is a mistake to lower language and write a third-period... As long as I mean of-illusion! That language already be so of the un-talent of me... Do I mean as the lesser-lexicon? Yes... Which is vicious too... My total-deconstruction never did get to creativity-as-language... Or, my "first-period," that did expand on the question of vocabulary so absurdly, and my "second-period," that, eventually, completely did lower that potential of an absurdly explosive language of unreadable... It was always a same-absurd, those two fake-periods, now as some complete-minimalism of language... As long as the "same" retain throughout... The philosopher philosophy and IQ without the question of writing/language, as infinite-regress, so as to create a strange absurdly-extreme contradiction as from Nietzsche/the best-great-philosopher to the philosophy he is to base essentially... As long as I am always first-best in what I write in philosophy... To better me was never necessary... (Those "assumptions," extremely in the way of me, always negated...) Or, that I have to be able to afford my philosophy... I write it as the safety of doing so... Writing billions of Einstein-smart genius-philosophies is an extreme-assumption, not a mild-value... Something had to combine those assumptions as the infinite-regress... Which is famous with my philosophy... The irrational-assumptions rationalized, seeing as my philosophy loves to rationalize... (The rational and IQ always had to contradict the best great philosopher...) And that it is so many bibliographies... (Heidegger...)

The zero-assumption/Einstein a priori/IQ philosophy always had to find a way to annihilate all those assumptions that my philosophy does assume... *The absurd of my philosophy!* Which is absurd/the-absurd-of-my-philosophy... (I can't be an absurd...) The absurd of my philosophy that is absurd... No absurd, nihilism or pessimism ever make it to my philosophy... Or, all three exchanging-in-my-philosophy... (Nihilism is to my philosophy pessimism and absurdism...) That I never differentiated... Meaning, something had to justify that an absurd suddenly does include...

(Naturally...) That the "idiot" to my philosophy always meant the nihilist *just as much* as what he believes to be annihilated... I am an Einstein-smart-philosophy... And that I am the between-rock-and-hard-place is that I am... (The "philosophy-part" never annihilates the optimism...) Eventually, one realizes that the German-philosophy part/philosophy-part doesn't necessarily exclude optimism from itself... The Einstein-combinatoric/IQ/optimism is the optimism-part of the philosophy...

I am sure that Wittgenstein will always be so great to my philosophy as my IQ... The assumption being whether I ever do get to that deconstruction of Dostoyevsky... Forever deconstructing/lagging Wittgenstein is against the original-plan of <u>On the Case of Italic...</u> Wasn't it to be like the rest I deconstruct? Like the rest I write in philosophy? A whole philosophy, that I have ready to write down as the first draft of final draft, *Dostoyevsky/Mozart,* so as to finish writing within the usual/three-month timespan as by simply writing down what I have ready in my head as that first of final draft? (I never should have deconstructed him...) Or something...

The IQ-part infinitely-prioritized... Or, a Wittgenstein, without the philosophy-part, as me, without the philosophy-part... Why am I constantly upping the IQ... That I and Wittgenstein used to score that same Einstein-IQ... As far as I know we now get to a sixteen million-nine-hundred score on the IQ test... (I have to find a way to stop with Wittgenstein...) Gets in the way of my lifegoal... That I search for two Einsteins, not two aliens... The two-professional-philosophers-philosophy, that is Einstein-smart, with all those usual billions of dependencies of my philosophy, must, somehow, revert back to itself... The Einstein-smart-part now being an alien-smart-part... *So as to write something constructive on Wittgenstein instead of a deconstruction on him...* I became a nihilist (a nihilist of my philosophy) ... Which I always hate, due to my strongest possible dislike of every possible nihilism... (I will write a "construction" on Wittgenstein...) Ten years/that-is-a-very-long-period-of-wait... Or something... (I can't simply be past my deconstruction of Wittgenstein...)

As long as it was a "constructive-deconstruction"/constructive-thought-as-deconstruction... (I don't have to regret anything...) And that it is an illusion... (Can be with or without the dream/film...)

Wittgenstein's ideal-aphorism, that I can deconstruct him ad infinitum, in that respect (as the mathematical aphorism), and that is be relative of the best great philosopher and best-aphorism/Nietzsche/best-great-philosophy... A-dream-come-true-would-be... (What is ideal of my philosophy will always be my philosophy...) It is not like Wittgenstein ever actually/absolutely competes with me... That nothing does get to me... As from sixteen bibliographies, to the best great philosopher, to the third-best great philosopher... The sixteen geniuses were my above in the prior-century! Meaning, all three extensions being so below me in the century I am in... What is now a friend/sixteen-bibliographies... (The usual Alzheimer's...) I get to be above the space that I am in, in the century I am in... (What is beyond space?) The round space was always so well defined by Einstein... Not that he ever gets to me beyond that space... (I and my mother...) I never regret being in the century I am in... And that I never related to a racism... (May black people always get to their century...) The usual difference of me and my mother... (I have nothing against the blacks, she always loves them...) That I am so infinitely an enemy of the century I am in probably meant the rest of the century... (A philosophical-nationalist usually means as hate of everything in that century I am in...) There always had to be created a three-difference: the philosopher, blacks and the century I am in... (Must be that something like the IQ of my philosophy compensated the irrational-value...) The philosophy already being so irrational-as-is/a-genius-of-philosophy-*Einstein-smart...* Except, I mean as a philosophy literally Einstein-smart of a genius of philosophy within a genius of philosophy... Literally... (It is a rational Einstein-smart philosophy...) Did the rationalism of the rational, of my philosophy, compensate instead? (*Rational* means *rationalism...*) That I never know how to propose my lack of racism... Must be a between-rock-and-a-hard-place to go with my between-rock-and-a-hard-place... Or, something is already between rock and a hard place... So as to film the visual-language/make-a-theory-out-of-my-philosophy... (Left-wing above philosophy...) Which was never all that possible too... (Left-wing to my philosophy being below philosophy...) The theory is IQ/mathematics, not leftwing... (Is it that everything, to my philosophy, become IQ in the context of theory?) Perhaps (theory is IQ to my philosophy) ... What is the difference of left-wing-theory and IQ to my philosophy? That IQ be the liberal concept of left-wing and right-wing... Doesn't my philosophy usually go with the usual-opinions on extreme? Absolutely...

Everything extreme, to my philosophy, being fascist with or without fascism... The obsession with Wittgenstein's IQ does come to an end at some point... Such a regret to deconstruct him... (Should have been Dostoyevsky *instead* of Wittgenstein...) What developed out of the deconstruction being an obsessive-compulsive disorder... (For next time...) As long as I continue searching for the fifth Einstein, as to how I view the psychology of the whole thing... It is my dream! The day I break off from Wittgenstein... (I guess I love me, Kafka and Bergman without Wittgenstein, and me, Einstein and Bergman...) That Wittgenstein won't ever blend in with the rest of the deconstructions and IQs... (I should probably re-deconstruct the first three deconstructions...) I usually love philosophy and IQ same... Or, the "IQ-part" never got in the way of philosophy... (A very strange-causing tiny text/Tractatus-Logico-Philosophicus, that can't stop to augment my love for IQ...) Which, also, it seems probably correlates with the augmenting IQ...

Bases on potential... Or, what potentially always has the never-ending ideal-potential of me... (Such a shame/had-Wittgenstein-been-a-purely-Continental-philosophy-as-that-Einstein-IQ-he-is...)

So as to augment my genius philosophical-potential or diminish the IQ... Wittgenstein, as the assassin of my philosophy, must lower his augmented IQ... Or something... (I write a philosophy as the two-professional philosophy philosophy, not as the known/that-nobody-will-ever-read-me-as-fact/infinitely-factually...) Some fatal mistake I make, in opening his Tractatus Logico-Philosophicus or deconstructing the text... The never-ending alien philosophy won't be read by an alien... (Do I simply discard with this essay?) Probably, as to how the whole thing probably solves in the long run... What lowers the IQ of billions of alien-philosophies is not thinking this essay/the last-in-the-series-of-alien-essays as possible of thought/simply-never-printing-out-or-finishing-to-write-the-lastinclusion... Either that, or simply throwing out those alien-essays out of my room/trashing-them... Or something... The infinitely overdeveloped-alien-IQ, an assassin of the philosophy-part and everything I wrote prior to that alien period/the-impossible...

That my philosophy always did base on the concept infinite-regress... Something antifoundational had to be intentional totally... Or, as the realism, of the problem-of-my-philosophy, seeing as I always appear so infinitely fascist instead of liberal... The infinite-privacy turned that fascism into liberalism in the century I am in... (And so, something made-sure/a-skepticism, seeing as I never did object to black people...) Or something... A total realist comparison of fascism, so to speak... (An add-on fascist-ant foundationalism, to sway away from the fascist potential of my philosophy, while comparing the two fascisms/fascism-and-ant foundationalism...) That it is a three negation (philosophy, the blacks and the century I am in) could have been mixed! What always helped being that I have nothing to do with the black people... (Or, as to how the racism of the whole thing always went...) Nothing against blacks, as the Jewish-German-French... That part about all those demographics that get the right to exist, finally, in the century I am in, was always the potential-assassin of my philosophy... Or, the infinite privacy, that is the potential-assassin, seeing as I always meant as the *perfect* of thought-out, perfectly, as IQ and the idea of thought-out and perfect perfectly exchanging... (Is it that thought and IQ didn't always perfectly-correlate?) Must be... In my philosophy a simple of rationalism and IQ... (Thought and IQ didn't have to correlate!) I watch *Enemy at the Gates,* last night, with my mother... As long as it be that I see that film again with my mother... (She never cares about film...) Or, so as to see a bad-cinema with her... (Which is mixed...) An entertaining film, as, probably, something completely-original/two-snipers, of the French-cinema as a Hollywood-entertainment... Is it a bad-film?

(Morality and a war-film...) This time as a "shifted-attention" instead of the self-conscious... (Or something...) A good-film... The evil-art-form doesn't care about the war-part of the war-film... (May it be a separate entertainment...) And that it is a French director/an-already-solved-thing-as-is... So as to augment philosophy over IQ... Which should easily solve the IQ of my philosophy as of late... (Except, that between-rock-and-a-hard-place being "itself"...) (The assassin has to shrink...) Writing a philosophy presently scoring sixteen-million-nine-hundred on the IQ test, as all that consumption of avocado, coffee and all that never-ending sleep, relative of my mother infinitely overreading everything on the planet there is to read, was never my intention... (I mean as two professional philosophers, not infinitely zero professional philosophers...) That my mother used to be so well-read, relative of my Einstein IQ... Now being an alien mother to create an alien son out of that Einstein-IQ... The equilibrium-corrupted and the equilibrium-infinitely-corrupted... (Like creating infinite-impossible out of an impossible...) Kind of infinite... (Why make the impossible Einstein-smart genius-philosophy philosophy a genius of philosophy alien-smart?) (Very disturbing...) France made it possible to synthesize Einstein and philosophy while retaining philosophy as the French-left... (What lowers an alien-IQ to an Einstein-IQ?) (Why is Wittgenstein not blending in with the rest of my deconstruction/philosophy and the three Einsteins?) Some really infinitely fatal mistake to make... (Or something...) I finished writing <u>On the Case of Italic</u> ten years ago... (It seems something has to tell Wittgenstein to go to hell...) Infinitely... (Or something...) Something infinitely un-fucked-off... Or something...

The thought-out always had to mean IQ... Or, what is my need for the squared/perfect? Does the idea of perfect imply IQ? Perhaps... Which is as Bergman... Or, I mean specific... And that perfect, as idea, always had the obsessive-potential as art/how-my-philosophy-defines-art... (The vicious/strange...) *Why does my philosophy care what art is at all?* Film and the writers, as the basic definition of art of my philosophy, as Webern... Always some strange-coincidence, that is probably true in any case, seeing as I mean art and science/philosophy as the emphasized science of IQ... (What is art relative of my science-philosophy as IQ?) That the science-part prioritized as IQ, not as science... The IQ will always be that same shared-possible of combining the three crowning achievements of IQ, as the theory/IQ of how all three can retain while combining... (Is it a fallacy to think art as possible of me?) Something antifoundational, in some respects... A mixed-category... The comparison of art to my philosophy being the bad writing... (I don't know how to write, seeing as I can be potential of art...) May Nietzsche always be that art potential of me... It is a potential-assassin of me, its name being art... (Isn't Bergman, always, the only artist, in history, to equilibrate art and an Einstein-IQ in a work of art, to my philosophy?) Truly so... (Like me and Wittgenstein in philosophy...) In some ways... (Philosophy scored one-fifty...) Or, that philosophy be a potential two-hundred anyhow, as the idea of everything/writing-on-everything... (Is everything everything?) The detriment to the IQ was always context/metaphysics... (Is philosophy Einstein-smart with or without the "art-part?")

What does the idea of thought-out relate as? Art and philosophy... Or, that my philosophy always correlated the rational with IQ... (Nietzsche is one of the three great philosophers and sixteen bibliographies as the best great philosopher...) Or, that I naturally complicated him... (There is nothing natural about him...) A philosophy basing on "potential," as the left-wing of liberal as apolitical, can be Nietzschean, not Nietzsche... Something to go with the fact that I do the first left-wing Nietzsche-philosophy in concrete terms... (He had to generalize...) Which was always great... (I become a philosopher so as to evade such stuff as Bergman in film...) That I was to go to a film school... That I would always have to make something like *Persona II* is impossible... I can't compete with something like Bergman... Infinitely as so... (That I became a philosopher was to solve the fact of that primitive/known-jealousy...) Which is irrational/What-changes-with-philosophy... Competing with the greatest genius of philosophy, that is Nietzsche, is just as impossible as making a second/sequel Persona-film... That the generalizing-fact, of my philosophy, of Nietzsche, then finally did solve both as the absolute-idea of happiness of generalizing Nietzsche s philosophy and a bibliography of general... How I think me a genius of philosophy at the same level of Nietzsche... With the help of the French-left to compensate the IQ-part of that genius-philosophy... Something had to compensate that I am a genius of philosophy that is Einstein-smart and a Nietzsche-philosophy Einstein-smart... Does the idea of coincidence finally actually-compensate the whole thing as one?

Perhaps/it-isHeidegger-who-will-always-be-the-best-great-philosophy-of-my-philosophy... And that all be simultaneous... (I write my philosophy so as to prove my Einstein-smart-IQ...) That I love my philosophy is that I be the only philosopher I write... (Where was the low self-esteem as relative of Nietzsche to begin with?) I am generalizing for absolutely no reason at all/I-mean-as-the-analytic-philosophies... (So infinitely mocking an analytic-philosophy will always be vicious...) Is that the next between-the-rock-and-a-hard-place too... I am sure that something like Continental philosophy will never get to my Einstein-IQ... And that being relatively mild as potential: a one-fifty Continental-philosophy IQ, as potentially, and my two-hundred IQ, absolutely... (Must be that I do love Continental philosophy as should be...) Or, the infinitely-complicating, to verge on a for-the-sake-of-itself/for-the-sake-of-being so/style... Relative of what? That my philosophy always did base on that realism too... To me something like a Continental philosophy can complicate for the sake of doing so/as-style... The strange fact of all my philosophy I write... All that Continentally-national philosophy, that I do write, that questions a "half" ... Doesn't all my philosophy, on the other hand, ask whether Continental philosophy gets past its reading-level-of-difficulty as style? Perhaps... (The impossible to read, that is style as that impossible level-of-reading...) The idea being to solve that rock-and-a-hard-place too... (Seeing as I base on the idea of the idiom, it seems...) I should film my philosophy of visual-language that is a film that is a philosophy... Art can include... Which was always the even-measure, as emphasis/science, as de-emphasis/art...

Didn't that always rest on my natural talents? Perhaps/Bergman-as-Wittgenstein, in that respect... Except, Wittgenstein being a philosopher... (Wittgenstein and me...) Except, Wittgenstein always being that uneven-me... I am the perfect-Wittgenstin instead of Wittgenstein! An excessive-Wittgenstein... As long as I do deconstruct the three deconstructions again, or write Relativity of the Half-being of Representation, again... Or, so as to find a way to generalize <u>On the Case of Italic...</u> (That never happened to me before...)

So as to generalize this essay... (Where is the deconstruction to go with the free-association?) Except, the essay serves to generalize so many such free-association constructive-essays as is... (There is nothing to generalize...) (I find it very obsessive-compulsive to be mentioning as that that is so...) Wittgenstein lags ten years... However, that that always annihilated as is... (He never stopped to rhyme with Einstein as Bergman and me, so as to retain the Einstein-smart third-best genius of philosophy...) Still the idea of a charlatan-Jew, of appearance, on that a Jew be a copy-race, as the race without thought, relative of philosophy and thought and the self-hating Jew, all so I mean illusion and a Jew, that the concept of illusion always imply metaphysics with or without a dream/extreme-illusion, so as to combine the actual point of my Wittgenstein... (That my Wittgenstein never gets to the self-hating-Jew as his philosophy...) It is an Einstein-philosophy, Continentally third-best... Or, the self-hating-Jew writing something as pure as one of the relativity-theories by Einstein... (What spoiled as should be?) That it is a third-best great philosophy... (As to some extent a self-hating-Jew...) Which perfected instead... (I mean as the Continental third-best great philosophy...) And so on... (A find...) Or, something I get to so excessively love coincidentally... (I usually don't open such stuff as analytic philosophy to read...) A deconstruction of Wittgenstein always became strange enough... (Must be that I love Wittgenstein's surname...) Something attracts as a *reminder* and *IQ/Einstein*... Used to be three Einsteins... Or, Wittgenstein then infinitely became the fourth Einstein... (Like nothing...) And that something like the worst great philosopher of my philosophy (Bertrand Russell) will, probably, always, eventually, get a "buying"/place-in-my-room... I, probably, will, at some point, in my life, start to read *The Principles of Mathematics*... (Why not read something last-best too?) And that I never did read a philosophy by Russell... (That he so clearly categorizes as the worst will always be the a priori of my philosophy/how-analytic-philosophy finds-itselfin-my-philosophy-with-or-without-the-a-priori-assumption...) Who knows... (Maybe Russell one day becomes Wittgenstein in my philosophy...) Anything is possible... That I so infinitely always mock the former is an a priori judgment/a-priori... (I infinitely mock analytic philosophy...) Or, the idea of analytic philosophy, that I hate enough/infinitely, so as for a priori to assume the role of a posteriori...

So as to assume that nothing changes in the way I do philosophy... *It is an illusion!* Or, what is the illusion? (That it is true...) It will always be the "general-mockery" (that I own the space I am in to mock that space) versus specific potential... In the twenty-first-century becomes same... Or, that I am in the century I am in... (I used to be very specific of mocking...) That it is now be that I mock everything... (What is the sixteen-bibliographies in the century I am in?) Something infinitely above me in the twentieth-century as fact... Or, a simple... What I used to be the infinite-slave of, now as what I infinitely master absolutely... (My philosophy always thought it a clear-difference to absolutely differentiate the two centuries, seeing as my philosophy does think the two centuries completely apart...) What my philosophy is, and that it is a philosophy... (Or, as to what my philosophy isn't...) I don't have to be in service of philosophy to be philosophy... (Or, that it is Einstein-smart is a between-rock-and-a-hard-place...) Nothing changes philosophically... (It will always be that I have to admire something like the absolute-genius of German philosophy absolutely/infinitely...) Something that helps the Serb be an actual-philosophy, while annihilating such potential in the very attempt to up a Serb to the German level of philosophy/a-half... (Never West or East...) A

Yugoslavian-Serb, of German-philosophy origin, without a world-region-difference of any kind, as the Western-Eastern twenty-first-century... (As to how the complex problem of my philosophy always went...)

So as to keep all those same-paragraphs apart... (What is the monotony of this essay?) Must be that I attempt some minimalist Webern-thing, as art, as question of art and my philosophy... Which was always mixed... (Webern, Bergman and Nietzsche...) I find a system to stop lagging Wittgenstein ten years... (He is not the only Einstein of my philosophy...) A subjective...

So as to find a keep... (To hide my philosophy from a thief...) What is my self-love? Infinite... (It would be sufficient that nobody can steal or change my philosophy...) Absolutely... (Becomes paranoid *every time...*) As long as I mean Jewish... Or, as long as such infinite-megalomania never grew fond of something like Wagner... How did my infinite-Wagner-philosophy always instead shrink to a Jewish proportion as Jewish, German and French? As Bergman, Nietzsche and Webern... Writing billions of philosophies, that are the one-philosophy, was always the infinite-danger of my philosophy... (I am not an anti-Semite or an infinite-anti-Semite...) That the appearance always grew in the direction of an infinite-anti-Semitism... Which was always that strange/the-philosophy-is-Jewish-as-IQ and-religion/Jewish... (How does something like *Jewish* and *infinite-anti-Semitism* compare?) As to what the never-ending extreme-difference, as from appearance, to essence, always meant, of my philosophy... And at the Jewish as the three races... (The France, to make possible the Einstein German-philosophy...) The anti-Semitic issue was a problem prior to that infinite-anti-Semitism... Is German philosophy anti-Semitic because of the plain-fact? Perhaps (By German philosophy to suppose philosophy-itself/anti-Semitism...) Philosophy, as the German profession, as the anti-Semitic profession... (That I always had an issue, in that respect...) I am not an anti-Semite, and I am the anti-Semitic profession... (The two had to combine in some way, while retaining the genius-level of German philosophy as the Serb writing German-philosophy...) That it will always be the impossible of my philosophy/philosophy... The Jewish philosophy (Einstein-IQ and Judaism as the best religion of that philosophy) ... How strange was that? Very (the philosophy aspires to the greatest possible genius of philosophy that is Nietzsche...) Is it that my Nietzsche always be so "Judaic," as every Nietzsche after Hitler, that is Judaic...

(Nietzsche already solved it for me...) That the greatest genius of philosophy will always be the Old Testament/Jewish... (The standard-Kaufmann...) The contradiction rested on the IQ/Einstein... (What to do with Einstein-IQ relative of that Nietzsche/Nietzsche...) That Nietzsche already so miraculously gets to the one-fifty IQ, from the clinical-depression/fifty... (Nobody ever hopes of a two-hundred as Nietzsche...) What does solve the whole thing? The subjective...

The location, of the free-association, always mattered... Isn't it, by this time, absolutely absurd what I free associate at all? Possibly... That I am so overwritten... Which was always just as absurd... (The Jewish in the place of Wagner...) I am underwritten... The nothing-of-language, as the zero-invention, means something...

Writing an absurd-essay is always absurd... (So as to find a next deconstructed...) I can't forever be doing a yin yang, of free-association... That the absurd and a yin-yang never made it to my philosophy... Especially the latter... (That I always mock everything *philosophy* outside Germany...) That an absurd was possible as impossible will always be the French-left of the second-best great philosophy/France... Which was impossible... (The French-left being something like Sartre and Derrida...) That it is impossible think my philosophy as nihilism, absurdism or pessimism, all three to my philosophy being nihilist... (The overwritten...) Why I do retain an absurd will always be the category/Wittgenstein... Or, I mean Wittgenstein's absurd... Or, my Wittgenstein was always possible of a specific-absurd... Or, that my Wittgenstein be a specific-absurd... Which was always absurd... (He is specifically absurd to my philosophy...) *What is so specific about a specific-absurd?* I mean a specific-absurd included specifically in Wittgenstein/something-specific... As to what all those billions-of absurd-essays that I write in fact are... (Isolating Wittgenstein's absurd from the early Wittgenstein, so as to analyze that absurd without his laterperiod...) A simple, so to speak... (The absurd, from Wittgenstein's early-period, as a free-association without my deconstruction...) The free-association being from my deconstruction... (A "three" ...) Irony... (Something past my deconstruction of Wittgenstein...) His absurd without his philosophy, as my free-association without my deconstruction... The never-ending excessive-Wittgenstein negated towards <u>On the Case of Italic...</u> Billions of regressive-essays, back to that deconstruction of Wittgenstein... All that never-ending lag, that is an illusion... (A nothing-of-language...) Instead of atheism... (The *nothing* being that self-negation/at-the-deconstruction-ofWittgenstein...) The zero-invention... (Must be something on the question of imagination and the century I am in...) That too... Relative of the Einstein-IQ... (Something psychological...) Imagination is a prerequisite... (There is no genius-IQ without imagination...) Intuition and IQ... (The IQ prerequisite: *I have an issue with writing philosophy in a century that is zero-imagination, seeing as my philosophy can't exist without Einstein...*) Or something... Talent, IQ and imagination, in a century that has nothing to do with all three... (Writing a philosophical-impossible in a century already so impossible of that impossible...) And that something like the concept of something won't ever fix the issue... (An Einstein-smart genius of philosophy that is Judaic-Christian...) The liberal-religion-part being the only thing to simply the problem to an extent... (Which never made me feel better...) Mixing the best religion/Judaism with the idea of liberal-religion never worked all that well... And that Judaism always was the best religion of my philosophy... (I don't mean Judaism and liberal religion...) An extreme, of my philosophy, that will always be that strange "add-on" relative of what I usually love as the IQ-race... Why is a Jew the religion-race of my philosophy? /IQ and religion are very clearly-unrelated... (The unknown of my philosophy...) Must be a right-wing problem, of my left-wing philosophy, that is a left-wing problem (a right-wing philosophy), as with the help of *religion* to add to a left-wing unknown as the right-wing-unknown and unknown/the-unknown-of-my-philosophy... (Isn't the unknown of my philosophy always something like Persona?) (I am not a Trekkie...) (As long as I am always expanding on an illusion-Wagner...) Must be that that fixed the issue... An IQ- and religion-race...

Maybe learn how to write... On how to add creativity to the free-association... (Better something than nothing...)

Doesn't have to be the IQ-kind... Or, adding the average-IQ imagination to my IQ-imagination would always help... When do I go back to my usual/the-deconstruction? Always... Which is vicious/I-never-stopped-to-deconstruct... (So as to get to the end of the deconstruction of Wittgenstein, so as to deconstruct Dostoyevsky next...) Did Wittgenstein, as the deconstructed, end? Wittgenstein, as the third-best great philosophy of the first-best genius of IQ, Dostoyevsky as the potential best writer of my philosophy and one of the best great great minds of my philosophy/second-best... The two geniuses are to combine... Which doesn't make all that much sense... And that both start there, at the primitive-category, so as to combine within a total deconstruction... (As me, Kafka and Bergman...) The deconstruction is the free-association of the absurd... (The unknown...) (That kind of a thing...) I probably expect for the reader to asume the role of the editor... Which is nothing new/my-philosophy... The strangefreedom... Or, something classically left-wing as communist/communist, as liberal of the apolitical... (A recontextualized "same-thing," on whether all left-wing be all left-wing...) Or something... Which never stopped to complicate... That I believe in infinite-freedom will never that I believe in infinite-freedom...

My infinite-freedom will never have the concept/thought (actual proposition on freedom) to think that infinite beyond the primitive/absolute fact of my existence... (Existentially...) I am the freest man that ever existed/infinitely-free, seeing as I am in a century infinitely zero-philosophy... Which never grew fond of such actual "infinite-freedoms" ... (The most private man that ever existed is infinitely free in the century he is in...) (Relative of the communist liberal-leftwing of apolitical as the problem of the three-freedom of my philosophy...) I believe in my philosophy, not in freedom or infinite freedom... (What does an Einstein physics-paper Einstein-smart genius of philosophy have to do with the two freedoms?) Freedom always assumed the role of Einstein... Or the idea of everything that is beautiful, that is Einstein, therefore liberal... (It will never be known what that liberal-value is as liberal...) And that Einstein never prioritized over philosophy... And that philosophy is the essential aim of my philosophy...

I love rhyming Wittgenstein with Einstein... As long as I make a same out of deconstruction, as deconstruction... (Dostoyevsky is always the next thing to deconstruct...) Something like deconstructing The Idiot will probably be way too great/such-an-idea... (Can't wait...) Wittgenstein being way too genius and one of the Einsteins of my philosophy... However, that being way too relative/a-third-best-genius-of-philosophy... (His IQ becomes so same of me...) Why does he lag ten years past my deconstruction of him... A subjective/I-never-should-have-deconstructed-him... As long as Dostoyevsky always be the next deconstruction for me to write... (All five deconstructions...) Me, Kafka, Bergman, Wittgenstein and Dostoyevsky do combine as the deconstruction... (I will always love to deconstruct The Idiot...) The a priori novel, without description/imagination, as the city-without-imagination, of the a priori Christ, etc... (All those categories...) Locating the a priori Christ as a priori/*a priori,* as the Platonic-forms, of the wrong category/Platonic-categories, as the wrong-thinking, all those characters to comprise the protagonist as representation as the wrong representation and that Dostoyevsky's Christ be more real than Christ-himself... (Etc...) *Everything combines into a Christ without Russia of imagination/Russia!* (Something I always appreciate...) My Continental-Dostoyevsky, of philosophy, as Shakespeare, literally that I don't have a favorite writer to rely on... (My philosophy, to love Shakespeare and Dostoyevsky same...) *Hamlet* and *The Idiot* will combine beautifully, as the literal a priori-combinatoric... (Two first-best writers of my philosophy, that will never be first-best or last-best...) And that the a priori-Christ as idea always matched... (What is next?/After The Idiot Hamlet always being the next deconstructed *naturally...*) On that film always be clear of my philosophy as category/best-lists relative of the strange writers-list that never combined... (The first-best Dostoyevsky and Shakespeare, of the second-best Kafka, Boll and Hesse, all so all five meant as *five best writers of my philosophy...*) Such-an-idea... (Naturally...)

Time to read Wittgenstein's late-period... *Can somebody solve it for me?* Will I always be lagging him... (It seems a catastrophe...) Dostoyevsky can't be the next-deconstruction... (What is so extra-significant about Wittgenstein?) Ten years of lagging... I can't stand it anymore... Somebody misrepresents the greatest genius of philosophy... (It is Nietzshe, not Wittgenstein...) That I am an even-fan of philosophy and IQ is not Wittgenstein.../Isn't he the third best genius of philosophy? (Einstein is one of the four Einsteins, relative of the three best great philosophers...) I "garbage" Wittgenstein... Or something... (What does it take?) I can't forever lag him past a philosophy I finish writing ten years ago... (I finish watching *The Girl in the Spider's Web* and Luc Besson's *Anna* last night...) So as to factually garbage Tractatus Logico-

Philosophicus... (With my mother...) I'll watch something feminist or "yummy girly"/Anna, to remind of the actress I ate in The Red Sparrow... (Or something...) (An actually major issue...) *Something can't fuck off as infinite regress, so as to be infinitely fucked off as the infinite regress itself...* (Or something...) An infinite-regress as an infinite obsessive-compulsive-disorder/a-never-ending-idiot... (What I usually don't watch...) (With my mother...) Or something... (I can tolerate it with my mother...) I usually hate infinite-untalented... (Some never-ending-pity, that I take on the two films...) Usually... (That I watch them with my mother...) Pitying, something, all the time, non-stop, is always a bit too excessive... (How of a never-ending-pity does it have to be...) I kill seven-billion people, so as to get to the planet that I am on, so as to, finally, be those five people instead of a seven-billion-world-population... (This time some really *infinite-regress* thing of obsessive-compulsive-disorder as infinite-regress-itself...) (Deconstructing Notes from Underground is impossible...) *Why do I wait to finish reading The Idiot?* Notes from Underground never interprets/is-the-effect-novel of self-conscious without hermeneutics or deconstruction as intention/intentionally... (Dostoyevsky didn't want to write something with thought...) Or, a novella that can't interpret or deconstruct *intentionally...* (Dostoyevsky assumes the role of Christ literally...) As to how I always interpret Notes from Underground... (Emotion is the effect without interpretation or thought/interpretation...) The self-conscious-man-himself... (My attempt to deconstruct that short-novel always being in the past...) I tried so many times... (Something confirmed out of experience too...) That the interpretation be that there is nothing to interpret never helped... And not like Dostoyevsky with me ever becomes greater than Shakespeare or the five writers... (Something would have to will, infinitely, a whole deconstruction, that is interpretation without interpretation...) I love philosophy and IQ! It will always be five writers and that I have nothing to do with a writer... I love Dostoyevsky to-an-extent as the idea/one-of-the-best-great-minds... (A writer has nothing to do with me...) And that Russia always be the greatest genius of mysticism... (What does Russia have to do with philosophy?) Which is doubly as-so... (I am meant to be respecting Russia for mysticism...) That I am Dostoyevsky and Tarkovsky, generally, once Russian was always a double antinomy...

The time it takes to comprehend my philosophy will always be infinite... Nothing makes any sense... That it is Einstein, or harder to read than Hegel, or an Einstein-smart philosophy more difficult to read than Hegel... Etc... Which is an understatement... (The German philosophy didn't have to be Hegel to be so impossible of Einstein or Einstein's IQ...) An infinite-regress... (As long as I always retain the illusion that I am writing something Wagnerart...) The hope always being in that illusion, of the two-illusion/art-and-Wagner... (As far as I know both always infinitely-shrank...) Wagner is a Jewish-philosophy of proportion, art the potential/film-and-writers... (Logic of mathematics as science...) That art probably, in all likeliness, be impossible anyhow... (The Einstein-IQ never changed...)

A philosophy to base on the concept of hope... (That I don't reference *The Principle of Hope...*) Everything mystical has very little meaning with me... And that never read that text... (The potential-appeal apparently being in the left-wing and mystical fusion...) However, that anything left-wing-mystical always had to be something like Persona/Bergman... (The rational, IQ, etc...) Bergman being the greatest possible genius of IQ like me... (What is the

"hope" of my philosophy?) I mean the ideal... Or, the famous fascist-appearance of all my philosophy... (The fascist problem of my philosophy...) *I hope I succeed in philosophy...* Which is, usually, infinitely-fascist instead of liberal as left-wing: *finding two professional philosophers, in sixty-three years from now, that are Einstein-smart...* The fascist-existence of my philosophy, as the fascist-success, of my philosophy... (The two-illusion, of all my philosophy...) (I never read The Principle of Hope/What does a Jew have to do with philosophy to my philosophy?) What does a Jew have to do with philosophy to any philosophy? Nothing at all... (It is an IQ-race, in my case combining with religion as IQ...) Something had to solve the mixed-problem of Jewry in my philosophy... (Completely non-contextual...) Or, I mean an illusion, that I am writing Wagner in philosophy... (It is Jewish since correct-proportion...) And that the IQ-a-religion problem probably already so self-solved... (Two Jewish Einsteins and two Christian Einsteins, as the absolute-religion of my philosophy that is relative as the concept of religion itself in my philosophy/liberal-religion...) Judaism is the vicious concept as the best religion of liberal... (The "Wagnerian" illusion probably being the skepticism of my philosophy...) Hegel can't correlate all four Einsteins as-Hegel... (Wittgenstein is the best possible genius of IQ, not the greatest great philosophy ever written...)

(Now is the time to discontinue the mode...) The illusion being metaphysics... (Not the time to stop with that illusion...) It turns out I have nothing against an illusion... And that the illusion be way too great to me/I-never stopped-to-deconstruct... (A fascist-existence/I-love-never-ending-Alzheimer's...) What is the minimalism of this essay? Irony... (Webern is art...) Probably a Webern-reference... Which is a famous-problem: one of the bibliographies, out of sixteen of them, and art and my philosophy/the-impossible-of-possible... Bergman and Nietzsche are a natural "Continentalism" as Webern... (The absolute-religion...) That I can know how the minimalist, as art, in my philosophy, can make it to my philosophy, and that I mean as mathematics of a logical-science/art already-did-integrate-with-ease... The IQ would always be in the way... (The hope...) (I text the prior-century, with the help of the twenty-first-century technology/a-cellphone...) (That it always be very base to assume that I can idealize metaphysics essentially-of-my-philosophy without asking how my infinitely metaphysical-philosophy does become metaphysics...) (Wittgenstein being the IQ-part as philosophy, so as for Nietzsche to interpret as Heidegger/the-last-great-metaphysician...) That Heidegger, always, in that respect too, became the second-best great philosopher of my philosophy... (What matches foundationally without foundation-as-question...) I fuse all three, with the rest of the bibliography and all-three... (A no-way-out (Nietzsche as the best great philosopher, because of Heidegger's political-participation), that Nietzsche will never be the ideal great-philosophy of my philosophy, had to be sixteen bibliographies and that I don't compete with something like the greatest genius of great philosophy...) The ideal/my-philosophy-always-loved-the-idea-of-perfect... (As the strange of my philosophy...) The concept of perfect will, in my philosophy, always be art, not philosophy... (An irrational-value...) Is it Nietzsche/an-irrationalto-match-Nietzsche-as-an-irrational/my-irrational-and-how-those-two-irrationals-are-to-compare-while-retainingNietzsche's-irrational?

What is the irrational-value of my philosophy? The polarity. (Heidegger is the second-best great philosopher, as the inclusion/*Hegel, Heidegger and Spinoza...*) And that, as the recent-vicinity, Hegel always isolated too... (It is now a vicious concept, as what excludes, as the inclusion, as the three evolutionary-participants of my philosophy...) Hegel is linear... As is Persona always the best film ever made... (How is Persona to relate as the other two evolutions/Heidegger-and-Spinoza?) *Is Persona a film on civilization to my philosophy?* Perhaps: a vicious-circle work of art, that never evolved or progressed/always-appeared-essential-of-the-history-of-art-ashistoryitself/history-itself... (Every either/or of every work of art and every art-movement...) *Truth-is-a-woman...* Or, Nietzsche delimiting something infinitely-essential... Which made sense... (A woman made a woman *anyhow...*) Every progress and regress as irony/art-instead-of-a-woman-and-metaphysics... The-relative... (The art-instead-of-a woman-part will always retain, so as for metaphysics to relativize of left-wing as the woman/become-a-woman...) The linear-history of my philosophy never annihilates! As the principal-value... Which is always so great anyhow... (Nobody can steal or change my philosophy...) What was always so great about my philosophy... The very idea/value meant never thinking the suicide-scenario... (It is never going to be a heart-stroke or suicide...) And that that Bergman-Webern-Nietzsche principal-value be so ideal of my philosophy as ideal/natural... (Something had to compensate the IQ-religion irrational-Jewry of my philosophy...) It is an illusion that I write *Wagner...* Bergman, Webern and Nietzsche, instead of Wagner, so as to make any sense out of the *IQ-religion-Jewry...* (I will film the language that is a film...)

Is Webern what always defines the minimalism of this essay? Perhaps... (Art being the percentage-participant...) So as for Webern to be possible... (The strange...) Or, that my philosophy never knew how to write, I am art and science, IQ being Einstein, and science being against my philosophy/is-empirical... Film and the writers always had to combine as art/I-don't-know-how-to-write and the IQ never matched art *totally...* (Film didn't have to compensate the "writing-part" ...) The language-philosophy, that will never know how to write, that is metaphysics, aesthetics and logic... (A philosophy of language as the three branches of philosophy...) Maybe as logic... Which was always vicious/I-mean-Continental-logic... (What is so *language-philosophy* about my philosophy?) That I was never good at language... In any way... (Perhaps as hermeneutics, as to how I see the whole thing...) The three-branch philosophy, hermeneutically to get to a philosophy of language, so as to be a language-philosophy as hermeneutics... That my deconstruction was never a deconstruction, and that all my philosophy synthesize/that-I-wrote-the-one philosophy... (It is a philosophy of language...)

So as to homage Webern's symphony... Or something... Or anything his-best... (His absolutely-atonal quartet, symphony or all those absolutely-atonal coral masterpieces...) I can't deconstruct him... That my first-period did think him as the major-reference/something-to-think... (So as to finish watching *Ryan's Daughter* with my mother, last night...) My mother probably wasn't necessary... Not this time... That that Lean-film probably be one of the only Lean films I can watch... Except, I know the film fully/did-see-the-film-so-many-times... (The actual-location *Lean...*) I never deconstruct such a thing... (Something would have to be worthy of me...) (What is the strange deconstruction I would write?) A percentage-participant will never be something like David Lean... And that my primary-bibliography be above that lesser-percentage... Or, sixteen-bibliographies...

I know how to read and write Continental-logic... So as to learn how to write first-order logic... Or, that I never learn how to write Analytic-logic... (Writing philosophy has to become a bore at some point...) *Why am I capable of writing billions of philosophies?* That it will always be the one philosophy I write... (Germany is Webern, not Wagner...) A Jewish-measure, as Webern... That the two Jewish "half's" (IQ and religion) will always be so vague... (Something had to write a clarification-of-thoughts/Wittgenstein...) Webern always being one of the sixteen geniuses... (The total-will, of *perfect,* had to strangely-match...) As art... Or, that art always be the irony of my philosophy... (A strange aspiration to Bergman...) That I am write a Bergman-philosophy...

A philosophy excluding of art, so as to include Bergman, so as to generalize the art-problem to begin with/make-mathematics, science and logic out of Bergman... (That it was always a strange three-relation...) (So as to watch Harold Becker's *Mercury Rising,* with my mother, last night...) She can watch the film, while I like anything with an autistic-child in it...

(Except, that being relative...) I love a "mild-autism"/Einstein... (So as to devise an absolutely-atonal system, that Webern did devise...) What is the point... Or, he did invent an absolute-system... And that the idea of perfect always go with art... (I don't mean philosophy and perfect...) As was the idea of a system already is vicious prior to the idea of a perfect... (A system-of-philosophy is Nietzsche/a-contradiction...) (That I always, *infinitely,* be above everything...) Which is not some primitive-desire, that I have... (Something naturally becomes that-concept *naturally...*) So as to be above space and the planet inside-that-space... (Infinitely...)

That I always be so strong on invention... Which is imagination/IQ, so as to know that I mean the IQ-imagination... (The rest being the lesser creative-possible...) What shares in my imagination-category? That I invent a whole new way to think philosophy or a system of philosophy... As to how my IQ always did get to the idea of imagination-ingeneral *first...* (Invention...) *The relative...* The total-will of my philosophy... (That I never minded talent too...) And who likes to be untalented? (The talent-part was always vicious...) *What do I care what becomes the same level of talent in my philosophy as IQ?* That philosophy to me never be above IQ... Or, do I really, in actual fact, like philosophy, so as to always, infinitely, praise Germany above everything? (A strange-relation of my philosophy...)

That I will always, infinitely, be mocking something like analytic-philosophy... (*Why?*) Isn't my philosophy Einstein-smart... (What is so Continental about my philosophy?) I probably mean an infinite-mockery of something like Russell... Which as just as relative... (The IQ-part/logic is the IQ-part/logic...) Do I mean an analytic continental philosophy? Is that what the between-rock-and-a-hard-place is? Or do I mean an impossible Continental philosophy? I never know how to define that in-between, seeing as it does always become an in-between... Or, it is a between-rock-and-a-hard-place... (As long as I don't mean *perfect* in philosophy...) The irrational-value may as well assume the role of the best great philosopher... Except, that such a thing never did make it to the irrational/imperfect as is... Nietzsche, as the coincidence first-best-great-philosophy... And that the vicious mean of Continental philosophy/philosophy... (What is so between-rock-and-a-hard-place about my philosophy?) The immediate appearance, that will always get to the essence instead... (I watch *United 93* with my mother, last night...) This time a strange-masterpiece, past the end of everything/a-film-made-in-the-century-devoid-of-everything... (My mother wasn't all that necessary...) As far as I know my favorite thriller-film as well... (As long as I watch it with my mother as the "apolitical-context" ...) Something way too expertly made as the ingenious-creation of technical-feat... And that the a-politic always match... (A docudrama...) Nothing better for me... As is my mother always fond of such apolitical-stuff, to base on politics, while retaining the political-potential... (The perspective-film, that is the

"airplane," within a docudrama so as to conclude anything or everything/*9-/-1-1...*) A masterpiece... Everyone, to participate, in a political event politically-or-apolitically, as the subtle-jazz the event-itself... (The greatest conspiracy in history, that was never all that good at hiding anything/*the-obvious...*) A chaos event, as the chaos conspiracy, subtly so, done in a bad-way... (So as to apply Clint Eastwood to 9/11...)

I did finish doing my philosophical masterpieces... (That I am so realist with everything I write in philosophy, that everything has to be the set-standard, will always be the obsessive-compulsive disorder...) I have to like everything I write in philosophy... (The doubly absurd...) Or is it the one absurd? Possibly: I write the "one-philosophy" ... The masterpiece will, always, be that one philosophy... (The illusion of substandard, that is this essay, being the absurd...) It seems I always loved creating irony... (Something against my philosophy, that is an absurdism, so as to create of-specific-absurd/Wittgenstein...) An irrational-value, as Nietzsche, that is irrational: the coincidental first best Nietzsche, of generalized-bibliography/*nothing-coincidental* and that I never mean to compete with German philosophy/a-coincidental-Nietzsche... Something had to solve in the three-fold sense/I-was-to-become-a-film director/make-a-sequel-to-Persona... (What so changes in the fact of being a philosopher instead?) Nothing at all... (As far as I know Bergman being just as infinitely-standard as Nietzsche...) Finishing to watch *Summer with Monika* last night, with my mother... (This time with or without my mother/the-mixed-potential...) The most perfect possible genius makes the "okay-cinema" ... (An okay film, as the first film to strip a woman...) Which was, then always, an okay thing to watch... Something as revolution, Sweden/mild, and the revolutionary/stripping-that-woman-naked... (Apparently/as-far-as-I-know...) And that it is a film of Fifties, as the Sweden and idea-of-revolution within something mild/Sweden... (That I, recently, finish watching Gary Goddard's *Masters of the Universe*...) Or, always so "fixing" the great first Star Wars trilogy first Star Wars film... (Such a chaos...) I can like it as the idea of *chaos theory*/anything-too-mathematical... (I will like the mathematician in the first *Jurassic Park* film...) Seeing as I never like that film all that much, and do love the first CGI special effects ever created... (That Spielberg to me always be *Raiders of the Lost Ark*...) An all-in-all untalented-Jew, in every-sense, so as to make that one film, finally... (That I am the natural-pity, on everything, will always be the century I am in...) Or, something to go with the specific mockery, that so generalizes in the century I am in... (I mock everything in the century I am in...) The problem of a nihilist/appearance of all my philosophy... What would always presuppose the absolute-nihilist, instead the infinite optimist, in the century I am in... (The Diogenes and the nihilist will always self-correlate, in my philosophy...) (*I mock-everything...*) (That it always be the greatest great mind that ever existed, as the greatest Einstein-IQ in history/ever...) My infinite-optimism proposed as the natural-problem of all my philosophy as philosophy, not as nihilism or the-Diogenes...

So a to make an analytic-philosophy-logic out of continental philosophy while retaining that it is a continental philosophy... The mathematician is a "logical-scientist," as to how that ever becomes possible at all... (The lesser "doing-part" of my philosophy...) Annihilating ethics and philosophy... Which never meant without-philosophy...

(Ethics is always the least favorite branch...) A "graphic" ... That it always be an irrational-value, as appearance, in an ultra-rational philosophy... The irrational being an illusion: Nietzsche, as that irrational and illusion (against Nietzsche) ... *Why do I annihilate the irrational?* Why else? /It is known why... (Something always had to generalize him as the coincidental-limit and that I never do intend on competing with German philosophy...) *Rationally!* That I am so German, in every way, is that I am a Serb/"a-German-Serb" ... I can be infinitely-German all I want... That it will always, in the end, end on what is an inferior race to philosophy and me... (My fifteen-percent two blood/German-Jewish blood flows through a man infinitely characteristic of Germany in every way...) Or, what makes me feel better, every time, is the lesser-percentage-blood that is two superior races... And that I outdo me as Germany... (The Jewish-part subsided...) As is that other lesser-percentage to me just as superior as the German lesser-part of that blood... (That there is no France to complete the total-issue is that I outdo all three superior races as Germany/the-superior-race...) And that France to me never gets to the actual superiority/Germany-and-Jewry... Why do I become French-left to begin with? So as to synthesize the two superior races, while retaining talent and IQ... (*Always:* so as to make possible the impossible that is impossible...) It is not like there will ever be something actually liberal or left-wing about me... (Something right-wing-left-wing...) That IQ and talent to me always be above left-wing... Or, I love philosophy and IQ, not the left-wing... (To me my philosophy, like any, already being so liberal in a fascist century to make my philosophy left-wing with or without the left-wing...) *Philosophy is leftwing!* Or, that, to my philosophy, philosophy be the profession that never based on the idea of polarity as is...The reader makes language out of the minimalism or edits the essay so as to do so... That it will always be that strange communist-liberal-left-wing-apolitical difference of unfinished-creation/the-reader-freedom as the intended communism that won't ever be getting to itself all-that-much... *It is a liberal-philosophy of apolitical...* The potential always meant something like my interpretation of Heidegger/my/any/left-wing-Heidegger, that he inspired all those French-left *Being-and-Times...* (Or something...) That it is true... That he means a second-best-great-philosophy limit will always be so literal/a-limit... (A "three"...) His philosophy being so apart-form-Hitler, so as for the man to join those bad-politics, so as for the difference, in my case, to, always, build on the extreme-difference instead/anactual-left-wing-philosophy-written-by-a-Hitler-advocate... (I am probably too ethically conscientious...) And that ethics, as philosophy, infinitely have nothing to do with me... As is the whole thing probably too moralizing/didactic... That my philosophy sometimes always becomes too anti-philosophical as ethics... Or, is that limit what emphasizes, naturally, my hate for philosophical-ethics? Perhaps... That being why Heidegger will always be the Nietzsche-limit... And that I mean something completely Jewish relative of Heidegger/not-just-Semitic... (I don't mean of non-anti-Semitic-philosophy, that is to delimit Heidegger due to bad political-participation...) The French-left doesn't mean to annihilate the "Jewish-part/IQ" ... (I am a heterosexual...) What annihilates as French left, as French-left, will always be that French-left... (That it always be a very violent/graphic philosophy as Germany and Jewry...) The French-left existed... Or, what rationalizes the irrational-value/Germany-and-Jewry-in-a German-philosophy... (That I am a Nietzschean will always be the rational-contradiction/rationalism...) A rational, left-wing, objective-reality philosophy as rationalism and the-rational... The analytic-philosophy-logic being the vicious/a-part-of-the-basic-vicious-circle-that-is-my-philosophy-that-is-philosophy... (To better my philosophy was never all that possible...) Those lesser philosophies, that I write, will always be just-as-great... (It is the one philosophy...) That there is nothing above me, inside or outside of the space that I am inside... (I love a double-triple confirmation...) Such a skepticism... Which was always natural too... (I build on the Nietzchean-contradiction as the Nietzschean...)

What to name the probability-theory? Something to correlate the total-theory of my philosophy/that-myphilosophy-always-infinitely-prioritizes-theory-over-the-rest? That Nietzsche always be the vicious concept as the best great philosophy as the vicious part of my philosophy? That I write my philosophy to prove my IQ and up my talent in philosophy to a German/genius level of philosophy simultaneously? That a probability becomes the theory anyhow? That such a thing never emphasizes the unfinished-creation/reader-freedom over the

IQ/theory part as Einstein? That Einstein and philosophy always be the point? Instead of left-wing? As the liberal left-wing of apolitical instead of left-wing/communism? (So as to rationalize the whole thing...) That I always move in the direction of something absolutely and infinitely antithetical... (That I have nothing to do with poetry or *potential*...) My philosophy, that is a film-poem/Persona, necessarily in need of a rationalization and annihilation of that rationalization... (To write a philosophy, that is Persona, was possible as the only Einstein-smart artist...) Maybe... Or, the impossible-anyhow... (The will being against art...) (An irrational-value...) How art, my philosophy and Bergman are to correlate "totally" ... That it always be the composite-argument... A mathematical philosophy, that is logic and science, as to how that had to ask what art and Bergman are to my philosophy... (What is the physicspaper/my-philosophy?) A representation... Meaning, so as to love science's IQ without science... And that Bergman always became that IQ of science too... And that Bergman's major talent won't ever relate to philosophy... (The philosophical was never genius as philosophy or the philosophical...) And that I can be art as the three-IQ relation/mathematics, science and logic... (And so on...) Always the total vicious-relation... (I watch Scorsese's *The Irishman,* last night, with my mother...) (As long as it is with my mother...) That I never related to realism-in-art... Absolutely... And as long as it isn't with my mother... (She can't watch realism too...) The least-favorite in art, so to speak... (Nothing worse...) We probably did get to the end of the film-duration because of the two Scorcese films we do watch: *Taxi Driver* and *The King of Comedy* (the lyrical-pond of Bernard Hermann's last film-score and something "complex" as comedy/funny on-comedy/nothing-too-realist-as-realism...) The problem with The Irishman being the film's length... Which is my issue/I-usually-hate-a-film-that-lasts-more-than-two-hours... (Or, art to my philosophy...) Everything has to be dry... (The film wasn't all that bad...) The antithetical/"dry" Italies become the film's duration... (And that one of the best films ever made to me/8 ½ wasn't ever all that warm...) It is a vicious question: liking Francis Ford Coppola over Martin Scorcese... (Which was always vicious...)

The mathematical-problem... Bergman did achieve making Einstein-smart works of art that are the greatest possible genius of film and greatest possible genius of art... (Why Bergman always becomes so essential in mention...) I am not the first to attempt a similar-thing/the-impossible... And that Wittgenstein always based on the similarity too... (Philosophy's IQ being higher by some thirty difference IQ score/one-fifty-instead-of-one-twenty...) Except, art being the one-twenty-limit... Doesn't philosophy usually score one-fifty? Perhaps... (On how to aggregate one-twenty and one-fifty...) As to why Bergman and Wittgenstein correlated... (Wittgenstein is the third best genius of great philosophy...) That he always reminds of me will always move in Bergman's direction... (That my philosophy never has a literal-relation...) Which had an infinite-confirmation/skepticism, just in case, to go with it... What is the meaning of sixteen-bibliographies? A skepticism, as irony, as Nietzsche... (I watch Michael Mann's *Miami Vice,* last night, with my mother...) As long as it is with my mother... That I can always appreciate the film's irony (the Eighties and Twenties) ... Which is never me suddenly switching to Mann's-film... (That I have nothing to do with a nihilism...) His cinema never appealed with my philosophy naturally... And that the idea of ultra-real never solved the problem of real or extra-real... (Anything in the real sense of real, real or extra-real, doesn't go with my philosophy as real...) Or, what is his handheld-camera-style? Real or two-negative/nihilist-of-real... And that that transposition to the twenties meant the label/never-liking-something-made-in-that-infinitely-untalented-andinfinitely-unintelligent-century... The-racist... (Which is nothing new...) I can't like something from a century that always thinks me the most retarded man in history, on the planet, that ever existed, non-stop... I am infinitely congenitally retarded to that century that I am in... (Naming the infinite-rhetoric, for what it is, was always a bit too dumb for me/a-retarded-feeling...) Infinitely/perhaps... Why emphasize what doesn't exist/a-rhetoric... Must be a category/that-philosophy-is-the-rhetorical-profession-that-reminds-of-a-rhetoric... (Or something...) Or, I don't know how to differentiate the two rhetorics... (Or something...) I love any form of rhetoric, seeing as I infinitely die in the name of my philosophy/a-philosophy... (Wasn't my philosophy always the problem of synthesizing the innocent-of-Einstein with the innocent-of-philosophy?) Absolutely... Nietzsche will always be that strange first-best great-philosophy place/Being-and-Time-will-always-be-the-best-great-philosophy-of-my-philosophy... That Nietzsche always had to build on irrational-values, so as to be first-best at all... Something had to be irrational as irrational, so as to be Nietzsche, so as to think the-irrational and Nietzsche and the irrational... (All that infinitetheory has very little to do with Nietzsche...) A complex argument/proposition, on Nietzsche... (I so infinitely go up in standard as the sixteen-bibliographies...) (Nobody ever competes with Nietzsche and I don't directly relate to the best great philosopher...) On-comedy... (I-made-sure...) An infinitely-self-loving-man instead of the low-selfesteem... (That I become a philosopher instead of a film-director...) Or, nothing solved in the question of the difference/Bergman-and-Nietzsche... That I do solve the issue is that I had to infinitely know that I solved it... (Or something...) (Comedy-central...) (It seems really fed up with it...) It took too much time... Writing something antithetical would always have to base on illusion... (On how to realistically propose the concept of illusion in my philosophy...) Writing a dream always being so funny/unnatural... Meaning, I don't know how to write... The rest being potential/as-mathematics, science and logic/possible... An irrational-value... Writing a Persona being naturally-impossible... The concept of nothing is always the appearance... (An ascetic-language essay, to appear atheist as the dream...) So as to measure the art-percentage of my philosophy... That I don't know how to write and I write the mathematically science-logic philosophy that is Nietzsche... (The impossible...) It is not like my philosophy, as the Einstein-IQ, can ever actually propose against art absolutely... And that the antithetical never becomes possible as the difference... (Nothing-antithetical-or-different, as to what the basic motto of all my philosophy will always be...) I have write a dream, so as to know that the essay naturally connects to the rest of my philosophy like the rest of my philosophy...

The reader solves the essay... (As by approaching it as problem-solving...) Which is beautiful/*matches*... Something to go with the Einstein-IQ of a genius Continental-philosophy, this time as the puzzle/IQ-test... (Irony...) Making the IQ-test out of an Einstein-IQ... A mathematical-problem, that is an entire *IQ-test,* as the one IQ-question... (Nothing changes with my philosophy as-should-be...) That it will always be the style over substance/Einstein-IQ, as appearance/illusion, *really,* so as to achieve that substance over style while retaining style-over-substance... Nietzsche is the first-best... The infinite-*complex/structure*... (The idea-essay, *cells,* of simplified-language of minimalism, as the analytic-philosophy/clarity, of atomic-propositions, is the absolute of this essay...) Bergman/the dream, as the antithetical-*analytic-philosophy*... (As far as I know never too-impossible...) And that Wittgenstein always did get to that third-best-great-philosophy place in my philosophy... As was something like the absolute mockery of Russell always relative/liking-the-logical/IQ-part... It is not like I will ever get to actually/absolutely mock that last-best great philosopher of my philosophy... (It was always a mild-thing...) Professional and common man philosophy, as comparison (Russell) and the IQ-part of his professional-philosophy that will always be so natural of me/anything-IQ-of-appeal-as-is... (Isn't every type of logic already so natural of me?) I love logic, mathematics and science... That I am the never-ending-German, always, as the infinite-standard of my philosophy, will always be that my Einstein-IQ never matched me... (What to name the Continental Analytic-philosophy?) A Continental-philosophy? (The most idiotic man that ever existed to me/Russell will always be logic/something-Ilike-as-is...) (Nietzsche has very little to do with Russell...) The suspension-points *mean-something*... I named it representation, as the unfinished-creation, as the unfinished creation of my philosophy and communism and my polarity... (Isn't communism atheist?) Or, the irony, that I always had to structure...

Made up of cells... (Does the essay go with something like my "first-period?") This time without "rotoscoping?" (I love my one-philosophy...) Or, something to affirm that I don't think a "period" as possible/the-fake-period... (I never depart from the beautiful-equation as the ultra-Continental-philosophy...) It was always the same between rock-and-a-hard-place... A comparison, of two opposites, to synthesize both... That it will always be the unknown of my philosophy... Whether the Continental Analytic-philosophy is Continental or Continental-Analytic... (To go with the mild left-wing, of my philosophy, that s liberal as apolitical...) Or, the two "unknowns," and whether the unknown of the left-wing be unknown/the-unknown as-category... (My dream...) So as to be able to equilibrate philosophy and the Einstein-IQ in a philosophy that is a genius of philosophy... (How do I always infinitely love my philosophy?) *The structural...* Suspension-points as the brackets... The cells base as the carriers and comparison/ "the-carriers" ... (Motifs without art...) So to speak... (Representation...) The logical-clarity/analytic philosophy, as the continental-philosophy/the-impossible-interpretation... (My-usual...) So as to comprehend the essay, to comprehend all the suspension-points and brackets, to synthesize all the suspension-points/brackets, to comprehend them, to comprehend the total-relation... (All the suspension-points and brackets and the essay...) *Isn't it harder to read than Hegel?* Absolutely... Which goes with the intention of all my philosophy I write... (Always the impossible...) An Einstein-smart philosophy, that is more challenging than Hegel, and so what that can mean as the genius-philosophy that is Einstein-smart... (Hegel or an extra-Hegel were, both, highly/factually unnecessary...) The mystery of all my philosophy... (An ideal irony and realism/the-ideal, as the shrinking/Jewish philosophy that appears of-Wagner/Hegel...) Except, Hegel never became the principal-illusion of all my philosophy... Or, on that

Hegel to me never correlated Wagner/isn't-a-fascist-idealism... (Or something...) That the mystery rest on the extra Hegel instead of Hegel, not Hegel... (Must be that I did search for a fascist-realism to the whole thing...) Or, the most private man that ever existed, to go with his infinitely-private philosophy... The extra-Hegel probably being the skepticism/just-in-case... (That it will always be that the black man get to his century...) Or, the century I so infinitely hate, that is the century-of-blacks... (Had to be an extra-Hegel, just in case...) That something like my race gets to its century too... (That I am so anti-Serbian and against the blacks will always be that I am liberal/have nothing-to-do-with-racism...) I approve of that black man in that century getting to his century... (It is that I have nothing to do with what I have no relation to...) The famous "neutral-liberalism" of my philosophy... (My natural talents never match...) Philosophy never has relation to that century... And that man grows retarded in that century... (Man is not as smart as he used to be...) The century being the wrong autistic-category... (A simplified-language does the idea with inventing a prolegomenon...) Which never helps/I-wrote-a-prolegomenon-to-my-philosophy-in the-past... (The illusion holds...) A double-illusion... Meaning, there is no reason to write a simple-introduction and that that simple-way to disclose my philosophy to the common-man is against the basic rule of my philosophy/against-the-logic... (The prolegomenon had to get to this essay, so as to connect to the rest I write...) ("Iachieve-much-in-philosophy" ...) As long as I am in that century that I am in... (The infinitely-ideal never mattered...) The philosophy being real instead... Or, the infinitely-ideal of me, not the infinitely-fascist as ideal... Something to go with the recent obsessive-compulsive disorder that grew out of me doing a deconstruction of Wittgenstein... Do I mean to match my favorite great philosopher *to some extent*... The-subjective... Or, I like my philosophy... Or, I like my philosophy... (I naturally infinitely fall in love with Wittgenstein's early period...) Which was self-evident... (How overpraised does he become in that deconstruction...) *The appearance/Wittgenstein-as-thefirst-best-great-philosophy-of-first-best-genius-IQ...* Which is absurd/untrue... (I always praise me just as much...) Or, my philosophy, that infinitely loves my philosophy... (That I love sixteen-geniuses will always be relative/below-my-love-for-me...) Which is *thought* too/natural/something-to-go-with-the-thought-out-genius-IQ-ofmy-philosophy... (I used to be a never-ending slave of all sixteen...) All sixteen friends now being the never-ending slave of me... (I love the idea of perfect/symmetry...) To the point of science... (Or something...) Nietzsche isn't the natural choice...

(Highly-unnecessary...) Why do I progress my philosophy with a third fake-period? Maybe since that meant the first two periods/that-it-is-the-one-philosophy... Or, that it will never reach-thatpoint/become-too-much-to-write-a philosophy... (Wagner will always be an illusion...) The autistic-category/Einstein... Or, a Jewish philosophy, as measure... (IQ and religion, and that that solve as the Jewish-measure-philosophy...) That Hegel never included in the problem-of-ideal/*ideal*... (I probably mean as the left-wing-Hegel, with or without communism-as-the-left-wing difference, and an excessive-Hegel...) Or, does too much of something go with what it is? (Does too much of Hegel go with Hegel?) I love the Wittgensteinian-tautology... Or, Wittgenstein's first period, that is too ideal of my philosophy as IQ... (Probably as to why he gets to be the illusion of a first-best genius of great philosophy of my philosophy...) Looks too real... Or, my Continental Wittgenstein (the *tautology* and *absurd* exchanging of the literal same-language/same) ... And that that had the ideal-value of indeterminate as is... The Continental Analytic philosophy that is Continental or Continental-Analytic... (Smart never existed to me...) My never-ending-pride... (Becoming or being a philosopher was always the impossible-task...) Which was always great... (What, instead, becomes the challenge of being a philosopher at all...) Philosophy ends prior to me, not at me... (Having that constant challenge/impossible, as the "second-simultaneity," of all my philosophy, always helped with something like the *Serbian-philosopher* and that philosophy, by the time I start to write my first philosophy, has no reason to exist at all...) As the century I am in and that philosophy already did achieve all the genius of philosophy there is to write before me... (I write philosophy since I am the most self-loving-man in history...) What, in the end, always helped the whole thing is that I love my philosophy... (It is not like I can actually love philosophy...) Art and science were never the measure for me... The IQ-part of science made science a priority over art, all so that meant art instead of science/shrinking-the-empirical-potential/hating-that-science-is-empirical... That science included in mathematics and logic... Meaning, loving philosophy, purely, will never be possible to begin with... (What helped is the general unknown/absolute-unknown...) How I do successfully mock something like those antithetical analytic philosophies will always be that something cheated the *perfect*-of-the-relation/science-and-art as by taking into account that metaphysics (philosophy) is everything/*can*-be-science-and-art... (Who ever said that the concept of everything means science and art being-combined?) I am a self-loving-philosopher and do love my philosophy over the rest of philosophy... (I would always aspire to great fame/becoming-a-great-philosopher-even, had I not began my first philosophy in that century that hates philosophy most of all...) (The will being to reach that stage/a-two-paragraph mention-in-Wikipedia...) Wikipedia one day includes my name, someplace, as an actual-article of limit/two paragraphs... (Is that like becoming a great philosopher in the context of philosophy in the century I am in/that-I-am so-hated-by-the-century-I-am-in?)So as to locate one more genius of IQ...

Wittgenstein is always spoiled by his "half-potential" ... (Too bad...) There was never a great philosopher matching of my philosophy and my IQ... I always had to propose three-of-them, so as to generalize, so as to end a bibliography on sixteen-bibliographies as the difference (great philosophers and the rest) ... And that that always had to be as philosophy, art, science, etc... It is sixteen geniuses, not three great philosophers... (More or less...) (What to do with the absurd of *Tractatus Logico-Philosophicus?*)

Bad-writing, as intention, differentiates that I don't know how to write anyhow... (That it is a postmodern style, always mismatching of the modern philosophy that writes it, will always be that I don't know how to write as should be/intentionally...) I have nothing to do with postmodernism! Or, that the postmodern be possible as the liberal religion... Which is impossible/*religion*... (The postmodernism of my philosophy being possible on the grounds of same-difference/whether-modernism-and-postmodernism-differentiated...) The Wittgenstein-Heidegger deconstruction being my philosophy... (As for example...) Something invented by postmodernism, that I regress to modernism... Which is my philosophy itself and whether I mean a Wittgenstein-Heidegger-Derrida deconstruction instead/"the-deconstruction" ... (An idea-Derrida and that deconstruction never invent itself...) Deconstruction never existed to begin with... Or, Derrida, as the "thetically-instead" ... (*Was there ever a next inspired/next deconstruction past Derrida?*) The movement being so postmodern without invention/postmodernism... (The-typical...) Whether, therefore, something like hermeneutics/religion be atheist... Which always, doubly, correlated with the deconstructive-problem of deconstruction/what-can-never-be-invented-to-begin-with... (Doesn't something like deconstruction to my philosophy always go with something like Persona?) Prior to itself... (Persona invents the deconstruction prior to Derrida becoming a philosopher...) Which was always as to how my philosophy thought Derrida or my deconstruction... (Kurosawa, Fellini and Bergman...) (Something like film invented the movement itself some twenty to thirty years prior to deconstruction/*Of-Grammatology* at *Rashomon*...) (Or, that my philosophy never did differentiate modernism from postmodernism as-hermeneutics...) Why something like an essential text on the essential/direct proposition on deconstruction, that is On the Case of Italic, always included that third/*mystical* part too... (It is not mystical...) The simple structure: Wittgenstein and Heidegger, then the forms/*absurd,* then Derrida... (The postmodern language of this essay always had to base on the modern as the modern philosophy writing something postmodern-style...) On how to define the language of my philosophy... (Isn't it postmodern?) *And too many bibliographies too...* Which is cynical... (The proposition-and-proof style/form is logic...) Or, The Einstein-smart philosophy, that is logical/analytic-philosophy, that is continental... (I never know how to think the difference, seeing as Einstein and analytic philosophy to me never relate to philosophy...)

What is so mystical about this essay... (The illusion...) Or, the total relation-to-illusion... And that the concept of bad-writing never had a clear way out... (It is mixed...) (As long as I am deconstructing without the deconstructed...) The rest being the next-imagination... Or, that I do become too much with or without the necessary-every-next imagination of imagination... (This time was a necessity...) Or, that I, usually, don't need to expand on the imagination-part of my brain... (The imagination always being the IQ/IQ...) And that my unimaginative philosophy needed to be without creativity as infinite-regress... I write too much, and don't concentrate on the success of my philosophy enough... (Or, I am trying to lower the potential of Wagner, not outdo him...) That the imagination, of this essay, always be the strange-part/an-excessive-evolution-in-my-philosophy... (I direct the film, that is this essay, of visual language...) The right-wing and imagination usually being two less-things for me to think... (Am I writing on the right-wing-inclusion and the specific-imagination of my philosophy?) Perhaps... That I was always the threeleft-wing and Einstein-IQ/*imagination*... Einstein was never possible without the concept/question of imagination... (Which is known to everyone....) And that the left-wing always divide... (Left-wing, the-liberal and the-apolitical...) (Something like Tractatus Logico-Philosophicus...) A visual-language-philosophy... Except, in my case that being the two first-best-philosophy... (Wittgenstein was always a major influence as his first-period...) (I make a film, as by writing a philosophy...) A Continental-Wittgenstein... The complicating... (That my philosophy already included something like analytic-philosophy as the Einstein-IQ...) Or, the Einstein-IQ and analytic philosophy correlated/hadpotential-at-all... (What does that "create?") That Continental philosophy never had that Einstein IQ potential to begin with... (This time as the illusion...) The difference/deconstructing-without-deconstructed... Which is the illusion... (The French-left of analytic-philosophy...) Two things solve the IQ-problem of my philosophy... As to how I always got to the greatest level of genius of philosophy/Germany... (It wasn't just-the-French-left...) The basic problem of my philosophy that I write... (Einstein-IQ and an un-talent...) I, obviously, never do get to like the latter... (Who likes to be untalented?) As far as I know the style of my philosophy never changed... (The illusion being the substance...) So as to resume to deconstruct Wittgenstein... (I can't forever structure an illusion that I am deconstructing...) On the other hand, that never being an issue... (It will always be same whether there is a deconstructed or an illusion-deconstruction...) I resume to deconstruct him since I do love to deconstruct... (All those deconstructions I wrote...) Or, it is much easier to deconstruct... I deconstructed so many times prior to Wittgenstein... (Why complicate?) Past my first deconstruction I wrote (that was an intended-effect of simultaneous (learning how to deconstruct and deconstructing)) was always the three-months it takes to get to the end of writing a deconstruction... (The three-intention, of my first deconstruction (deconstructing, learning how to do so and inventing a new deconstruction without doing so), was never in the way in those latter two (Kafka and Bergman) deconstructions...) Why do I complicate?

The language, that is for filming... (On how to add imagination to my philosophy...) Which is vicious... My philosophy never suffers from a lack of imagination... That I probably mean irony/adding-the-opposite-category... Or something... An essay on a realist comparison of imagination/creativity and the imagination of all my philosophy/IQ... (As long as I don't foul up the literal-continuity/the-one-philosophy...) I love a challenge... Which is ancient/I-always-wrote-the-impossible-infinitely-impossible... Something always had to shrink the infinitely-ideal, to get to the ideal, to shrink to a Jewish-relation as the French of German... The extreme-tendency of my philosophy always being something like the infinitely-ideal as idea... (The illusion of all my philosophy I write...) A never-ending-*ideal,* that is Jewish-instead, so as to compare a realism of Germany, Jewry and France and that all three races combine as German while retaining the *Jewish*... And that that always had the analytic-philosophy problem to go with the excessive/unreal France of French-left... (So as to complicate...) Which was always more like making doubly-sure... (France and analytic-philosophy...) Einstein, analytic philosophy and Continental philosophy as France... (The point being Continental philosophy and Einstein...) (Seeing as why exactly/especially France...) Something, to make the impossible possible, could have been anything/something... (I double the problem for the sake of a *lame/anything...*) That I direct France to analytic-philosophy... To complicate is to simplify... (A "mixed philosophy" ...) Or, *philosophy...* Meaning, Germany... (Meaning, may Jewry complicate Germany...) (Had Wittgenstein been German-philosophy absolutely...) Nothing does become the best great philosophy of my philosophy... (Nietzsche will never be my IQ, Wittgenstein being my IQ without my genius philosophical level in philosophy...) Generalizing the best great philosophies of my philosophy always made sense... (My Einstein-IQ probably being why I became a philosopher to begin with...) Writing something that proves my IQ... Which was always the impossible task... (Nothing simplified me omitting what it would take to become a physicist or a mathematician...) *Is it much easier to write an Einstein-smart philosophy or get a degree in mathematics?* Perhaps writing the never-ending-IQ philosophy... (Is it that hard to find a way to make the impossible into a possible?) The French-left always being so philosophically second-best as the first-best left-wing... And that analytic-philosophy be the last-best philosophy all in all... (Worked out beautifully...) (The total-cardio (Germany, *Einstein-IQ,* France and analytic philosophy) probably never gets to be as tough as me going back to high school, to qualify for a mathematics-degree, so as to get a degree in mathematics...) And that it is an unnatural/*absurd* self-taught-man was always the twenty-first-century and two professional-philosophers... (The self-taught-man-part always annihilated...) An Einstein-smart two-professional-philosophers philosophy... In the century I am in intended for two-of-them tome... (Or, a philosophy intended for zero professional-philosophers and common-men...) That it is two professional philosophers and zero common-man-readers was always a coincidence... (Wittgenstein appeals as my IQ...) (Kind-of-okay...) Expanding the IQ-imagination to creativity... *Very original...* From Jewish to Christian-art/art... Which serves beautifully: IQ and art always compared as the Jewish and Christian... (In my philosophy...) Or, something as the Jewish-Christian relation of my philosophy... That my philosophy always goes with that view... (*Christ-is-art...*) That Christ never did get to IQ... Not to my philosophy... And that that be what my philosophy goes with... (Something like Dostoyevsky competes as the great-mind...) Or, the two great minds that I always cite as the greatest in history (Einstein and Dostoyevsky) are always IQ and art... (Do I name me the greatest great mind above both?) That Einstein was to me always greater than Dostoyevsky... Which is the two "separate-comparisons" ... (*The best genius of IQ and the best great mind...*) As to what the nature of my philosophy is as the idea of a great-thinker as well... (All three, in my philosophy, divide...) IQ, great-mind and great-thinker... It is to me not the same language... (That Dostoyevsky always be one of the best writers of my philosophy, as that I don't have a favorite writer...) Naturally (he never got to be above IQ) ... (*All very relative...*) I am so infinitely tough to comprehend as the "irony" ... (A never-ending-Hegel and Hegel, again...) IQ and Hegel... And that that IQ already couldn't think itself within a German-philosophy... (Wasn't it always a *three?) Isn't Tractatus Logico-Philosophicus to my philosophy an absurd-text?* Why do I lag something, past deconstruction, that is "absurd?" Why lag anything past ending a deconstruction? (Excessive is subjective as Nietzsche...) Is it on-Nietzsche? (As far as I know Wittgenstein rhymes with Einstein, so as to be me and Bergman...) *And that it is three great philosophers and sixteen bibliographies...* (Wittgenstein is third- and first-best...) (I, this time, subjectify the objective-deconstruction...) Or something... (A subjective to compare Nietzsche and me to a subjective as the two "subjective" ...) Must be that I will never deconstruct Nietzche, seeing as my Nietzsche doesn't deconstruct... (Seeing a shrink...) Expanding a whole deconstruction, that I write, to a subjective-lag, so as to compare Nietzsche and me as the subjective of Nietzsche... (Something usually very-unreal...) Which is great... (That being so original about the whole thing too/*What do I have to do with* unreal?...) That my philosophy always appears so French-left will always be at the level of appearance... The style/*French*, doubling on itself... Maybe as the style that is appearance... Or, the style didn't have to double... (Is it the style of my philosophy that makes an Einstein smart German philosophy possible as substance?) That my philosophy always be too "stylistic/French" to be German... Or, why Einstein-IQ... The point being that that be skeptical/analytic-philosophy... The unnatural-potential (an Einstein-and-philosophy philosophy) naturalized... (The tautological-philosophy I always write...) (No great philosopher becomes the best great-philosopher of my philosophy because of the continental/analytic difference...) That I write a Tractatus Logico-Philosophicus that is a first-best genius of IQ as the first-best genius of philosophy will always be that my philosophy be the best great philosophy of my philosophy... Which is natural too... (Everything is below my philosophy...) That all sixteen geniuses be so below... (Isn't that how I also solve that issue with Nietzsche/the-best great-philosopher?) That it is always an awkward/coincidental relation will always be due to sixteen-bibliographies...

That is how... (Symmetry...)

As long as I never stop to deconstruct... Such an imagination! A deconstruction without the deconstructed... And that deconstructing Dostoyevsky will always make me feel better... *Doing a deconstruction of* The Idiot... *What could be better?* The awkward (a deconstruction without a deconstructed) ... ("Three" was never a problem for me...) As art... And that Dostoyevsky always be one of the best great minds of my philosophy... (Something like The Idiot already does have the whole philosophy ready in my mind...) A deconstruction that will take three months to complete... (To go with my deconstruction of Kafka and Bergman...) That my total-deconstruction does have the two intellectual-connectives... And that I did change my deconstruction in the name of the missing *deconstructed...* (It wasn't all that tough to do...) Without a deconstructed is a different deconstruction... (The same always remains that same...) Or, the philosophy of "same" ... (The hypersensitive...) The Jewish-measure, as the illusion/Wagner... That that solve the IQ-religion Jewish-problem of my philosophy... Or, why I do the Jewish-measure as idea to begin with... (It is meant to be IQ!) That I never know how to think the best religion of my philosophy and that it is the best religion of my philosophy... (Something in the way...) Is it that I think science as religion? That there is no difference to me between the two? Perhaps/absolutely... The four Einstein-IQs (Einstein included) meant science or religion... (Something-like...) Or, I don't believe in science... (Thought is to me symmetry, not Nietzsche...) *How is that possible?* (I should have been that greatest possible Heidegger-fan without the rest...) As long as my coincidental-relation-to-Nietzsche does make sense... (It is a coincidence...) That Heidegger isn't first-best is that no great philosopher becomes the first-best of my philosophy... (How Heidegger never does get to that first-bestplace/my-philosophy-will-always-be-the-first-best-great-philosophy-of-my-philosophy...) Philosophy is just as below as the rest/sixteen-bibliographies... Which is perfect/I-am-in-the-century-I-am-in... (There is nothing in that century that I am in, or philosophy in that century, or anything in that century...) That I so love that the black man gets to his century will always be the lesser-potential... *Didn't that always so perfectly-divide?* I have nothing to do with racism or the blacks... (Absolutely...) (I write a tautology...) Or, the absurd... Which is absurd/has-nothing-to do-with-my-philosophy... (So as to find something my first-best two-genius philosophy/just-as-great...) So far nothing measures up to my usual-standard throughout... (Something that is sure to ban Wittgenstein from my philosophy...) And that I did deconstruct me... (A sequel...) (A very tough thing to write...) Something on top of the usual impossible of my philosophy... How impossible does writing my philosophy become now?

Wittgenstein was the ideal thing to deconstruct the IQ-match/the-deconstruction-and-deconstructed... Now that I am sure that I did get to the end of that deconstruction him is whether I finish to read The Idiot any time soon... The deconstruction without the deconstructed and deconstruction without deconstructed are a tautology, though... When do I stop to write billions of tautologies? Never! They are always infinitely too-ideal-of-me... And that they be language/the-absurd... How that always translated is the logic, as analytic-philosophy, of the same language/absurd/hermeneutics and language matching/a-categorical-absurd... (The imagination-IQ, Einstein and German philosophy as tautology...) There is nothing absurd about my philosophy... (That it is a tautology will always be absurd instead!) The philosophy is not "everything"... Or, the infinitely-ideal *value*... Everything matching without doing an *everything* without metaphysics... (My deconstruction, that is my first-period/the trilogy...) And that Relativity of the Half-being of Representation synthesize with the deconstruction/isn't-a-deconstruction-intentionally... (Science doesn't deconstruct...) Or something... Or, a deconstruction without the deconstructed too... (To go with this essay, that literally goes with the rest of my philosophy...) (The "charlatan Wittgenstein"...) Wittgenstein is made to rhyme with Einstein... (To my philosophy...) Why do Interpret his Tractatus Logico-Philosophicus as the "substantial-thing"/an-*Einstein-smart*-to-come-with-substance-as-the-"stylephilosophy"... As long as <u>On the Case of Italic</u> didn't spoil him/stayed-with-my-interpretation-of-him... (He can't be on the self-hating-Jew...) Not to my philosophy... (Nothing too self-referential...) Or, that his philosophy, as idea/copy, to resemble all sorts of things, while homaging, never did get to that stage of a proposition on a Jew, thought and philosophy... (That he meant a Continental-potential, not an actual-thing/something-actuallyphilosophy-as-Germany-without-the-French-left-of-absurd...) As far as I know... (My Continental potential with him will always delimit as France of French-left, as the German-philosophy...) Or, he is never at the level of German philosophy... (That he wrote in German will always be what is German about his philosophy below the German standard of the best philosophy there is historically and world-regionally/totally as West and East...)

The language-philosophy... (Wasn't that always "specific?") Or, what is so philosophy-of-language about a philosophy that has nothing to do with language, doesn't know how to write, and doesn't exceed in a study of language/isn't-linguistical... That I mean hermeneutics... (Probably...) And that the "writing-part" probably already somehow provides for an absurd... (I don't base the question on "simple"...) Hermeneutics, without art-of-writing, as the specific/metaphysics, aesthetics and logic... And that the philosophy be against philosophy/Einsteinsmart/impossible... (*That is how...*) (I watch *The Seventh Seal,* last night...)

With my mother... Which is always an intermediary-value... (The film goes with my mother *more*...) That the best film-director of my philosophy always did do that expressionist-period of "right-wing" first... Which, to me, never made all that much sense/to-me-can'tcompare-to-his-Sixties/"minimalist"-period-as-extreme-difference... (I can like the film as the gloomy cinematography of irony/gloomy-theme...) And that he is my favorite director... (Relative of that expressionist period as the two films I can like from that period/The-Seventh-Seal-and-*The-Magician*...) (It is not like Bergman ever gest to left-wing in-actual-fact...) I like The Seventh Seal... Or, that I can like the film... (That his next period to me so extremely outdoes the prior-one will always be something the perfected-greatest—dream-ever-made-, that he is one of the Einsteins of my philosophy, etc...) Something the-rest *categorically*... (I usually don't categorize The Seventh Seal for the greatest possible genius of IQ/the-film-is-usually-with-me-relatively-"lesser-intelligence"-ascompared-to-something-like-Persona...) (I don't agree that The Seventh Seal easily-dates as the film of simple that is too simple/simple...) (For the sake of imagination...) Mentioning Bergman, again, relative of my deconstruction of him I wrote some ten years ago... (For the sake of literality...)

(How do I shoot my philosophy?) In black-and-white without the "gloomy?" Possibly... (Isn't the first rule of all art-house that it be in black-and-white?) It is not like film naturally became an art-form... (The banality needed the black-and-white cinematography...) So as to up film to the level of imagination/the-writer, or lower the potential/apparent-lack-of-imagination... In my case the theory I go with... (I never did need to film a film in black-and-white...) What does the dream do in the meantime? Make the film director a writer... (The film-theory I always go with...) The conundrum of my philosophy defining film as black-and-white... (The gloomy black-and-white being just as superfluous...) I have nothing to do with depression/I-am-an-optimist... And to homage Bergman was just as trivial... His famous-label, with me, always being mixed or impossible... (The Kafkaesque and Bergmanesque were to me always that Bergman outdo Kafka's IQ as the "depression" ...) The clinical-depression writer and the genius IQ film-director, as to how I always related to both... And that the man himself/Kafka always meant clinicaldepression... (I don't categorize Bergman for a clinical-depression-work-of-art...) That my interpretation of Bergman never did get to the usual/universal label of him... (Einstein-IQ instead of clinical-depression...) That he be just optimist as me... Or, something Einstein-smart being the extreme-difference... (How can something an Einstein genius of IQ be clinical-depression?) Which, obviously, doubled doubly... From a fifty IQ-score, to a two-hundred IQ-score... (I mean doubly-impossible...) The literality/the-literal of that fact... (It is a fact to my philosophy...) A study in psychology... Or something... (*Studying-psychiatry*...) Kafka gets to one-twenty as the impossible... (How I always differentiated from the usual-label...) Bergman's art being optimist... Which is always an extreme difference... (I watch the famous *Friends* TV-show last night with my mother...) (As long as it is with her...) She finds the series very-talented... I, though, naturally, being the German-Jewish-French-man... Naturally... Nothing too capable of a sense of humors, as the potential/*Jewish*... (Always very awkward...) The German-philosopher, to comprehend something-funny on the planet... Which was always strange... (My mother being German-Jewish Spanish...) How does the difference compare? / Something makes her comprehend the comedy... (That it is true...) I can relatively-like my mother... That she has nothing to do with philosophy or IQ... Meaning, I strongly-dislike my mother... (My relative-love for her always being in the racial-fact without question of talent or IQ...) I love that she is talent too... (The classical-music composer and a philosopher...) We get to preserve each other...

As to what that mutual-love, between, always existed as... (Primitive, though very useful...) I don't find her all that genius... And that she be infinitely-atypical of philosophy or IQ... (The actually-genius member of my family always being my father...) The greatest genius of flute-playing/my-father... (Talent-wise...) How that always categorized... To me probably just as talented as me in philosophy, to compare something like my Einstein-IQ to something like my uncle's IQ... Which is potential... (The above-average IQ of my uncle never gets to my Einstein limit/comparison...)

The ancient family-comparisons of me... (Something like my genius-level had to be my IQ-level...) Which will always be the impossible-challenge/why-I-exist... (Something originally-*negative,* very great as the challenge of the genius-level...) What makes me so infinitely-untalented will always be how I become the greatest possible genius there is... (My genius-level never did compare to my Einstein-IQ...)

The deconstruction of The Idiot is going to be so great to do... On the other hand, this essay being a deconstruction... (No deconstructed was ever above my deconstruction...) My deconstruction being my philosophy... (The clinically-depressed language being the illusion/an-illusion...) As the logical-series/a-set... (I am trying to be funny...) Or, what appears like an attempt at a difference without difference/differentiating-my-philosophy-itself... Which would always annihilate the very philosophy itself... That I delay the deconstruction of The Idiot some ten years isn't bad for me... What will that deconstruction always be? The rest of my deconstructions... Meaning, my total-philosophy... (Me, Kafka, Bergman and Wittgenstein...) It is not like one of my deconstructions ever exceeded above the rest... The difference would be less appreciated than usual/impossible... And that my philosophy doesn't categorize a writer as the best/first-best... And isn't Dostoyevsky to me the second-best great mind? Absolutely... (I love IQ, not a great mind...) That a great mind and a great thinker to me always swayed away from a great IQ! (I don't regret anything...) Dostoyevsky and Shakespeare *literally,* as Einstein/the-first-best-great-mind-of-myphilosophy, relative of something like Bergman, as Nietzsche, Kafka, Heidegger, etc... (Relatively...) Naturally... (Dostoyesvky always becomes "included" ...) That I am a philosopher can't ever go with Dostoyevsky as the finallimit/above-everything... Which is natural/I-am-a-philosopher... (Germany being above the planet that I am on...) Germany is above everything...

I don't mind... Adding creativity to the IQ-imagination, as by extending my usual imagination to the right part of the brain, is original... (The deconstruction never suffered...) And that a deconstructed never becomes greater than the deconstruction... That Dostoyevsky has to wait ten years always shrank to the inconsequential-proportion... (The right-hemisphere, extending to my left-brain/IQ...) (I never exceeded in writing before...) Irony... And that never change the original-idea of the one-philosophy/the-one-philosophy... (It is an illusion that I suddenly learn how to write...) (The aim being combining Dostoyevsky and Shakespeare...) Which is the illusion... (A writing, that is both writers, as an illusion...) (Difference as an illusion...) Which is the obvious-context, as to what I try to structure as the "same" ... *Difference,* the difference-as-an-illusion, Derrida and my deconstruction... *Does the concept of difference retain in my deconstruction?* The ideal/positive-negative deconstruction, that is my philosophy/ant deconstructive... Isn't my deconstruction on left-wing/the-left-wing-itself... And that being as the specific category/a-three-left-wing, as irony/ on-technology/ a-general-metaphor-on-the-problem-of-philosophy-in-thecentury-I-am-in... (That there is no philosophy in the century I am in...) Which is a metaphor as comparison as from negative, technology, to know the positive, philosophy... (*Language...*) Something to regret... The very language appearing-technologically as the primitive-idea... Or, that I have no regrets... (Primitive idea as language...) The idea of a "positive-negative" being obvious/primitive, as to what I mean... (I am not trying to structure an irony...) That it is technology as the negative-technology of positive-philosophy is *primitive-technology... What is the technology?* (It is not a realism, that I try to "represent" ...) To me technology naturally/infinitely being below philosophy, seeing as politics and science have very little relation to me... That I find it so great that a black man gets to his century will always be that I be so atypical of a black man... (My zero-racism not being sufficient to like the century I am in as the two extreme opposites of philosophy and technology thinking irony as possible...) Which never hurt thought wise... (It is not a contradiction...) I live in a fascist/potentially-totalitarian century... What is against imagination, IQ and all that is beautiful in this world, is fascist... Which is fascist... (Whether the synthesized-planet ever takes place as fascist is inconsequential...) The "first-fascism" ("political-science") is fascist/potentially-gets-to-the-secondfascism/fascist-media-of-absolute-control-as-the-synthesized-planet-of-fascism... Something without-talent-or-IQ... Meaning, a zero-creativity already so fascist as the zero-imagination as potential... (Thought is liberal as imagination/liberal...) Or, what is liberal? Thought... Meaning, the thoughtless century being so fascist as the zerothought century that is fascist... (It is a fascist century since zero-thought, since a zero-imagination century that is zero-thinking...)

It hurts me to know what the century I am in amounts to... On the other hand, that being that I never do get a degree in philosophy... It is my favorite century! (That there will never be anything essential about the self-taught-man of my philosophy...) How I stay at that level of infinite-happiness... Two professional philosophers make that happiness possible... The infinitely-happy, that is my degree of happiness as relative of my philosophy (that I so infinitely love my philosophy), in the century I am in to remain that-happy as happy... Never-ending-happiness... (I don't go to an infinite clinical-depression from that infinite-happiness...) That being so great as IQ too... I never got to fifty as from two-hundred... That I always be at that Einstein IQ-level, as by staying there/at-Einstein... (One of my basic prides/why-I-exist...) The clinical depression would mean something doubly clinically-depressing of my EinsteinIQ... (I have nothing to do with the right-hemisphere in the brain...) Wasn't my brain's right-part always the skepticism/that-I-don't-believe-in-science-or-a-brain-science? Absolutely... Especially those brain sciences, that now so assume the absolute-role of absolute... (*It is a mystery...*) Seeing as I always go with the IQ-theories of psychology that claim that it is necessary to think the necessity (tabula rasa, imagination and idea) ... (It was never possible to isolate the right-hemisphere from the IQ-part in the brain/left-hemisphere...) Not to me/the-psychologytheories-I-go-with... (The nature of thought...) Or, something is liberal, so as to be thought, so as to mean imagination/the-liberal/possible... (A fascist to me being a never-ending idiot with or without the liberal-polarity of the liberal...) (*I'll call the elevator infinite number of times...*) Something to go with Einstein... (*As long as it is creative,* as to how Einstein would always think a genius of IQ...) A genius IQ without creativity is no genius IQ!

Why is my philosophy so "skeptical?" To get to this skeptical essay... (It was truly great to deconstruct something *my-IQ...*) And that I never deconstructed a great philosopher before... Or, on how that counts/I-am-to-me-the greatest-great-philosopher... (I mean the famous-great-philosophers...) Which probably rests on the potential self hating/Einstein-smart philosopher, as to how I think me the best great philosopher... Which was never all that true too... That I love my philosophy above everything on the planet, all-in-all, is the self-loving-philosopher! (I don't mean an untalented philosophy that is Einstein-smart, I mean a genius of philosophy at the same level of Einstein's IQ...) I mean the greatest genius of great philosophy, that is Einstein-smart... (As long as I do get to that philosophy genius-level that is Germany...) (That-happy...) Which will always be the happiest man in history... I never minded my infinite-happiness at all... The ideal-brain, that is Einstein-smart and Germany/German-genius-of-philosophy... (My self-love never does get to a limit/a-*delimited...*) (How does something like Nietzsche become the best great philosopher of my philosophy?) As coincidence... I infinitely hate a clinical depression/must-be-that-I-mean-asphilosophy/great-philosophy/as-far-as-great-philosophy-goes... Or, Nietzsche to me being the "optimist philosopher" ... Or something... My mathematical genius being so infinitely optimist! Meaning-and hermeneutics/hermeneutics...

That I get to be so hermeneutical is Nietzsche... (The-strange...) My philosophy being purely-hermeneutical... (One more necessary-Nietzsche-contradiction, for the sake of me and Nietzsche...) Don't I read Nietzsche as contradictory-necessity? Absolutely... That Nietzsche to my philosophy exists for the sake of *contradiction...* As the subjective/What is the limit of Nietzche's total-contradiction? The rest being natural/the-coincidental-*first-best* great-philosopher... The absolute-hermeneutics were never a mistake to think absolutely... (It is a limit...) Nietzsche and Heidegger... Or, Heidegger always being the most natural great philosophy to think as the best-great philosophy-of-my-philosophy... *How ideal does something like Being and Time get to be of my philosophy?* All those Jewish participants of my philosophy, that never allowed for Heidegger to outdo Nietzsche... (Had my philosophy been Semitic without the Jewish...) Mathematics... (The unrelated-to-Nietzsche...) On the other hand... What always had to be the mixed-potential... (A deconstruction relates to Nietzsche without hermeneutics...) When do I take a rest from writing philosophy? After Covid-19... (My philosophy, that is always the writing- and sending part...) Once I resume with the professional philosophy, that I send my philosophy too after the pandemic... (As long as there never becomes something-too-excessive about my one-philosophy...) That I can write philosophy ad infinitum... *It will never be a transcended-Jewry...* The monotony being so literal... (Like writing billions of similar/same things...) That I would, one day, reach a Wagner-limit never takes place as the known... (I take a break from the writing-part as by selecting something to read...) My philosophy, always so high on being written without the well-read... That it is true/I-am-intentionally-never-all-that-well-read... Which is the very essence of my philosophy... However, that I have to read something/to-some-extent... (I don't mean literally-illiterate as the never-ending genius of IQ...) That I am a philosopher, with or without the cynical-value of my philosophy/IQ... (The cynical never matched my philosophy to begin with...) I am trying to retain philosophy and IQ in a philosophy, not both in an IQ... (It is my goal to become a genius-philosopher at the same level of Germany as genius...) The cynical was always ambivalent/one-of-the-unknowns-of-my-philosophy... (A reading-list has to equilibrate to some extent...) I can't literally write a physics-paper that is philosophy... (So as to read while I wait/they-are-saying-that-the-virusis-nearing-an-end/*almost-there...*) And that I did select what appears to be okay-to-read/okay-of-me, relative of all that, that is me, that I read... I read everything there is to read... Now being the-question... (What is a second-best list of writers and philosophers to read...) Seeing as I did read everything related to my philosophy, as philosophy and the-writers... All three (philosophy, writing and film-directing) did come to an end ten years ago... (I saw everything and read everything...) Now being the primitive-task/selecting-second-best-lists... (Something like Hegel, Kant, Spinoza and Leibniz...) What holds as idea, as a natural extension of the best of my philosophy... (Something like

Russell isn't potential of me...) Not yet...

The IQ always matched... However, that the genius-level of philosophy never does get to me... (I don't regret deconstructing without a deconstructed ten years because of the illusion of the whole thing...) Or, that it be a deconstruction with a deconstructed *anyhow*... That it is some ten-year-lag, of Wittgenstein, is what is so bad about the whole thing... Or, there is nothing bad at all/it-is-an-anti-deconstructive-illusion-to-go-with-the-lag... Nothing changed... Presently a free-association as the lag... (Mixes...) (Once or twice...) To see-the-language never changed...

That the theory of language of my philosophy go with Wittgenstein as my theory of him... (That one part literally stays-same/never-changes...)

(Time to read Wittgenstein's second-period...) So as to stop to write philosophy, for the time being... (Getting to the end of The Idiot is the major-aim...) Which is inconsequential... (I never stopped to deconstruct...) And, again, that my deconstruction be the one-philosophy too... (What is going to to be so great about a deconstruction of Dostoyevsky?) That there be nothing above my philosophy... (I deconstructed billions of times...) (The atheism/*nothing* of those anti-deconstructive deconstructions always being the illusion...) *I am not an atheist...* (Nietzsche is the best great philosopher relative of great philosophy...) Moving on to the next/*system* Wittgenstein is allowed... (That a system-of-philosophy be against me *insofar...*) Nietzsche being contextually the first-best... (Sixteen bibliographies...)

The extension-category... There is nothing all that great about Dostoyevsky to my philosophy... *Isn't he Shakespeare to my philosophy?* Absolutely... That my philosophy never names a writer the first-best... There will never be anything tragic about the ten-year-delay... Dostoyevsky being relatively-inconsequential and my philosophy being above everything/the-greatest-thing-on-the-planet... (I was below those sixteen bibliographies in the prior century...) The illusion/metaphysics of my philosophy probably being the natural reason, as to why

Dostoyevsky can't be Dostoyevsky... Philosophy/Germany to me being metaphysics... (Why mention Dostoyevsky?) That it is the "contextual/*German*" Dostoyevsky will always be that he is one of those sixteen friends I always mention relative of my philosophy... Something as Continental philosophy, of Germany, as Walter Kaufmann, of Einstein, as Wittgenstein, Bergman and me/Einstein, etc... My Dostoyevsky always being some "infinitely-composite-thing" ... Has no end as the extension... (He is literally Shakespeare...) And so on...

(Naturally...) Must be that I think my philosophy as "science" ... And that no writer ever got to my philosophy, therefore... And that I mean IQ instead of a great mind... Relative of philosophy (*metaphysics*) ... Meaning, Germany... (What does Germany have to do with Russia prior to Dostoyevsky?) And that the total-challenge base on that simple/philosophy-and-genius-IQ-in-a-genius-philosophy-at-the-same-level-of-philosophical-genius-that-isGermany/the-only-philosophy-there-ever-was-on-the-planet... Dostoyevsky becomes naturally relativelyinconsequential/I-have-nothing-to-do-with-Dostoyevsky... Why I exist will always be Germany/I-am-a-philosopher... (A two-professional-philosophers-philosophy has very little to do with him...) And that it is a physics paper intended for two professional philosophers... (It is good to do an introduction/preface from that deconstruction that I will do on Dostoyevsky ahead of time...) A preface, from that deconstruction, that is to deconstruct him... (What is this essay/*a-preface* and that deconstruction of him...) (That my philosophy eternally never-changes is a system of philosophy...) That Nietzsche always, naturally, require the justification/why-he-is-the-best-great-philosopher-ofmy-philosophy...

A very metaphysical-language... Probably as to how I synthesize that it is a language-philosophy as aesthetics and logic... The philosophy of language being very hermeneutical... Which becomes generally traditional, so as to relate to metaphysics as tradition/that-metaphysics-be-the-traditional-profession-of-philosophy... Or something... (I never know how to solve the language-philosophy-part of my philosophy...) And that my philosophy be a philosophy of language *entirely...* (A total mystery...) As the unknown of my philosophy... (Or something...) Something to go with the general-*unknown* of my philosophy/it-is-not-like-my-philosophy-ever-knows-what-its-unknown-is... Wasn't it always an unknown-*unknown...* The unknown being what the unknown is to begin with... (Left-wing, the-liberal, the-apolitical and a-left-wing-center-polarity-as-left-wing...) All four being left-wing... *What is the left-wing of my philosophy?* (Below every-next-paragraph being every next paragraph above...) Do I mean picture-thought as a visual-language to reference Wittgenstein's first-period and how I do read Tractatus Logico-Philosophicus? Absolutely... I always wrote doubly-*first-best* Tractatus Logico-Philosophicus, so to speak... A visual-language philosophy, to go with the picture-thought of it, to go with my Tractatus Logico-Philosophicus... The language theory being something like structural, without belief-in-language, so as to compare structuralism and poststructuralism, so as to achieve a post-structural style relative of a completely structural/theist philosophy that can't go with its style... Which was absurd... (My philosophy doesn't believe in language...) As structuralism always impossible... The style does match... Or, that the style never-match... And that that absurd be out of place... (My philosophy has nothing to do with an absurd...) And so on... What always had to be absolutely structural, while equilibrating both movements, while absolutely making an equilibrium out of both... (Always the composite argument...) Something already complicated by Wittgenstein and that never was a clear a difference between structuralism and post-structuralism... *My philosophy is liberal-religion...*

The post-structural freedom will always be structural... (So as to name Wittgenstein "psychology"...) What was that part, always? That my Wittgenstein be his Continental potential... Which is nothing strange (I am always the Continental-nationalist...) How that correlated, as me, as him, as his Continental-potential, will always be the self undermining-text, as to how I interpret Tractatus Logico-Philosophicus... (The picture-thought-part would have to self-undermine...) Or, the visual language, of that text, that can't be post-structural, that is to inspire poststructuralism, as the principle of picture-thinking in that period of Wittgenstein, as psychology of the visual language and picture-thought... All three include to my philosophy... (Clearly defined in <u>On the Case of Italic...</u>) Something like Tractatus Logico-Philosophicus inspires Derrida/deconstruction... As to how the structural-text of early-Wittgenstein assumes the post-structural potential with-me... As by assuming the "structural-role"/positive*Mihajlo-Bugarinovic...* (I mean as the self-conscious, that is to create the self-conscious-language, as my structural deconstruction that is my structural-philosophy and that structuralism be potential of post-structuralism, as to how the liberal-religion of the whole thing is to retain as "post-structural" ...) The difference is the differance itself... (Something deconstruction-without-deconstruction...) How I always simplify the problem of my structural deconstruction... (Being and Time is the best great philosophy of my deconstruction and my philosophy...) Which is nothing new/logical... (Nietzsche is coincidentally-the-best-great-philosopher...) Or, that I base on perfect as thought/the-infinitely-thought-out... (I mean rationally...) Not as an *irrational* as Nietzsche as the-irrational... (The relation will always be as-far-as-great-philosophy-goes and as-far-as-the-bibliography-goes...) Nietzsche, as the coincidence, as the best great philosophy/Being-and-Time, as far as great philosophy goes and as the sixteen bibliographies... (I am not comparing my irrational with Nietzsche's irrational as the-irrational: the irony of my philosophy...) *It will always be-clear...* Philosophy will never be a priority... Which is absurd... (*How can an ultra-German philosophy be a general bibliography inclusive of philosophy?*) That it is irony... (Probably...) So as to correlate the impossible-Einstein with the impossible-bibliography/that-philosophy-is-below-philosophy... (That is how...)

(When do I read Derrida?) That I never did get to the end of his Of Grammatology... (He is one of the French-left participants of my philosophy...) That my deconstruction be completely-unrelated... Which was never a reasonable justification... (Has to do with the unreal-deconstruction/that-a-deconstruction-never-invents-itself...) Or, nobody invented a deconstruction... (Not yet...) And that I always do finish reading what my philosophy *is*... (I am at the potential of my philosophy just-now/recently...) That I used to read the absolute-genius of my philosophy... Which came to an end... (Derrida can always be the next interest/reading...) Mainly due to the French-left-idea of my philosophy... French-left never gets past the idea of idea in my philosophy, as to why... (As what intends on simplifying the impossible/philosophy-and-Einstein-in-a-philosophy...) And that both French-left philosophers of my philosophy be *idea,* in my philosophy, as is... (I have nothing to do with communism...) The analytic philosophy-part was always the irony/*strange*... (Why make a Continental-potential out of something infinitely Continentally-nationalist?) Since there is nothing all that Continental, at all, about an Einstein-smart-philosophy...

(The Continental can't correlate as the greatest genius-IQ magnitude...) On how to make infinite-un-talent a never-ending genius... (The-irrational never intended as the irrational...) Or, the ultra-rational philosophy, that is Nietzsche as philosophy and philosophy... (Wittgenstein being too uneven for me...) The idea being from the start/the-very-first-thing-I-write-in-philosophy... How to achieve the impossible/a-Wittgenstein-first-best-asphilosophy-and-IQ-absolutely... As to what the principal claim, of all my philosophy, will always be... That a first best-genius-Wittgenstein, that is Einstein's IQ, can achieve German-philosophy to go with that Einstein-IQ...To base a relative-philosophy on the idea of one would be just as absurd... *I correlate my IQ with Einstein as the relative too...* Which always relativized... (That my philosophy never believe in science...) And that the Einstein Solomon comparison always be relative... (*It is all relative...*) Or, what does such a statement achieve? Nothing at all... (Einstein is the famous IQ since relative...) Or, that the question of Einstein always go with the question of liberal/relative... Meaning, Einstein wouldn't create a vicious-circle as question of relative... Doesn't Einstein epitomize that "psychological-question" of Einstein/the-imagination-and-IQ/that-imagination-be-IQ... (Idea, tabula rasa and imagination...) The relative was never a problem for Einstein... (It is the fascist who, always, had very little to do with IQ that is imagination...) (So as to compare this essay and Webern...) Or something... What is the minimalism? That I would always imply Webern... Which was always indirect, direct without the least favorite/Philip-Glass... (Or something...) And that I can imply Bergman and Nietzsche generally as Webern... (My favorite Bergman-films always being so minimalist...) It is not like I directly-copy a Webern-system... The idea being the minimalist... And that I be the mathematical-science of logic... (Is art a direct value of me?) (The ultrarational comparison...) The self-copying and the minimalist... (I achieve something as by combining both...) (That I hate everything "uneven" in art...) Which was always strange... It is not my tiny-percentage-art-philosophy ever got to art... Not in actual fact... (What do I care what art is?) That I can care in the context of an honestaspiration/achieving-the-greatest-possible-genius-of-Continental-philosophy... Or something... (That art did get to the Einstein-IQ, that one time, with the help of Bergman...) Or something...

Without being able to deconstruct Nietzsche is that something has to write on him or as him... Which was never an issue... (All my philosophy that I write does have the clear indicator...) It was never necessary to create a next extent... Some things, of my philosophy, won't ever deconstruct... Like Nietzsche... Which goes with Einstein... And how does one deconstruct music/Webern... (To go with Notes from Underground...) And that I, probably, never get to deconstruct Heidegger... (*I already deconstructed one of the great philosophers of my philosophy and one of the principal ways to think my deconstruction prior to deconstruction...*) The value being clear... What can't be deconstructed shouldn't be deconstructed... (The psychological-question...) That I should direct a film/enter-a-film school... Which stopped being the interest prior to me becoming a philosopher, after I stop to be music... (It was a question of what to do after...) That I would have to be making a sequel to Persona... Which is always impossible/itis-infinite-that-nothing-competes-with-the-film... (My IQ matched...) That I, famously, compensated the fact of becoming a philosopher/the-absurd... (The sixteen-bibliographies...) I could have done the same as by becoming a film-director... (Including film bibliographically instead of including philosophy bibliographically...) As to how it is possible to be a film-director instead of a philosopher... (To match the visual language of my philosophy...) It is never too late... (I hate being untalented...) And that I do love being an absolute-genius... (Why not do the same with film?) Because I did do same with philosophy/I-excluded-philosophy-from-my-philosophy... (I can do the same as by becoming a film-director...) To exclude film from film would be too similar... (Or something...) And that film did bibliographically include in my philosophy... (It is same whether I am a philosopher or a film-director...) (Very base in-question...)

Writing a deconstruction without a deconstructed is possible... (Looks like a post-structural structure...) A minimalist language, made up of parts-of-language, the reader-freedom... Which is like copying Persona... Which is great/intentional... (My philosophy was already the post-structural-appearance...) The reader-freedom always being an Einstein-IQ and all that "the-rest" that always mystified what my philosophy, in actual fact, is... Which is simple/the-philosophy-is-structural... That the philosophy appears post-structural never meant a post-structural tendency as the philosophy's appearance... The post-structural being the appearance... (The becoming always being that hybrid/Hegel, Spinoza and Heidegger...) That Hegel (recently) became the fourth-best great philosopher of my philosophy... And that Heidegger was always the second-best great philosopher of my philosophy... And that I never read Spinoza or Hegel... Meaning, Hegel can't suddenly include in my bibliography... (Why is Hegel the fourth-best great philosopher?) (The clarity of this essay, that is against the structural-essence of the essay/the-

Continental philosophy...) Does the essay mean as the analytic-philosophy-irony of my philosophy? What is the never-ending simplified-language of minimalism? Something to go with the strange of analytic-philosophy in my philosophy infinitely-strange that is just as strange? Perhaps... (The logic, *analytic-philosophy-aspect...*) Logic, as one of the branches of philosophy I always wrote, was always half... A strange "double-confirmation" ... (Why do I include analytic philosophy in my philosophy?) As far as I know, France solves the impossible-difference... (Analytic philosophy being the skeptical part of my philosophy...) Or something... (Why not make doubly-sure?) Or something... (As long as my bibliography *included* Wittgenstein...) Or, the third-best great philosopher... And that it is as-far-as-philosophy-goes... Which is sixteen-bibliographies... (I didn't include analytic philosophy...)

Wittgenstein always being Continental with-me... (It is an "aspect" ...) Or, something infinitely-indirect, it seems...

(That I so infinitely-mock analytic philosophy doesn't change all that much...) Nothing changes... The dumbest invention, in history/ever... The never-ending clinical-depression (that a German invented analytic philosophy) will always be the never-ending clinical-depression... (As long as I am infinitely-happy...) That infinite-*clinical depression* being way too infinite for me... (Very-musical...)

Piecing the post-structuralism is as the post-structural-illusion of all my philosophy... Which is vicious/the-readeris-expected-to-assemble-the-personal-truth/subjective... Something probably aided with the help of Nietzsche... (A Nietzschean subjective-post-structuralism...) As the objective/as-far-as-philosophy-goes Nietzsche always vicious... (Persona being the first thing to come to mind...) A Nietzschean structuralism, that is a post-structural-illusion... Had Persona been something like mathematics, logic and science... And that that "vicious" always meant one of greater unsolved-problems of the film/what-is-so-infinite-about-that-never-ending-genius-of-art-and-IQ... Nietzsche, as the atheist, would mean something like the atheism of post-structuralism... Which never matches as polarity... And that a structural-Nietzsche be impossible as religion... Which never appeared absolutely-impossible to begin with... Meaning, what about the "religious-Nietzsche?" And so on... The "infinite-regress" of the film always naturalized as Nietzsche, structuralism and the post-structural-illusion... (It is the simple of the film instead of the potential infinite regress...) That my Nietzsche always be "theist"/representation-atheism... Or, representation and atheism can't think *simultaneously...* (Very-musical...) Something infinitely-intuitive as appearance... (Something like Bergman would always be the most ideal possible category of my philosophy/I-write-the-mathematical-science-of-logic...) I naturally mystify the whole thing... The unknown... Or, what is something like mathematics, logic and science as art or without art? An unknown, as the left-wing-unknown of my left-wing, as the left-wing-known, of my left-wing... (Why am I homaging Elfriede Jelinek?) That I have nothing to do with postmodernism... And that I never read her prior to my actual/last-extent old-age/at-some-point-in-fifty-years-from-now... (Is it as a fake/structural homage?) The "music" being structural... (I don't homage her...) (That is why...) Very strange/music-isn't-one-of-the-artforms-of-my-philosophy... (Is it as some strange-relation/that-Webern-never-excluded-as-one-of-mybibliographies...) On Webern and my philosophy... (Or something...) Or, the impossible-Webern, possible as the total-question/art... (Mathematics, science and logic as art...) Or something... (Film and the-writer are never the pure value...) All three crowning-achievements-of-IQ being possible of art as "combined" ... (Are all three all three?) Or, all three being one/"all-one" ... (The never-ending genius-IQ never annihilated...) Or, that something be impossible of art as IQ...

Isn't the word *vicious* my favorite word? (No unsolved-problems of philosophy...) As far as I know I do remain national of Continental philosophy... So as to mystify what the IQ of my philosophy means to say... Which is never mystical... IQ probably being why my philosophy exists/what-is-so-original-about-my-philosophy... (I love German philosophy, not Russian mysticism...) (Potentiality...) In my philosophy as Heidegger... (Something always had to be liberal instead of communist...) And that my interpretation of Heidegger always rested on left-wing as liberal... (His French-left popularity is in my philosophy just as strange as his political-polarity...) *Doesn't something like Being and Time to me read relative of something like Persona?* Or, why the extreme difference of him, in my philosophy, always relativized/based-on-mild... The communist "Hitler-man" being my polarity... (Being and Time to me being right-wing or left-wing...) (I do mind the question...) Music-isn't-one-of-the-art-forms-of-my-philosophy... Or, the rational... (The problem of Heidegger being so genius to my philosophy being rational...) Something I always needed to rationally/clearly-propose, relative of the ethicalissue of Heidegger-as-a-man-and-Heidegger-as-a-philosopher and that the composite question be as Jewry and IQ and religion/what-was-already-unclear-as-is... I don't mean Jewish philosophy, since I do mean the IQ-race... Meaning, what was the best religion of my philosophy meant to say as the IQ relative of the Hitler-*liberal-left-wing-philosopher* and that philosophy be the German profession? (A homage?) (A strange, to base on that a Jew never write philosophy and a German always invent the profession of philosophy itself to me and everyone else...) (Does the fact that a Jew be the IQ race change the religions of my philosophy?) Something can't be the best genius of IQ and best religion at the same time... *Or, can a race infinitely ideal of IQ be the best religion at the same time?* As long as I relativize the whole thing as the structuralism of philosophy and *obsolete/ancient...* (The question being whether I mean structurally as the outdated to date the obsolete-profession of philosophy as structuralism...) The structural-philosophy being an irony... (Does a two-obsolete value help with the completely new way to think philosophy past Derrida's death/end-of-philosophy?) Perhaps... (Structuralism and post-structuralism were already so ambivalent-of-each-other as ambivalence...) Except, that irony being as the total-religion of my philosophy... (The structuralism is for the sake of religion...) (A subjective-value...) To compare Nietzsche and my philosophy as the two-subjectives... (Maybe...) Which is subjective... (The great philosophy of my philosophy always being as-far-as-philosophy-goes...) (A-fake...) Or, as how the concept of artificial, in my philosophy, always existed... (Has to do with the concept of a self-hating-Slav...) Which is natural/no-Slav-race-ever-got-to-Germany... And is vicious (a homosexual to me always being the infinite-alien...) An infinite-difference, that never made sense/isprobably-an-irrational-as-Nietzsche... (Or something...) Seeing as the German-fact of my philosophy never changes relative of France and the Jewry of my philosophy... (What will always be the strangest infinite-contradiction infinitely *contradicting?*) How does a never-ending philosophical-nationalist remain a never-ending-heterosexual? A Serb, writing a philosophy infinitely *German-philosophy,* that is heterosexually the heterosexual-polarity, as the heterosexual race... And that an "irrational" never did object to my philosophy/Nietzsche-is-one-of-the-sixteen-bibliographies... (*To name it the irrational-value of my philosophy...*) (A "three," to me, on the other hand, being the *"whore-religion"* ...) I always justified it as the heterosexual-polarity, as to how I always think my impossible-sexuality...

That my Nietzsche always read as-every-next-reality/metaphysics... Which is relative/Heidegger... (Last metaphysics...)

That it is famous that Heidegger's Nietzsche be the first correct-way to read Nietzsche prior to Hitler, in my case some "extreme"/the-best-way-to-think-Nietzsche... (I do the literal fact of last-metaphysics, as by arranging everything Nietzche wrote within a metaphysical-reality/rationalism-and-metaphysics...) Or, a rationally "metaphysical-Nietzsche" as a

"rational-Nietzsche" ... Everything he wrote being the rational-parallel in a metaphysical-reality... (Which is "thought" ...) Or, which matches in the perfect sense of perfect/rational as my theist-Nietzsche of Nietzsche/liberal-religion...

Lagging a deconstruction of Wittgenstein is doubly-absurd... (One of the sixteen bibliographies and that I am to me always the better-Wittgenstein than Wittgenstein...) *Why not deconstruct me instead?* And that I to me be above Wittgenstein and the bibliography... (The triply-absurd...) (*Because I am writing the non-deconstructive deconstruction that is a deconstruction...*) The lag already "rationalized" ...

The "above-paragraph," to come with meaning... Must be that the system of this essay mean a theist-message and twenty-first-century/lacking-imagination... (On art, my philosophy, theism and the minimalism...) And as the polarity too... The "hypocrisy" ... (Being against the century and free-associating...) How do I include in a century that ended everything? As unimaginative man, who never needed to nurture imagination, as the IQ-imagination and that he is expected to develop the right/art/pure imagination too, because of psychological-definition of great-IQ... Which is strange/Freudian-as-the-basic-system... Must be that I suddenly can't create a "potential-imagination"/invent-that-shouldwrite-on-the-opposite-Jew, as the doubly absurd... (What has nothing to do with Freud...) Or, what I mean by the oppositeJew being Jung just-as-much... (That I have nothing to do with psychology or psychiatry...) The former, always, being the greatest genius of psychology/a-writer, relative of my primitive psychological-potential/primitive-psychological-talent... (Psychology and psychiatry can't a science...) Not to my philosophy... And my potential, in terms of psychology, always being something as primitive as the self-conscious-man or the self-conscious/a-left-wing-and-right-wing-*self-consciousman*-comparison and the regressive that is primitive/in-the-nineteenth-century/Dostoyevsky-and-Nietzsche-as-the-leftwing-in-the-twentieth-century-and-that-Dostoyevsky-and-Nietzsche-be-so-essental-of-that-favorite/twenteth-century-ofmine-as-the-right-wing... (Dostoyevsky, Bergman, Tarkovsky and Nietzsche...) How my philosophy always delimited psychologically: the greatest psychologist in history, the psychological-competition, something almost just as great as the psychological-competition and the essential-intellectual-tie to the greatest psychologist that ever existed, respectively... A self-conscious-creation/minimalism...

How is a language-minimalism to go with my philosophy? *The philosophy isn't minimalist!* That I am cynical of philosophy is what is so original about it/German...

Meaning, Webern, Bergman and Nietzsche, as my philosophy, *generally...* Why? Simply as-to-why... (Or something...)

Or, so as to lie, as illusion, of appearance, that it is the total-bibliography of my philosophy... Which, directly, relates to Nietzsche, as to what the in-itself-problem then becomes... The moral-lie, metaphysics and idealism... (Generally...) Or something... (And-the-anti-Christ...) Or, the problem of Nietzsche and anti-Christ in my philosophy/Nietzsche, that he be the best great philosopher, the mild-metaphysics (a-last-metaphysician) and idealism... There is nothing impure about my philosophy and Persona at all... (Why is Nietzsche/mild-metaphysics the best great philosopher?) I mean a dream, not an illusion... (Must be that my philosophy does affirm Persona as a total-contradiction/a-film-too-composite-to-comprehendas-the-dream...) (Or something...) That I categorize film purely will always be the composite-category of Persona, a film to me that great as the rest that the film has to offer too... What is the simultaneity of the film? The best dream, best IQ, second-best-psychology, best religion, the second-best-religion, etc... (Something categorically-infinite, as to why I, *probably,* never get to a clear list with the writers-side of my philosophy...) (So as to locate an aphorism from Tractatus Logico-Philosophicus that I didn't deconstruct...) Which is subjective... Now that I did deconstruct one of the great philosophers of my philosophy is that start doing a deconstruction of one of the two German-ones... (Nietzsche and Heidegger will never be deconstructed too...) Which is, always, such a shame... Nietzsche, as the rational/metaphysical reality, Heidegger, as one of the ways to think my deconstruction/the-unimaginative... (Etc...) As long as I make the whole thing feel better with the fact that I deconstructed the best great philosopher of my philosophy/my-philosophy... (That probably being why it becomes self-evidence that I will never do a deconstruction of the first two great philosophers...) That I am relatively-cynical of philosophy as the total-bibliography... (Something had to solve the cynical-value/IQ of all my philosophy I write, as to how the bibliographies and IQ combined, to retain the nationalism of my philosophy that is German philosophy as the only philosophy there ever existed to my philosophy...) That too... (The French-left as the excessive-bibliography...) Relative of Judaism/that-a-Jew-can't-be-both-principal-simultaneous-categories-of-all-Jewry... All those categories that make possible that my philosophy is the greatest genius of philosophy possible and the greatest genius of IQ possible... (The minimalist-style/language never shrinks its flamboyant-philosophy...) As to what the next form, literally, this time, is... On whether it is possible to write the *how*-as-the-*what* philosophy without the how-*part,* and how that question relates *essentially* to my philosophy of the total-question of modernism and postmodernism of my philosophy... (Was the style always postmodern?) Or, was the *how* a doubled-effect or doubled-negation of postmodernism as postmodern... (Something famously-impossible...) A style, of my philosophy, that never believed in language, as the modern-how to correlate the modern-philosophy...

My love for "category" always being the infinite-regress... (Something to aid with the problem of left-wing...) (Locating a free-association is always the major-aim/why-this-essay-exists...) So as to compare something like my favorite Jews and Judaism to something like the imposible/Freud/the-least-favorite-Jew... And that being on the relative of the whole thing... *Judaism can go with Kafka, as my interpretation of the writer,* while the rest of the favorite-Jews never matches as will... And that Kafka be the ambivalent-concept of my philosophy: the second-best writer, relative of the second-bestwriting of my philosophy, that a first-best writer never existed to my philosophy prior to a second-best list of writers, that Kafka get to the one-twenty-score on the IQ test as from a-fifty/clinical-depression (never competes IQ-wise with what means to be essentially Jewish about my philosophy), etc... Judaism is my-Kafka, so as for Kafka to be one of the favorite Jews as ambivalence/potential... Relative of Judaism as religion to complicate what complicated... (Religion isn't mathematics/IQ...) And, finally, as the ambivalent-antithesis *as is...* (I hold something personally against Freud since I love Freud and Jung/hate-both...) And so on... (As to what the meaning of the free-association, that is this essay itself, is, so as to go with other-meaning too/the-twenty-first-century, that I am a philosopher, lack-of-imagination-in-the-century-Iam-in and the problem of total-imagination of my philosophy and IQ/Einstein/imagination...) And so on... Why am I a philosopher in a century infinitely against philosophy? Because I am not against philosophy and my philosophy being twoprofessional-philosophers as magnitude... And that my philosophy simultaneously preserve my Einstein-IQ... And that that *totally* be as the interesting-challenge/a-Serb-aspiring-to-become-the-greatest-possible-German-genius-of-philosophy/thegreatest-possible-genius-of-philosophy... On top of which will always be that I never minded the art-science difference of philosophy... (Kind of mild, thought absolutely true...) And that the philosophy match religiously too! (The modern/liberal-theist philosophy, to go with the first half of the greatest century in history to me...) I am not an atheist! Which, in the ancient-way, mismatches the other half of the favorite century... Meaning, I doubly never get to the century that I am in... (In-plain-English...) My dream (to succeed in philosophy) will always be the infinite-magnitude/twoprofessional-philosophers... (I film the language...) So as to achieve a Bergman or Nietzsche level-of-success, as by negating what is always so-in-the-way/the-infinite-genius, as by *including* instead of *negating...* As to how always solve the infinite-jealousy... And that Nietzsche was never an issue as is/coincidentally-the-best-great-philosopher... (It was always the Nietzsche-Heidegger limit...) And that I am not a film-director... (All that infinite-genius always shrank as infinite-regress...) And that Bergman be one of the four Einsteins of my philosophy... (Etc...) (Me included...)

What is the other-meaning of this essay? (Or, that I, fully, make a primitive-exegesis...) There is no other meaning... The essay being the continuity, like anything/everything I write in philosophy... (The lesser-continuity, that never existed to begin with...) Or, all those free-association-essays I wrote, that are never written/my-philosophy-itself... (As to how they were possible at all...) Writing something "psychology," that isn't the self-conscious, self-conscious-man, Dostoyevsky and Nietzsche and left-wing and the twentieth-century/modernism, is never possible of my philosophy... The primitivepsychology will always be the same composite-potential/the-primitive-*composite-psychology*-of-all-my-philosophy/thesimple/"idee-fixe" ... That I be so bad at psychology... Meaning, I don't believe in such a thing... Meaning, Dostoyevsky, Tarkovsky, Bergman and Nietzsche/I-do-believe-in-psychology-in-art-and-philosophy...

Who is the free-association intended for? (I assume the role of a psychologist/psychiatrist...) Must be a form of irony... An essay to utilize free-association on-someone... (Must be yet-again as-from-a-negative, to-know-the-positive...) As my antithetical technology-deconstruction/irony... (The ideal/German deconstruction, that is my German philosophy...) Or, is it a proposition... So as to question what Freud without Jung is in my philosophy... (Am I great to Freud without Jung?) Or something... (A technology-psychology/psychiatry, as the *positive* of comparing the positive and negative, to know the positive as from a negative-positive...) And how that compares/"represents" ... (On technology and psychology, and that both be negative of my philosophy...) (Dostoyevsky, Tarkovsky, Bergman and Nietzsche as Freud and Freud without Jung...) I am fairly-traditional/modern... Meaning, stay at those early theories of psychology prior to the twentieth-century in the second-half/postmodern...

All my philosophy, that is a positive-negative... Wasn't that always the absurd problem of my absurd philosophy that hates absurdism? The philosophy being categorical, not absurd... Or, a philosophy "absurdly-categorical"/German... Something absurd can't be infinitely-categorical... (What is the positive-negative of my philosophy?) Mocking technology? Absolutely... Which is natural: *What could be more antithetical to my philosophy than technology?* Meaning, what could be more antithetical to philosophy than technology? (The hypocrisy rested on owning a Wii...) Which is probably true instead... (I own a Wii without hypocrisy...) Meaning, what will always be the infinite-boredom/the-nonhypocrite... That my room becomes so technological will always be that technology be the most popular thing in the twenty-first century that I am in relative of two professional philosophers that I aspire to find as the least popular thing in that century... (A psychoanalytic essay...) Or, the essay that hypnotizes the reader... (So as for the reader to use the essay on its patients/hypnotize...) Which will always be a strange essay on hypnosis, correlating the exact number of freeassociation essays I wrote... (A strange German-relation/Werner-Herzog...) Or something... Which is never strange as the total-bibliography, strange as the lesser/greater German, as one of the potential Germanies of my philosophy... (Germanmysticism, a half-German/Croat-German, German art and surrealism have nothing to do with me...) Why is he one of the bibliographies of my philosophy? And why do I write so many "hypnotic-essays?" (A German work of art meant the two German writers and Herzog...) Meaning, "inclusion" ... Or, that a writer be unrelated to my philosophy as the related filmdirector... (The absurd...) Why is Herzog someplace at the genius-Hollywood of my philosophy? (Germany isn't art to my philosophy and that art have very little to do with my philosophy too...) Is it some "vicious"/that-art-included-in-myphilosophy-and-that-art-can-include-in-my-philosophy?   Perhaps... Something having to do with the vicious question of IQ in my philosophy/the-three-crowns and that science be one of the three IQ-crowns of my philosophy... (Isn't a mathematical science of logic very-artistic while retaining the IQ of all three crowns as one?) I found a way to simultaneously think art and IQ... And seeing as Bergman already provides for a coincidence/is-one-of-the-Einsteins-ofmy-philosophy/was-Einstein-smart...

Writing billions of hypnotic/psychoanalytic essays is very-absurd... And that they are idea instead of free-association... *I don't know much about psychology...* Or, that the free-association never hypnotize... And searching for the idea-word, from the prior-paragraph, as the system, will never achieve free-association or hypnosis... (The essays are on creativity and the century I am in...) Or, on the problem of imagination and Einstein and the twenty-first-century and IQ... (Imagination, Einstein, the twenty-first century and IQ, and that I go with a theory of psychology/that-imagination-be-the-IQprerequisite-with-or-wihout-the-prior-*one-twenty-score*-IQ-of-the-creating-arts/creativity...) Herzog is not the representation of those essays... Or, something Freud as Herzog being the unreal/appearance/mistake-to-mention... (Something like the performing artist never gets to the one-twenty IQ...) (As the most retarded people possible/thesinger...) And that a painter be just as retarded as a performing artist... (Which always competed with politics: the mostretarded man in history, on the planet/George-W.-Bush...) And so on... (The usual list...) Everything that is at a zero-score IQ or scoring below zero on the IQ test... That least-favorite, of me, on the planet, totally, usually intends as politics and law... Which will always be relative... (What about all those performing artists, singers, painters, etc.?) Logic, mathematics and science being so infinitely-natural of me... (That something subjectify...) Either an infinite-regress, or an infiniteregress, or the infinite-regress/those four categories of the lowest-possible-IQ: a politician, a performing artist, a singer and a painter... Which will always be subjective... Something like a signer outdoes all-four... (Is an infinite-idiot to me infinitely-idiotic or infinite/the-infinite-itself?) (Technology retained...) (Technology without psychology...) Which is technology without technology... (The "hypocrisy" being absurd/unreal/*appearing*...) I don't side with my enemies... The problem of my-anitheses will always rest on something like the limit/my-bibliography/that-it-is-a-relative-bibliography-offreedom... A relative-bibliography and a freedom-delimiting/reader-freedom... Or, both... (Or, the one...) (The relative bibliography is the reader-freedom...) Relative of the slavery of my philosophy/that-I-am, infinitely, not a slave of anything... The concept of the infinite-master-of-everything... My sixteen-friends are a slave... (Which is whether that makes them an antithesis of me too...) In the twenty-first century everything changes... Infinitely...

Referencing Herzog is too-general/probably-impossible... (That he will never assume an actual-significance with me...) And that I be the four geniuses as psychology/Dostoyevsky, Bergman, Nietzsche and Tarkovsky... (What do I have to do with actual psychology or psychiatry?) I mean of the triply-defining/science, psychology and psychiatry... All three have very little to do with... That I am science will always mix with logic and mathematics/isn't-*mathematics, logic and science... The challenge being to retain the crown-IQ of all three while synthesizing all three...* Or, the question being whether the three IQ-crowns retain when combined... (Billions of *idea-word* essays...) (What am I expected to do anymore with the idea?) That it be hypocrite to write philosophy so much i the shrunken-magnitude of the literal every-next-formof-same/why-my-philosophy-is-clearly-Jewish... (The IQ and religion will always be the mixed/irrational definition...) Something like the IQ-race always had to be the religion-race... Which is never rational/doesn't-make-any-sense... That Christ is to my philosophy never IQ, *clearly*, will always be that the Jewish, on the other hand, be the mixed problem as IQ and religion... (The second-best-religion of my philosophy always had an issue with the fact that I am Jewish/Semitic...) The basic-definition (Jewish-since-IQ) was always ambivalent... (Hence, something like the idea of *Jewish-measure/real,* to aid with the Jewish-Christian problem of my philosophy...) (Christ got as far as the greatest possible great mind/Dostoyevsky...) Which is never IQ and never becomes the greatest great mind of my philosophy/Einstein/IQ... (Does the fact that I am the greatest great mind of my philosophy solve the issue too?) I infinitely love my philosophy... The greatest great-mind of my philosophy always being the IQ-kind/Einstein... (*Logically...*) Einstein is never the best great mind too... (I mean the greatest genius of philosophy possible, in a greatest genius of philosophy possible, as the greatest genius of IQ possible...) Philosophy can mean the greatest genius of philosophy to me... Meaning, that IQ never be above philosophy to me... (As far as I know I always, purely, mock something like analytic philosophy *infinitely...*) Something like Bertrand Russell always exchanges the question of talent and IQ... Or, the most retarded man in history, on the planet/Bertrand-Russell... (One of the major candidates...) What is always an infinite-dumbo to my philosophy... (Wittgenstein being the third-best great philosophy of my philosophy as the first-best Einstein-IQ of my philosophy...) It is a coincidence... (So as to always paint a picture of the world, as the visual language, of psychology and pictogram, as Wittgenstein/my-representation-of-Wittgenstein's-Tractatus-Logico-Philosophicus...) Which is true... I wrote billions of Tractatus Logico-Philosophicuses that match my needs/are-as-to-how-Wittgenstein-would-always-become-the-best-greatphilosopher-of-my-philosophy... Everything I wrote in philosophy... My total-philosophy/one-philosophy, I always write, that is a first-best-genius-of-philosophy-and-a-first-best genius-of-IQ Tractatus Logico-Philosophicus... (Why my philosophy exists...) My total-philosophy...

How does my philosophy "suffer?" At the expense of language... Which is too little language/at-the-expense-ofIQ/logic... A strange-suffering, as the sadist-philosophy, written by a sadist... (Something Christian as the anti-Christ...) And that the anti-Christian mean of Jewish/Judaism as the liberal-religion of my philosophy... (What is so Judaic about a liberal-religion-philosophy?) A masochist-language, that I never know how to think as Judaism and Nietzsche/my-JudaicNietzsche... Which is too great *anyhow*... (As to what, *apparently,* solves something entirely else...) That always paint-aclear-picture/am-bad-at-art, as the picture thought of Wittgenstein and that Wittgenstein have artistic-relevance/havesignificance-in-the-world-of-art... (As Schopenhauer...) Or something... Which was always the mixed-problem: Nietzsche and Wittgenstein, as Heidegger... (Schopenhauer has nothing to do with me...) The ascetic-language... (Something like Bergman's *Winter Light...*) Or something... (Why?) Didn't I finish doing a deconstruction of Bergman eleven years ago? That I be past Bergman eleven-years... (As far as I know Bergman prioritizes as the best possible bibliography of my philosophy...) Or, Bergman is not the only best-bibliography... *Why does he prioritize?* Isn't he the best film-director of my philosophy, as the four best films ever made of my philosophy/Persona, *Andrei Rublev, 8 ½* and *Rashomon,* as Nietzsche, Heidegger and Wittgenstein, that the writers never clarify a best-list, as the best classical-music-composer of my philosophy/Webern and the best great philosopher of my philosophy/me as Einstein, Wittgenstein and him?

Absolutely... The best-lists being so-many... And that Bergman be the two-inclusion of film/a-two-best-list... And so on... (It is a composite-question...) There is nothing clearly first-best about Bergman... Meaning, he being doubly first-best...

(My philosophy is sixteen-bibliographies with or without the relative delimiting...) (A "three" being the lesser religion of the two religions of my philosophy...) That I do know that my interpretation of Bergman be Jewish as IQ and religion/theJewish-problem-of-my-philosophy and that he is one of the Christian churches of my philosophy... However, that being

Christian-Jewish... (An *excessive* too...) I can't be past Bergman and Wittgenstein... (A strange obsessive-compulsive disorder...) The eleven- and ten-year span, that sin;t annihilating, as of late... (Sixteen bibliographies is not two "emphases" ...) (Bergman and Wittgenstein correlated as IQ, as far as I know...) That the double two-genius of Bergman (the best film ever made and the best Einstein-IQ) can't be the mixed-Wittgenstein... And that Bergman be overpraised *philosophically*/be-from-Sweden-has/very-little-to-do-with-philosophy and that film/art can be philosophy to me without reaching my list of best great philosopher... (Bergman being the filmmaker and an artist...) That Bergman never compete with Wittgenstein *philosophically*... (That Wittgenstein be third-best is not Bergman as the third-best great philosophy...) (As to how that always mixed...) That my philosophy is Einstein-smart will always be a Continental philosophy national of Continental-philosophy/impossible-to-read-for-the-sake-of-being-so/being-impossible-to-comprehend-as-will... (I never feared the stylistic-potential of Continental philosophy...) Or, I don't go with such opinions/infinitely-have-nothing-to-dowith-Analytic-philosophy...

(Wittgenstein always rhymed well as the literal fact/rhyme of Einstein...) However, that being so general/me-andBergman-too... And that Wittgenstein coincidentally makes it to my great-philosophers best-list as a coincidence... Doesn't my philosophy hate analytic philosophy *purely?* (It would always have to be some miracle of infinite-coincidence or the half-Continentally potential to be potential at all/to-begin-with...) A subjective, that is objective... Or, something subjectively-okay as Nietzsche... Or something... And that Wittgenstein wasn't an issue as Nietzsche to my philosophy... (Tractatus Logico-Philosophicsu means to consciously-copy all sorts of things, at the same time, simultaneously...) *Why the text exists...* (As the primary intention of the philosophy, as to how my philosophy always read that early Wittgensteinperiod...) Jewish identity and the self-hating-Jew, to annihilate both as the indifference/Einstein-IQ... (The Einstein-IQ being cynical of philosophy/there-is-nothing-self-hating-about-the-early-Wittgenstein...) *Can be Jewish-identity...* (*As...*) (I watch Aisling Walsh's *Maudie,* last night, with my mother...) As long as I watch it with my mother... Everything comes to an end twenty-one years ago: that it is an okay-cinema to see as the Irish-director... (Something like Ireland would compete with Russia in art without the Western-part of Ireland...) However, that film does end being possible at that time/twenty-one-years-ago... (Ireland probably never helps...) And that I never have interest in Canada... *What does Canada have to do with me?* A zero-talent and zero-IQ always meant zero-interest as is... (Can be possible as the general/infinite outer-space that I live in, that is my infinite-slave...) Or, by now completely-same... Or, everything being the natural slave of me inside a never-ending outer-space... (That Canada used to be specific...) What used to be Glenn Gould, as the only thing to come from Canada, to achieve genius, if nothing else... (That IQ never does reach a level of potential/stays-at-the-zero-IQ-IQ-prior-to-the-century-that-I-am-in...) Something a "theme," as the film with a story to tell, was already the negative-value: two brain-damages make for one Canada... Or, two insane/deformed people, categorically anything/everything, as to how Canada always solved the problem of insanity... (Both *are* insane...) Or, both *are* physically-deformed... Or, both *are* "psychosomatic" ... Meaning Canada/*the-psychosomatic...* A very great film, in that respect, absolutely, as the two-simuletnaeous... That the major definition of Canada always rested on the down-toEarth/*concrete* or a mildly-insane/mild... (What becomes so different about States/*the-concrete?*) Or, Canada being

"one"/there-is-nothing-simultaneous-about-Canada... (A film in the century I am in and that that "theme" never becomes possible of me...) That film ends at the extended year that was twenty-one years ago, at the tiny-masterpiece/*CasinoRoyale*-in-two-thousand-and-six... (*The actual end-of-film will always be that film, probably...*) Which is very inconsequential... *The Man with the Golden Gun* being the best action film and the best James Bond film, of all time, to my philosophy, as far as I know... (A mildly-ended-thing...) (An-opinion...) The context, always, being that I am a philosopher/do-affirm-philosophy-as-the-philosopher-and-the-philosopher-fanatic-about-philosophy-being-philosophy... An opinion will always be below to me... Or, that an opinion be below as infinite-regress/infinitely... (That was always an issue with me/my-philosophy too...) The anti-Semitic Jew/Semite... (How does one think such a thing?) That philosophy, as self-loving, always be the anti-Semitic profession of Germany/the-German-anti-Semitic-profession-that-is-antiSemitic... I hate an anti-Semite, as far as I know... (Absolutely...) How does my Jewish-Nietzsche, as the second-best liberal-left-wing Heidegger, become the fanatic German philosophy that I am? (Never matched, so to speak...) *As an impossible of my philosophy probably too...* (I love a challenge...) Which is a bit too infinitely-challenging... And that that I am a Serb was the-challenge... (I infinitely complicate...) A Serb writing the greatest possible genius of philosophy already being so infinitely-impossible to think beyond everything/beyond-a-beyond-itself...

An analytic-judgment... (Of the a priori-kind...) Kant was, always, possible... That my philosophy never objected to Kant as-idea... Which was always literal... Which was always intended/the-problem... Something to go with the French-left, of my philosophy, as irony and left-wing and right-wing... (The-comparison and that my left-wing be essentially against French-left first/right-wing...) Or something... All those homage-deconstructions I wrote: the name, of them, collectively... (*How is deconstruction Possible?*) As to what the title, of my total-deconstruction, will always be... (*How are synthetic a priori judgments possible?*) The homage of the title, and what that title always represents... Which is the "homage" ... Or, a homage as comparison: a homage, the left-wing, the right-wing and my left-wing, as my total-philosophy... (What I title is my philosophy itself...) Which was always included in the title/homage too... (How is my deconstruction possible as my philosophy as my philosophy?) (The Einstein-IQ of my philosophy will always retain throughout/in-every-philosophy-Iwrite-and-in-every-philosophy-that-I-am-to-write...) That my infinite love for my Einstein IQ always be in the way... (It is why my philosophy exists...) On how to annihilate my IQ, while retaining it, while including it in a genius-philosophy a German-genius-of-philosophy... (I write philosophy so as to prove my IQ with something that I will preserve/succeed-in...) (Probably...) (So as to watch Raiders of the Lost Ark, last night, with or without my mother...) The best Spielberg-film ever made to my philosophy... (Must be that iconography, as measure, as the "measure-film" of fascism as the right-wing film, always appealed...) A successful right-wing-symbolic-exchange... Or something... (The quadrilogy's third entry always being the contender, as to how I judge those four films...) The antifoundational film and that I am not antiSemitic/can't-be-proposing-those-films-anti-foundationally... Which was always mixed... (That I am Semitic never meant liking all Jewry...) Isn't Spielberg to me usually an untalented-Jew? (I make a hypersensitive issue out of the whole thing...) The third Indiana Jones film always being *almost just as great* as the first one... (Sean Connery, the funny-comedy and the comedy-of-measure/double-comedy always complicated the issue for me...) That I, famously, love everythingcomposite... (Or something...) My German/philosophical nature... (The funny double-negative aspect of the third one: something fascist used to be fascist, to become excessively fascist as a funny/infinite fascism of prior comedy and the comical/infinite-fascism...) Einstein, Wittgenstein and Kafka always being the best Jews of my philosophy... (What do I have to do with Spielberg?) (So as to complicate...) Or something... (The cheap-prostitute/Spielberg...) Why do I mention him... Must be that he does make the best Spielberg-film... Or something... Which is absurd/excessive... (The best Hollywood directors of my philosophy being concretely-specified...) Is it because the delimited-*unlimited* bibliography of my philosophy? Must be... (I am so liberal/relative with my enemies...) A best Hollywood and best Jewish director will always relativize... (Kubrick...) Or something... Or, something recently added to my best-lists... (Or something...) Something having to do with how I otherwise define Kubrick in my philosophy... (A snobby Polish left-wing-art, that is l'art-pour-l'artistic/snobby...) That he was, recently, so upped in my philosophy as the Jewish-fact and, probably, as the director's total-blood... (Or something...) The spoiled/Polish-Romainian ancestry being as Jewish and Austrian... (As far as I know...) As to why I (probably) make him a relative potential of standard of my philosophy/a-greater-lesser-geniusabove-Spielberg... (I used to never realize what the self-conscious/autobiographical *totally* is...)

A hypersensitive-essay... (Retaining deconstruction without deconstruction...) The philosophical-object being a constructed, not a deconstructed... (How is it possible to retain the idea-word without a deconstructed while retaining the deconstruction as the prioritized idea-word?) I lag

Wittgenstein... (Or something...) And that the language shrink so much... *Isn't it Webern?* A minimalist-language, of my deconstruction, now *so infinite...* (As my first-deconstruction/thedeconstruction-of-me...) Or something... That I, initially, did think language as possible relative of my deconstruction... (Learning how to deconstruct and inventing my deconstruction *simultaneously...*) And that the idea-word-essays be the

"fragments"/Persona of structuralism as the strange reader-freedom of illusion/appearance... (I name a lot of stuff related to my philosophy...) That too... The bibliography, as a clear-delimited and clear mention to begin with, solved the problem of the construction/that-I-am-not-deconstructing... (Kind of like combining two things against the basic rule of all my philosophy...) Nothing can be constructive without deconstruction and it is impossible to define what the bibliography of my philosophy is... (The minimalist-language being the skepticism, not what solves the constructive fact of the constructive/idea-word essays...) (I like to be sure...) Or, that I absolutely don't like a construction in the place of deconstruction... (The constructive-deconstruction will always be a constructive-deconstruction...) There is nothing constructively-*constructive* about my philosophy... (That the problem of my polarity never switch me to right-wing...) Not actually/absolutely... (The right-wing of my philosophy must stay at the level of potential...) I don't mean right-wing since left-wing of liberal as apolitical... (That my philosophy be so mixed as polarity will always be exact/the-polarity-that-Iam...) (I never exchange my bibliography with my polarity...) (The Austrian philosophy being German...) Or, that I be the total *three-potential...* (A North in Germany, as Germany, as Austria, as that German-north...) Going around the problem of Bavaria will always be the total-Germany, Austria and that I can't be Austrian/untalented-in-philosophy... I am, to me, always, the proud-German/a-Serb-at-the-same-level-of-philosophy-as-Germany... (Austria has nothing to do with philosophy...) Or, that Wittgenstein coincidentally become the third-best great philosophy... (That I was always antiSemitic, in that respect...) Something like Hitler, to me, always being the infinite Down-syndrome as relative of the superior race/Germany... (That I am left-wing was always an issue for me...) Or, that I am the three-left-wing will always be way too great to me... (Something clarity as thought/of-thought...) That I love everything-rational... (That I am the infinite-German/a-philosopher-as-infinite-regress always had the rational to go with the pure value/an-infinite-issue-to-gowith-the-German-definiton-of-me...) My Semitism will always be IQ and religion... Or, that that I am Semitic will always be irrational as my definition of Hitler and Germany/*the-separate...*

What is the idea-word of the day? (That my lack of creativity relate little to the fact that I write billions of philosophies at the same time...) A Hitler-philosophy as appearance... (It is three major Jewish categories that help with the anti-Semitic Semite/Jew/a-Jew...) IQ, Judaism and measure... (As far as I know I am not anti-Semitic...) That Hitler always be the antiSemitic problem of me... *It is a Semitic problem...* (And that something match as thought...) I am half-Christian... (Or something...) That I name a Jew the *IQ, religion* and *measure* race should be Semitic enough... (I probably mean aproblem-with-the-Jewish...) (A Semite is not a Jew...) Or something... (The problem of Semitism and thought...) (It is kind of "Down-syndrome-like" to be so rhetorical...) That the idea of *rhetoric,* on the other hand, be my philosophy's generalpotential too... Always the Nietzsche, rhetoric, mockery, irony, the Heidegger-limit Nietzsche, question of direction of the mockery, that my philosophy loves philosophy-conceptually/is-anti-Nietzschean, etc... And something as *sense*/a-child... (That my philosophy always did self-propose the issue of

Einstein/IQ and philosophy...) That realism, of my philosophy, never hurt too... A traditional philosophical-rhetoric, that always appears so-childish-in-my-philosophy, and the IQchild/Einstein... (Einstein has nothing to do with philosophy...) (My self-respect for me...) That it is known that I infinitely-love-me... (Is my never-ending unpopularity bad for me?) As long as I mean no popularity of any kind at all... (I am neither popular nor unpopular, as to how that "Hitler" issue of my philosophy always solved *beautifully...*) I don't like the Hitler-art-scenario as philosophy... (Can be a half...) That something is popular/recognized will never all that much...

Which is usually an "art-thing" ... (I define philosophy "half-artistically" ...) What is so great about my philosophy... (Nothing popular or unpopular...) And that I am unpopular is unsuccess... I am infinitely-unpopular as-should-be... (The neo-fascist appearance of all my philosophy...) (A constructive-deconstruction...) The emotion that always self-healed will always be the lack-of-success, not the most unpopular man in history... (There is nothing popular or unpopular...) And that the success always rest on those two professional-philosophers/be-two-professional-philosophers... (As to how both never-ending "clinical-depressions" annihilated...) The essential infinite-extreme of my philosophy... (The infinitely happyman and the infinitely clinically-depressed-man...) So as to explain why I always reach that level of happiness that is infinite-happiness...

The idea of a beautiful-equation/IQ... Which isn't unlimited... (I mean Einstein and Wittgenstein...) *Can be unlimited* in the sense of the three-crowns/mathematics, science and logic... Or, Einstein, Wittgenstein, Bergman and me... Which generalizes, in all likeliness, as the three-crowns... (Some shared-potential...) (Reminds of my bibliography...) Freedom and IQ... Which is true/I-always-go-with-the-*traditional-definition...* The theory of psychology always being the creativity-prerequisite/freedom... (Freedom and imagination will always be necessary...) That it is a *delimited* is skeptical...

(The most popular-psychology of the question/what-I-side-with...) The "hurt" being at my relative-philosophy and that the idea of *relative* was to be IQ with or without Einstein/*relativity...* (The New-World-Order never-ending-idiot/idiot-fascist always relativized as the general-indifference of the very question...) Or, the apolitical as left-wing of the liberal, of my philosophy... (I hate the absolute-power New-World-Order in the sense of creativity/freedom/all-that-is-beautiful...) Which will always be IQ instead of left-wing... (An Einstein-smart left-wing has nothing to do with left-wing...) That it was always the "half" with me... Which never changes... (Naturally/I-am-apolitical...) The politics being the Einstein-smartIQ... Which is apolitical... (My hate can retain as the simulatenous-question of Einstein, philosophy and left-wing...) Does the Einstein-IQ philosophy retain that hate? (More like mixed instead of half-potential...) Or something... (The never-ending-idiot is the never-ending-idiot...) What usually means to be on-both-sides/same does subjectify/objectify... (Something mutilated by New World Order would usually mean the New World Order/New-World-Order-mutilatingitself: *something on the planet,* that miscomprehended that I mean actually the half...) (I hate the never-ending-idiot...) Something infinitely gets off my back... (I infinitely love me...) Meaning, *I infinitely love me...* (That I kill anything in the way of my infinite love for me...) (I watch the third Indiana Jones film, last night, with my mother...) With or without my mother/the-film-probably-being-almost-just-as-great-as-the-best-Spielberg-film-ever-made... An Austrian-waltz, of the wrong-category as intention (American-Austrian-waltz) will always be great as the out-of-control fascism of excessivefascism/the-liberal, as to what always gets to be so *masterpiece* about that film... (India, as the out-of-control, as idea, is back at the original-root of *Aryan* of the Indiana Jones series...) How always got to like the film-series on the whole/generally... To me the total-joke followed-up... (A measure-film, followed by an out-of-control one as idea, so as to create the next measure-film of same as the out-of-control/combine-both as the over-the-top/comedy of the doubly-*funnyfilm*...) (My mother...) Or, that similarity-too... (Indifference of New World Order, as the difference of New World Order...) And that that did always go with the *slavery*... That I infinitely-fart-the-never-ending-outer-space was always an issue for me... (My mother does the same...) Or, she would have to be included in the fart... Which was always vicious... (Do I include her as my IQ and my philosophy?) That she has nothing to do with IQ or philosophy... Which probably always helped... Except, her IQ being potential of my Einstein-IQ-level... That she scores one-twenty on the IQ test will always be vicious/relatively-potential-of-my-two-hundred-score-on-the-IQ-test...

So as to, finally, film my philosophy... (Every philosophy I wrote...) That the theory becomes that-literal... Which is always an issue... (My infinite love for IQ...) As long as I *don't* film my philosophies... (I am aware of the fact that I lowered that "infinite-theory-potential"...) Or, it is just as philosophy as IQ... Or, my philosophy being the German-genius of philosophy... (My mother is infinitely doubly-atypical...) Which is okay... (She is just as Christian as Jewish, as to where things become possible between me and her relatively...) And that she be German-Jewish-Spanish in nature... (Racially and religiously...) So as to live with her to-some-extent... (That I have nothing to do with classical music or her classical music...) That Webern is always the best classical music composer of my philosophy... Or, I never discard with classical music *absolutely*... And the "utility" of the whole thing being way too great... *What do I care what my mother's music is?* As long as she preserves me/I-preserve-her... (After death...) Which is natural... That my philosophy always based on the idea of posthumous-fame/Spinoza *naturally*... (Two professional philosophers...) (I love my mother's music...) So as to solve the whole slavery-problem of me... (My mother never included in the "outer-space-fart"...) Or, I will be her infinite-slave/may-she-be-my-infinite-slave... (Very-practical...) (It is never a new-thing to, suddenly, revert to my original-mode of philosophy...) That my philosophy was, as the best I would write, in those first philosophies I did write, the double-*avante-garde*... (As art and philosophy...) Or, a work of art, that is philosophy... Which is always so avante-garde... And the work of art being so avante-garde... As to what was always the major/infinite contradiction of me in philosophy initially... (I love my infinitely-impressive first-three-philosophies/first-philosophy-I-wrote...) Something science, as he double *avante-garde-potential,* that was never a contradiction/a-problem... (The science being idea...) Or, the science that is IQ as the IQ-part of science/logic-and-mathematics-as-science... A physics-paper, that can't be science, that is Einstein-smart/a-physics-paper-to-begin-with... And as an ideal Tractatus Logico-Philosophicus/the-TractatusLogico-Philosophicus-that-I-do-absolutely-love... That my philosophy, to me, always, be the infinite-masterpiece... (How great is it that I mean as two professional philosophers?) Those two-infinite clinical-depressions were way too infinite, it seems... (That my philosophical always grew political as left-wing...) (Can a left-wing be apolitical?) All that imagination and IQ being in the way of politics... Which was always simultaneous/a-mystery...

The art of my philosophy/*writing* always being the un-talent of my philosophy... (As should be...) That-literal does the art-part, *initially,* be in my philosophy... (The difference is too extreme with or without the mathematically-logical of my science...) A "mean" ... Bergman "made" so many physics-papers too... However, that that always be that infinite coincidence/the-impossible... That my philosophy is the "half-art" will always be that I write literal-art... (A work of art actually-art...) Which is infinitely impossible... (It is not like I, *initially,* wrote a *Thus Spoke Zarathustra*...) The work of art is actually-literal... (As long as Nietzsche meant a philosophy a smaller genius of writing to go with the greatest possible genius of philosophy...) As to how that always compared... (I never had to worry about the irrational art-part of my philosophy...) And that the avante-garde be doubly *as-so*... And that I never write a science-paper without mathematics and logic to go with the science-part of science... (Finally...) (Nietzsche, as the art-philosopher, of the regular one-fifty philosophy-IQ, can't suddenly be smarter than me...) I don't mean an *irrational* between me and Nietzsche... (Nietzsche's irrational is as my irrational...) Or, my irrational being as Nietzsche's irrational... Or, my rational-philosophy, that is Nietzsche as a coincidence... (Something Einstein-smart can't be Nietzsche...) (The-possible...) That too... (I am too liberal to be Nietzsche...) Or, the liberal-problem... (How is Nietzsche one of the natural categories of something like Persona/Bergman?) (I infinitely love-my-mother...) Somebody does preserve my philosophy... (Does that always heal the coincidental-Nietzsche of my philosophy?) That I be more Egocentric than the infinite-regress itself... (The Christian contradiction of my Jewish-Nietzsche never retained...) It seems... (The skepticism of my philosophy...) Or something... (Just in case...) Making Nietzsche the absolute best-great-philosopher... (I have to *lower* the Nietzsche-potential of my philosophy...) The outer-space-fart... *How does my infinite mastery over outer-space relate to my philosophy's Nietzsche?* As by discarding with the fact that I am so infinite/sixteen-bibliographies... Which is untrue... The avante-garde philosophy was always *half...* Or, is Thus Spoke Zarathustra an absolute work of art? Possibly... Or, that Nietzsche was a genius of writing... (The problem will always be so ambivalent...) The philosophy, that is a work of art, is a genius piece of writing/actually-art... (As long as something like Thu Spoke Zarathustra be the lesser-greater Nietzsche...) Something third-best from Nietzsche... (*Beyond Good and Evil* and *On the Genealogy of Morals* always being Nietzsche's best to my philosophy...) And that Nietzsche be Nietzsche's best to my philosophy... (My Nietzsche being the metaphysical reality of rationalism composing everything he wrote as every-next-extent-of-reality/rational-reality and last-metaphysics...)

(Nietzsche and Spinoza...) The basic idea of the success of my philosophy/posthumous-fame... (Relatively...)

That it is true... (A very irrational essay...) And that being doubly as-so... (Relative of Nietzsche, again...) Which is always great... I never deconstruct my favorite great philosopher... That I deconstructed Wittgenstein will never have a deconstruction of Nietzsche to go with Wittgenstein as the deconstructed! And that thinking Heidegger in the sense of *deconstruction* being the bore/probably-just-as-impossible... Heidegger is one of the ways to get to my deconstruction too! And that he be one of the great philosophers of my philosophy... (It is actually-literal, that my Nietzsche doesn't deconstruct...) Meaning, I would have to be deconstructing everything he wrote *simultaneously...* (Naturally...) A fact I always like as interpretation of Notes from Underground... (Except, the difference being plain...) Or, that Notes from Underground have nothing to be outside-of... How my Nietzsche and my interpretation of the Dostoyevsky "effect miniature" always compared in my philosophy... *Isn't it an irrational-itself?* (My Nietzsche does interpret...) Or, the half... (My Nietzsche doesn't deconstruct...) As to how that always went with

Notes from Underground, in my case... (What compensated?) The fact that Notes from Underground have the general-interpretation in the place of a specific-possible...

(The effect is interpretation as the novella's two halves/Two-Testaments...) Or, that a dialectic be in-two, as the dialectic that isn't a dialectic/in-two... (The famous Nietzsche/Notes-from-Underground greatest possible-potential of intellect/intellectual-tie/Kaufmann is true with me too...) As to what the Kaufmann, between the two, in my philosophy is: the-basic... Making IQ out of philosophy is always untalented... *Why is my philosophy Einstein-smart? Or, why do I aspire to achieve un-talent in philosophy? Philosophy can to me a genius of philosophy...* That it will always be the strange irrational-value of my philosophy... Or, what appears as-irrational in my philosophy... (The smaller the better...) Why am I writing a philosophy that is a "preface?" Will I achieve the usual page-count with it?

The "appearance-language" never changes... Now as the irrational... (It is relative what I mean by the "relation" ...) Wittgenstein as Nietzsche? How a third- and first-best great philosophy compare as the first-best genius of IQ and me/the-first-best-genius-of-IQ and the first-best genius of great philosophy... *Which is irrational...* (Whether an irrational of my rational philosophy goes with Nietzsche's irrational and whether my rational-philosophy can be irrational at all...) What is the principal rational-value of my philosophy? A three-rationalism... (Is my philosophy potentially irrational as the rational-philosophy that is my philosophy?) It is a "two-rationalism:" something like French-left and philosophical rationalism/Descartes... (The very "being" of my philosophy...) (So as to deconstruct everything Nietzsche wrote...) Deconstructing Heidegger has little to do with imagination... And that the concept of imagination always be the prerequisite... (The strange idea-word essays...) (Are they original or strange?) A dialectic on the irrational... (The completely original...) Or, that there be nothing strange... That I will never deconstruct Nietzsche... (Something had to invent...) So as to invent philosophies that homage Nietzsche! (I can't deconstruct him or interpret him...) What was the initial way-out? Writing a philosophy that interprets him without a deconstruction deconstructing him... Which is same of the homage... (I can't traditionally interpret something...) That my philosophy be left-wing with or without the rest/category... How I solve the whole thing being ideal... (The homage being the only possibility at all...) The idea-word essays are completely original... (There is nothing strange about them...) And that the "skeptical" second-parallel of them (originality, imagination, philosophy and the century I am in) aid... (Both parallels annihilate the essay as both...) The point being that I didn't write those essays to begin with... (The theme being *illusion* instead...) Or, that they be on the metaphysical problem of my philosophy... Or, that they be that I am metaphysics... (Or, that they be that I define philosophy metaphysically essentially as metaphysics...) On that Heidegger would always mean as the best great philosopher... (On that metaphysics is the only in-itself branch of philosophy to my philosophy...) Which is what? The problem of illusion, dream and illusion/illusion-and-a-dream... On the problem of the mild-value/an-illusion... Do I mean illusion? Meaning, are the essays on an illusion or a dream? (An illusion is not a dream...) And that a dream/*film* be the illusion of my philosophy... (An illusion is not the illusion of my philosophy...) Film always becomes the essential artform of my philosophy... (Is it on the problem of Persona/the-best-film-ever-made-to-my-philosophy?) Or, on a left-wing film that is a dream/not-left-wing... Which is unoriginal... Which is original/*I-deconstructed*-Persona-*eleven-years ago... Are the idea-word essays original?* Or, what should-be-okay... (I deconstructed the film eleven years ago...) And that my deconstructions never become significant-enough... It is the total-deconstruction that becomes so fascinating as the page number/great-philosophy as idea and left-wing and great philosophy... (The deconstructions I write will always hold up as the "context"/the-total-deconstruction-and-the-total-philosophy...)

Nietzsche... (An illusion would be impossible, in my philosophy as the last-metaphysician/*Nietzsche*...) The problem being in the extra-illusion/next-extent... How does that always solve in my philosophy? As the left-wing-dream/left-wing metaphysics... So as to "parallel" ... (That my Heidegger always be something like Persona...) And that he is the secondbest great philosophy next-to-Nietzsche... (I build on perfect-thought...) It isn't a contradiction that I aspire to... (It is so great to be inventing a way to compensate that I will never deconstruct Nietzsche or Heidegger...) (In all likeliness...) Heidegger always being so potential-of-my-deconstruction... Which is philosophy and deconstruction... (Is it known that I will never deconstruct Heidegger?) An irrational-essay... (The strange/*irrational* always justified...) An illusion-language... (It is the appearance-language of my philosophy...) Something vicious of my metaphysics/the-dream, linear as the leftwing... (The best dream ever made to my philosophy is Persona/left-wing...) Or, that it was never a dream or a best dream... Which is vicious... (Isn't the best dream ever made the best dream *anyhow?*) Or, the left-wing being liberal as apolitical... (The dream does correlate as left-wing...)

The impossible-philosophy, impossible to read... *I get to outdo Hegel!* Does the impossible (impossible-to-write), of my philosophy, correlate as the impossible-to-read, of my philosophy? Possibly... (I am always harder to read than Hegel...) Which is always absurd... Which is always the double-absurd: *What do I have to do with Hegel or an extra-Hegel?* All in the context of Einstein/the-absolute-genius-of-IQ... (All in the context of the sixteen bibliographies...) The limit is unlimited! Or something... And that Hegel does, recently, become the fourth-best great philosopher of my philosophy... (So as to solve-my-philosophy...) The problem-solving... Or, creating an IQ test out of a philosophy Einstein-smart... (Augmenting the cynical-value/*contradiction*...) So as to subjectify the cynical of my philosophy and that it is a cynical philosophy... (Paralleling an extra-Hegel with the Einstein-IQ...) Isn't that always a *total-parallel?* And what is the problem-solving problem? An IQ-test or an IQ-test-question/specific? Augmenting the dream-come-true philosophy could be either... (I love an IQ question...) Which is too specific/I-love-the-IQ-test... Which is unreal or relative/I-don't-believe in-the-IQ-test... An IQ test to me being the aggregate/potential/psychology... (I, Einstein, Bergman and Wittgenstein score the Einstein-IQ-score on the IQ-test as the fame/talent...) To me... (I don't believe in the IQ test...) It is relative what the mood-swing of the IQ-test is... (Daily...) (I write my philosophy, Einstein wrote the relativity-theories, Bergman makes the best film ever made as the best film-director and Wittgenstein wrote Tractatus Logico-Philosophicus...) The rest never interested me... (The four Einsteins being the four Einsteins...) I don't care what the psychology/IQ of all four is... (Which always goes with my opinion on science...) Psychology is, again, art and philosophy, to my philosophy... (The building philosophy...) Something literally-structural... Which was always irony/the-strange... (I mean-structurally, not as fascist/right-wing...) It is the-irony... Or something... A right-wing-realism and the fascist-problem/realism... (Relative of the fascist appearance of my philosophy...) I am liberal in the century I am in... Which is, *infinitely*, dependent on the century I am in...

What do I mean by it? (An IQ test that scores two-hundred on the IQ test...) And that it be philosophy, again... (The IQ score was always in the way of the philosophy of the philosophy prior to the IQ test...) An essay on the IQ test? Something on what I would mean by my opinion on me in terms of IQ? Perhaps... (The IQ test scores the highest possible IQ...) Meaning, that the IQ test know itself prior to itself... (How does an IQ test know the lowest possible IQ?) Or, something... That I mean all four Einsteins as what they do/write without the IQ test that is so subjective to my philosophy... (Which is irrational...) *The irrational, again?* Nietzsche and my irrational, as IQ/question-of-IQ too? Possibly... (That I never deconstruct Nietzsche as should be since I will never deconstruct him...) Except, what is the actual/total-irrational of my philosophy? The rational... Art (the irrational-potentiality of my philosophy) will always be philosophy and science/as philosophy-and-science... And that science and art be as philosophy... (The philosophy is all three in a philosophy, not all three...) That my philosophy never included an irrational... Meaning, as to why any irrational selects to begin with... Or, why I select any irrational value in this essay... (It is same what irrational is to compare to Nietzsche/s irrational?) *It is an absurd-irrational... Science is mathematics and logic...* That I always be fascist towards an irrational... Which always rested on the limit (Nietzsche and Heidegger) and the sixteen bibliographies and philosophy, art and science in a philosophy... (Hegel...) The most impossible thing to read/comprehend, in my philosophy the extra-Hegel/my-philosophy... (The dependency is infinite...) Something to go with the billions of dependencies of my philosophy... I watch *Grey's Anatomy,* with my mother, last night... Was my mother really necessary? Or, that something like film come to an end...

Which is never a series/TV... (What does that create?) That I don't like a TV-show is that I be a fan of one made in the century I am in... (Or something...) (The problem-solving...)

So as to locate a fifth Einstein... (I can't forever lag Wittgenstein...)

So as to invent a new "location-philosophy" ... The idea-word being so overused... (This essay, and the rest of the continuity/idea-word-essays...) Wittgenstein is the first-best genius of IQ... (Why he becomes the third-best great philosopher...) (Isn't he always of great help?) In case an idea-word doesn't propel the essay forward! Or, something like Wittgenstein, to have next to the laptop I use to write philosophy... (What was the deconstructed, now as imagination...) The idea can come from the previous-deconstructed too! (The unnatural-lag does pay off...) Or, that I can't just *idea word...* Something simply not enough... I am trying to exchange my deconstruction with the idea-word essay... Or, that the idea-word essay be my deconstruction... Literally... The idea being to structure an illusion/that-I-stop-to-deconstruct... (That I forever deconstruct *naturally...*) That it is never too much of my philosophy... (It is not like my philosophy ever reaches imagination without IQ...) The question being whether I ever invent something past deconstruction... (Making a literal-same out of my philosophy doesn't have to be the two-periods...) That can always evolve to a next same-period... (It is same how many periods I invent...) The philosophy will always literally tie to itself/the-period... (The idea-word- essays always had something next to the laptop...) Locating something in my philosophy will always be my philosophy itself/the-one-philosophy-I-write... (That the problem of measure always be a major Jewish-category of my philosophy will always be one of the Jewish categories of my philosophy too...) IQ, religion and measure always combined in my philosophy...An overuse of the idea of a philosophical-system... The philosophy means to be Nietzsche! Which is okay/the philosophy-means-to-be-against-Nietzsche... And that the so-called system always subjectifies... (The idea-word and something like Wittgenstein...) As for example... And that it is never a system that is all that *system...* The system being in the fact of the previous-paragraph... An order-control, relative of a chaos-thing... (More like a New-World-Order irony...) Or, probably something more on the half of my philosophy... (I am against New World Order, I am for New World Order...) Or, something on my love for such stuff as Einstein, imagination, IQ, genius, etc... The generally against-NewWorld-Order, as the wrong polarity, of the right polarity... (Or something...) *I don't care... And* irony... Which is a wrong irony... (There is nothing ironical...) Something to go with the system of my philosophy... Or, that my philosophy always was a system-of-philosophy as the continuity/literal-*every-next-form-of-same... Something usually art and philosophy, as Nietzsche, Bergman and Webern is, instead, a philosophy science as mathematics and logic...* (Those deconstructions of mine become very-monotonous more than anything as everything...) (In history...) As to why I name my philosophy the system-kind... And that it is true... (The one philosophy I write did start somewhere/at-the-first-thing-I-wrote...) A Spinoza circle-philosophy of Hegel and Heidegger... (A very strict-system...) Which is nothing "emphasized" ... (Everything I write in philosophy is the professional-philosopher/a-physics-paper...) The professional philosopher knows how to read it... Meaning, a system-of-philosophy as is... (Generalizing Nietzsche is a system/absolute...) (Sixteen bibliographies...) In that respect sixteen-of-them absolutely... (The liberal-value/limit being in the way...) Does the limited-unlimited help with Nietzsche too... (What used to be art and philosophy...) Now as science of mathematics as logic... (I finish watching the longer/Alan-Smithee version of *Dune,* yesterday...) (How do I usually judge that film?) Or, what is usually a bad-film to my philosophy, now as a *Blade-Runner/2001- -:-A-Space-Odyssey* comparison, now that I have the film on Blu-Ray, DVD, can watch the extended-version, bought the film's score, etc... (A film in my room, for the first time...) Something to do with the concept of nonsense in art, that, in Dune, to me never synthesized: an art-film, a Star-Wars film and a science fiction art-film... And that the expensive-special-effects to me always look obvious/cheesy... (Probably so as to fix those bad special effects...) Or something... And the rest becomes possible too... (Something like my hate of surrealism, now a three-/four-synthesized film...) (I am trying to add one more film to the five-Hollywood-list: 2001: A Space Odyssey, *A Clockwork Orange, The Godfather II, Apocalypse Now* and Blade Runner are the best Hollywood films ever made to my philosophy...) Why not add Dune to the list? Not that it matters all that much... (It is not like Hollywood ever outdoes the best films ever made and the best directors...) (Bergman, Tarkovsky, Fellini and Kurosawa are the best film-directors...) And that Herzog mix with the three best Hollywood directors of my philosophy... (Isn't Herzog to me someplace at Kubrick, Francis Ford Coppola and Ridley Scott...) *Same-magnitude...* (The genius-Hollywood becomes relatively inconsequential...)

A mine-of-ideas... (Irony...) An idea-essay, to go with all those ideas/idea-words... Or, that my philosophy already was the idea/an-idea-philosophy... Something ideal as the a priori of IQ/Einstein... Meaning, Germany/idea/German philosophy, as Einstein/walk-of-ideas... (The appearing cheesy-relation...) Germany and the Einstein-IQ... (The emphasis of my philosophy...) *Writing a German genius of philosophy that is science is not a German genius of philosophy!* (I hate analytic philosophy...) Or, why did my philosophy always have that analytic-philosophy-aspect to go with the philosophical nationalism of my philosophy/Germany? Probably since I mean a total-mix/mild-value in a mild-philosophy that becomes-extreme/builds-on-the-most-negative-value-to-become-the-most-positive-philosophy... (The logic is Continental as Analytic in a philosophy completely-Continental and logical as the philosophical-branch...) Or, that it be an illusion... (My philosophy doesn't include an analytic-philosophy-aspect...) Philosophy and IQ being in a German philosophy.... (Nothing changes *philosophically!*) And that it is

Wittgenstein who matches Einstein IQ-wise... (Is the rest of the analytic philosophy Einstein-smart?) Analytic philosophy being potential of Einstein's IQ/IQ, not Einstein's IQ itself, as far as I know... (It is a relative...) Art, science and philosophy in a philosophy... And that science be logic and mathematics... (That is why...) Something made sure... (Analytic philosophy can include in my "German-nationalism" ...) (I am the best philosophy and best IQ...) The becoming (Spinoza, Heidegger and Hegel) always synthesized both as the best philosophy... And that IQ never suffered... And that philosophy never suffered... (I always film the language...) That I should go to a film-school, so as to learn how film my philosophies/the-language-of-my-philosophy... (The "mix" of my philosophy always saved my philosophy...) (As long as it be an irrational-essay...) Something way too great to me/I-will never-deconstruct-Nietzsche... My philosophy, that is Nietzsche, now "directly" ... And that it is an impressive-thing/a two-irrational-comparison... Which doubly-impresses: *Is it a two-irrational-comparison?* (An overuse of monotony...) That I am tying Webern to Nietzsche... (Or something...) Which is irrational... Or, that being what is so irrational about the essay... Nietzsche is the irrational-inclusion!

To base a philosophy on a *why* doesn't go with Nietzsche... Not all that much... That it is philosophy/a-why... And my philosophy being so rational... Why? Or, that rationalism always fascinate my philosophy as the rational-profession... *How can something like rationalism exist to begin with?* (Relative of Nietzsche...) How can the irrational be a rational profession... As to how I always synthesized the rational-problem with the irrational-philosophy of Nietzsche as by synthesizing both... (And that Germany/the-irrational go with the irrational/Nietzsche and invent the rational-profession...) (A French-problem...) As to how I, probably, synthesize the rational and irrational... (The doubly-rational/the-irrational and the rationally-irrational/the-irrational...) Which is excessive... (An analytic-judgment...) *Is it* a priori *or a posteriori?* Or, the absurd/impossible question... *Everything I write in philosophy being factually-a priori/Einstein-smart/IQ...* And that my philosophy already be so a priori as Christ/the-Christian... Or, my Christ/the-a priori... (The inferior religion, as one of my two religions of my philosophy, as the superior religion as a priori/an-inferior-religion-a priori-wise...) The problem being that that was never enough to categorize for an actually a priori philosophy... (My philosophy always based on two religions...) And that Christ be the inferior one of the two... The philosophy had to be IQ so as to be a priori... A mine-of-ideas... I guess I mean the-reader! Or, the post-structural problem... The reader is expcetd to realize the reality of the essay out of the idea that is the essay... Which is impossible... The essay never becomes real naturally... Or, the liberal left-wing of apolitical... It is not like the reader is required to make a communism out of apolitical-liberalism... Or, I don't mean a communist-philosophy of the reader-freedom... (It is a contradiction...) Or, an appearance/lie as appearance...

(Something to purify the impure Nietzschean potential of my Nietzsche philosophy that isn't Nietzsche...) The suffering philosophy... *Or, what are the pure categories of Nietzsche in my philosophy?* That my Nietzsche never be a pure-category or category... Or, Nietzsche has nothing to do with a category... (The rational to me never contradicted the irrational or Nietzsche...) It is an irrational-mockery... Or, attacking everything is criticizing everything or creating a self-mockery out of an antifoundational mockery that is irrational... Which is irrational... Isn't Nietzsche meant to be irrational? (The irrational-mockery being rational...) (The irrational-inclusion...) How does Webern compare to Nietzsche? *Or, what is Webern relative of Nietzsche?*

The philosophical Austrian music is no philosophy/Austrian... And that the Bach left-wing homage be unrelated/has-nothing-to-do-with-Nietzsche... Is it possibly Nietzschean as the transparent/rational? (Against Wagner...) Or something... (The anti-nationalist...) Or something... Except, Nietzsche being the irrational... And Webern being classical music... Which is possible of Nietzsche/natural-of-Nietzsche... In some ways... (As the wrong classical music/the-rational, Nietzschean as the anti-national/against-Wagner...)

Is the essay subjective as irrational? (A guessing game...) As long as it is a game... (An IQ-game, IQ-test and Einsteinsmart-IQ...) The three combine... And separately... (So as to fascinate...) The philosophy has to base on the idea of imagination... (An absurd-appearance...) A lie/illusion... Or, a lie (Nietzsche) to go with the illusion (Christ) ... Always the vicious-potential... Isn't my Nietzsche Jewish/Judaic? Absolutely... Except, something never annihilated in the Christian sense of *suffering* and Nietzsche... And that Nietzsche never becomes the "anti-Christ" as the liberal-Christ/somethinglike-the-Orthodox-Christianity/the-concrete... As is my Nietzsche generally possible of the general-liberal-Christ generally... (Anything liberally-Christian never objected to Nietzsche *as* the Orthodox-Christianity!) Nietzsche, as the possible "Catholic-philosopher," absolutely liberally-Christian, as the anti-Christ and that my-Nietzsche always meant Judaism *absolutely!* (All-that, and the optimist-Nietzche, that is my Nietzsche, that is Nietzsche...) Meaning, without the absurd... (*That my Nietzsche never be nihilist, absurd or pessimist...*) Meaning, all three exchange in my philosophy as pessimism... Meaning, all three exchange, in my philosophy, as all three... And that the concept of nothing "or" atheism never make it to my Nietzsche or my philosophy... (The philosopher who invents pessimism is to me always Judaic/theist and Judaic...) It is the greatest possible irony! (Nietzsche invented the philosophical-atheism and atheism!) How extreme does that always grow in the direction of Judaism... (It is inconsequential that Nietzsche invent both-atheisms!) (Very...) (As long as it be true that he didn't invent atheism...) *I was never interesting for the sake of being so...* And that I don't invent the Judaic-interpretation... (And that that be the professional-philosophy...) Something doubly-triply to shrink the interesting-appearance of my Nietzche that is fantastical/fantasy as appearance... (The fantasy-genre...) (Science-fiction does have potential in my philosophy as film without the-writer, as far as I know...) What I actually hate, in art, most of all, will always be fantasy, not science-fiction... (Science-fiction gets to the "idea," if nothing else...) Or, the banal/obvious didacticism of science-fiction never hurt as idea... (And that 2001: A Space Odyssey, Blade Runner and, now, Dune always make an art-house science-fiction film separate-of-the-writing-they-base-on as the natural question of film/the visual-art-form...) The visual-effects... (Except for Dune...) And that Dune sufficiently and recently fixed the cheese effects with the aid of the rest healing with the longer-version, sharper-resolution, separate-music, etc., in my room... That I am always Austrian... (What care do I have with a Hollywood cinema?) Except, I being German, Jewish and French as Austrian... And that it is a philosophy too "liberal" to be German... Which never annihilated Germany... (Must be something out of pity...) Or, an impossible, again... (Something to go with philosophy and the Einstein-IQ/the impossible...) The philosophy-and-Einstein-genius-IQ is not the only impossible of my philosophy... (Or, that I had to locate other *impossible* too, to make the principal-impossible possible at all...) Do I buy Hollywood out of pity? Possibly/absolutely... Except, the question of pity being so absolute/infinite with me... I pity everything... Meaning, that I mock everything... (Must be that I am in a century I pity *totally...*) Except, that being so relative too... (Pity what?) Pity the IQ of science and left-wing question of politics? And that the black man to me get to his century...

(That I have nothing to do with a black-race doesn't mean a black-race-potential...) And so on... (That my absolute-pity always relativize...) Or something... The-relative...

Anything is everything... On the question of subjective in my philosophy... *Who buys that I am a philosopher?* Which will always be irrelevant... (The never-ending clinical-depression annihilated...) My philosophy being so nihilist of a clinical depression... (The Einstein-IQ has to retain!) Which was always so relative... (Nietzsche scored one-fifty on the IQ test...) Which is absolute/I-do-have-to-think-about-such-stuff-as-positive-psychology-when-I-write-philosophy... No clinical depression scored two-hundred! (One-fifty is not two-hundred...) (A hurt of some kind...) (I make it in philosophy...) Such a great thing to be writing... (Something intermediary/a-solved-problem...) An irrational-essay... It is bad that I can't deconstruct my favorite great philosopher... (A *nothing-essay...*) A total-irony... (Or something...) The nothing would be atheism... (Relative of the irrational of the essay...) That I affirm Nietzsche's irrational, while denying his atheism... Why? Or, the illusion that I, *also,* write an atheist-essay... (The real and unreal of the essay...) Which always becomes metaphysics/*real-and-unreal...* And that it is a nihilist-essay as an illusion... (As long as something *principally* prioritizes as the irrational, as to how I read the essay...) The potentially-bad about the essay always being that *mix...* (That never happened to me...) I am writing something I potentially dislike/throw-out/never-print-out-or-publish... *What happened to my never-ending self-loving-philosophy/my-never-ending-love-for-my-philosophy?* Must be that I did finally reach that limit... Or, I overwrote with or without the one-philosophy I always write literally...

Depressing philosophy and language... (An irrelevant-essay...) The irrational being so great... However, that that irrational include in an irrational/itself... I don't know how spoiled this essay gets to be... As long as it is irrational... (Or, what is my irrational?) That no irrational be an irrational possible of me... (There is nothing to spoil...) Or, selecting an irrational... (Does a three-rational-value/my-philosophy create an irrational?) Which is a bit too excessive... (My philosophy is rational!) Who cares what the irrational, relative of Nietzsche's irrational, in this essay is... It is any irrational as should be... (I don't omit adding this essay to the rest of my philosophy...) (The nihilist being an illusion...) The question of the mixed-category being irrational... Or, that the initial irrational be the included irrational...

Some desire to spoil my philosophy... Or something... (The reader is expected to rationalize the irrational...) As long as it be a structural-irrational... That I am a never-ending Nietzsche as the infinitely self-loving philosopher/man doesn't need a spoil... (The essay is structural, as far as I know...) I do initial everything I write in philosophy... This essay does go with the rest of my philosophy... (I change my name...) That my philosophy never suffered at the expense of my name... (An essay subjective of me...)

(How can structuralism be irrational?) (Isn't something like post-structuralism the actually irrational potential?) Which rests on the question of irrational and religion/atheism... That something like post-structuralism to my philosophy always be irrational *anyhow...* (My structural-philosophy always had the irrational-potential of atheism/post-structuralism as the double irrational-value of post-structuralism to my philosophy...) As the strange structural *un-belief-in-language...* Which is the only post-structural contradiction of my philosophy... However, that being as the liberal-religion... My philosophy does take atheism into account as-possible... Judaism, as the best religion, will always be strange... *It is liberal-religion...*

Something like religion is, possibly, responsible for all the bad... (The meaning of Judaism in my philosophy being that it *is* two religions...) Or, Judaism is not the only religion of my philosophy as the best religion... (Or something...) The usual... (Fixing-categories...) IQ and measure generalize the idea of Judaism/the-best-religion, to make that a best-religion be as an inferior-religion and two-religions! (The desire being to generalize that *best* and *superior* religion...) A never-ending-philosophy as idea... Or, that that infinite-philosophy be idea... (To my philosophy...) A two-idea negates idea... (To my philosophy...) (No change in pace...) The "*differance*" being in the fact of the irrational-essay... (So as to compare my difference-deconstruction with a different essay...) My deconstruction, that always based on the idea of difference without deconstruction, relative of the different/irrational essay... As long as something essentially-ties... *It is a same-essay...* Or, on Nietzsche and my deconstruction... (I found an easy way out/a-way-out...) That I can't deconstruct Nietzsche is that I write an irrational essay that is a rational philosophy... (How would that be?) A subjective... (I name me the best great philosopher...) Whether my infinite self-love solves the issue of Nietzsche in my philosophy... (The self-love, that is the self-hating-Serb...) *Am I a self-hating-Serb?* Possibly/absolutely... Except, that being that relative... (What is a

German-French Jew?) A Serb? Except, that being the mixed-problem of the German, Jewish and French... Or, I mean Jewish and German as French... (Is it three or two ideal races of me?) Except, that being the one race of Germany... (To me...) Or, that I to me always be the same genius-level of philosophy as Germany... (Does France solve the IQ/Jewish problem of my philosophy?) Am I a Serb at the same level as Germany... (Except, that also being as the general question of talent and IQ...) Or, that a Serb to me exceed in making the best food on the planet/Chinese-food/my-favorite-food... And so on... (So as to name my philosophy a left-wing, not a philosophy...) Does that solve the question of talent/my basic-fear? Possibly... That I always fear un-talent, the certainty of my philosophy being my Einstein-IQ... Maybe I should stop categorizing me for philosophy... So as to simply name me a left-wing... (That way I can know that I am the greatest genius-of-philosophy and Einstein-IQ at the same time without constantly asking whether the French-left-part means that I am an Einstein-smart German-genius of philosophy...) I should have been something purely-left-wing as left-wing. (An infinite genius, an infinite genius of philosophy and an infinite genius of IQ...) (As long as I like a challenge...) Or something... (Such a regret...) What could have been so many times easier to write... (Which is same...) As long as I do achieve a philosophy a never-ending genius of philosophy and never-ending genius of IQ... (Who cares what the magnitude of effort/the-impossible is?) And why do I respect philosophy so much? (It is not like a blend of art and science ever purified...) That I love art and science same will always be subjective/I-love-science-more, seeing as I dislike both, seeing as I like science's IQ... (It is not like my care for philosophy ever purified/becomes-absolute...) I love *my* philosophy, to subjectively-love-philosophy... (That my mockery of something like analytic-philosophy be absolute...) Or something... Or, I do purely-love-philosophy... That I always mock analytic philosophy infinitely... (My philosophy always names Germany the greatest genius of philosophy possible, historically and world-regionally...) Meaning, my philosophy does categorize philosophy for genius... A genius of art and a genius of science always meant a genius of philosophy/that-therebe-a-genius-of-philosophy... Or, there is such a thing/a-genius-philosopher... (How I praise the genius-circle-vicious of German philosophy, as for example...) *There are no unsolved problems of philosophy...* Or, Germany, as the only race to realize what philosophy/the-vicious-circle is/as-the-only-race-to-realize-that-philosophy-is-a-vicious-circle...

(The question of art and science is the only thing to specify in the context of philosophy...) The question being everything and nothing as art and science, as to why I do love my profession/am-a-self-loving-philosopher...

I stop writing this essay... *When?* That there is no deconstructed... Or, maybe split the essay in half, in the place of my usual deconstructive-proportion... Those deconstructions of mine always assumed a same magnitude, following the first in the series/the-deconstruction-of-me... *Something stabilized!* Now the irrational-essay on irrational and Nietzsche... However, that that "difference" always be indifferent, again... *I assume the usual deconstructive-proportion! Purifying the irrational-essay is irrational... There is nothing to purify...* (I am not mocking my philosophy out of boredom...) And that I don't mock my philosophy... (Nothing changes...) The-potential... (What is the rest?) I eat my favorite food/the-planet that-I-am-on... Which is nothing new... (I eat the outer-space that am in...) The never-ending-difference... Something like the outer-space to me always being so infinitely-inconsequential... Except, that being like exchanging Chinese-food with a fart/my-fart/what-I-infinitely-fart... And is it infinitely a favorite food that is Chinese food... (I mean Serbia and France to go with China...) *And why name my favorite food a fart?* I ate the infinite outer-space/doesn't-have-to-be-my-favorite food... (So as to invent a different metaphor...) The outer-space, as the fart, my favorite food, as my favorite food... Meaning, me and my favorite food without the never-ending outer-space... (What exists to me will always be my philosophy and Chinese food...) I annihilate the outer-space, so as for both to exist without that outer-space... Which has to complete as sex... (Do I love food or fucking a woman?) It is not like I am a food-lover/I-probably-mean-my-philosophyand-the-woman-I-infinitely-fuck... (Something like my favorite porn-star...) Piper Perri... Except, that she never does all the sexual positions... (Not my favorite porn star...) What used to be my favorite porn stars... Which was a long time ago... (I don't know how those new girls look like...) (So as to create a nostalgic-feeling...) Something more of the first three things I write in philosophy: a poem, the Avante-garde, an Avante-garde work of art, an Avante-garde work of philosophy, whether those philosophies were, in fact, artistically-Avante-garde and an Avante-garde-essay... (Generally...) And as the science of mathematics as logic of those three things I write principally, as the one-philosophy, as the first philosophy that is my philosophy without all three... (The irrational-essay is a homage/a-fourth-sequel to those first three things I wrote...) That my philosophy already knew that I will never deconstruct Nietzsche once I do get to the secondperiod/deconstruction... (Something foreshadowed...) Except, this essay being the irrational/without-mathematics, logic and science... (Except, all my philosophy being all three crowns of genius-IQ...) It is a homage... Or, it is a direct sequel... (Something strange to do/reversing-to-the-first-period...) Which is infinitely nothing-strange, the idea of a *period* in my philosophy always being that illusion... *I write the one-philosophy!* Suddenly writing something my-first-period is like suddenly inventing the second-period *suddenly-now...* That my philosophy will never base on the idea of a philosophical system... (Not in that respect...) The philosophical-system being the one-philosophy, not a differentiated-philosophical period... (Such an effort to "differentiate" ...) (Wasn't it a literal every-next-form-of-same and the one-philosophy?) Didn't Nietzsche essentially tie his philosophy as the one-philosophy too? What about Bergman and Webern? *That I always annihilated that my philosophy be Nietzsche, Bergman and Webern in the context of repetition...* Every next form of same is not what is Nietzsche, Bergman or Webern about my philosophy...

A mockery, that attacks-everything/my-philosophy... (I am typical of my-Nietzsche in the century I am in...) Except, that that mean the limit-of-mockery/always-the-realist/*Nietzsche*... It is an irrational-mockery, in my case rational...

All that I am typical of... (An atypical-illusion...) My Nietzsche never changes... (It is a constant...) Something relative, though... (Philosophy, art and science...) And that be philosophy... Which is mathematics, logic and science... (How does one work out the "total-relation?") What appears of a total-mockery too/an-anti-foundation... As long as I be the best great philosopher of my philosophy... (Is Nietzsche the best great philosopher?) I mean A Wittgenstein-of-subjective... (How excessive is it?) As long as I mean as anything/something-to-boost-the-unimaginativeness, relative of the idea-word/the basic-idea-of-the-essay... (I am not deconstructing him...) I can't write an Einstein-smart-philosophy without the imagination-part/prior-creativity! The primitive psychology of my philosophy (the-self-conscious) will always be that I do go with a psychology: the self-conscious and IQ-prerequisite, a to how that always worked psychologically in my "anti-psychological" philosophy... *It is philosophy!* Which was always okay... My philosophy to me being psychologically-apt anyhow... Or, that psychology be art and philosophy *to my philosophy*... The primitive-psychology, that is psychology itself, to my philosophy... (Must be something one my dislike of scientific-psychology...) Which was always strange: the IQ psychology-theory on IQ was always the science/actual-theory-of-psychology-that-is-science, as far as I know...

(Primitive-language and primitive-psychology...) Something primitively-philosophy too... Or, the three-primitive essay... (So as to combine the self-conscious and the IQ theory of psychology...) It is not like I know that that is an actual theory of psychology, that a whole theory exists to support in an actual way that creativity is the IQ-prerequisite prior to Einstein's IQ... (It is like me assuming that I am writing a free-association...) Which is general... (*The essay is hypnosis/boredom...*) Which is an assumption too... (Philosophy isn't made to be interesting...) And to hypnotize a philosopher would mean a completely obsolete-thing/writing-something-for-the-sake-of-doing-so... (The essay is my philosophy/the-one-philosophy...) The boredom/outdated of my philosophy will always be the revolutionary system of philosophy... Which was already excessive-enough... (Or, the completely new way to think a philosophy...) Meaning, a

Serb writing a German genius of philosophy... (Why did I need to invent a new system/philosophy?) The art of writing has nothing to do with my philosophy... (Nietzsche has to be a contradiction/one-of-the-three-as-one of-the-sixteen...) Or, that my Nietzsche always be mild/mild-of-me-as-the-best-great-philosopher-of-my-philosophy... That art included... Which was always as mathematics, logic and science... (Which was always as philosophy and science...) (The problem of IQ and art...) Or, that my philosophy never objected to being art as Bergman... Which is a bit too limited/Bergman-as-the-only-artist-to-reference... That my philosophy can be art in the context of Bergman... Or, in case Bergman used to be the only artist, ever, to score an Einstein-IQ score on the IQ test... (As two Bergmans...) (The boredom...) Something I always write... (That I am not an artist creating a work of art that is Einstein-smart...) Art has nothing to do with me... Which was always subjective too... The philosophy is philosophy and IQ... Which was always objective/the-IQ-never-shrinks... (That it is a philosophy-and-IQ philosophy is always a philosophy-and-IQ philosophy...) As to what the basic claim of the philosophy is... (Something can be a genius of philosophy and a genius of IQ at the same time...) That the philosophy becomes the greatest possible genius of philosophy never shrinks its Einstein-IQ/the-greatest possible-genius-of-IQ... (A mean, to include, both, while being the one, while including both in the one...) Jewish mathematics become German... Or, a German, suddenly a genius of mathematics... (I watch Persona, with my mother, two evenings ago...) This time really unnecessary... *Why do I watch the best film ever made to me with my mother?* And that it be to the end/the-whole-film... Something usually intended as impossible with my mother... (She finds the film great without the greatness of her favorite Bergman films/The-Seventh-Seal-and-*Fanny-and-Alexander*...) And that Bergman be second-best to her... (That the best film ever made to her always be Andrei Rublev...) Meaning, Tarkovsky is the best/the-first-best-best... And that I am watching the best film ever made... (Why is she watching Persona with me?) I don't need her to make me feel better/make-it-possible-to-watch-an-infinite-un-talent-instead-of-the-best-film-ever-made... (Really strange...) That my mother never relates to an Einstein-IQ or philosophy... Meaning, the IQ of Persona, that has nothing to do with my mother... (Probably as to why the film is so less potentially of my mother...) Something okay to appeal as the structuralism... (The film appears *post-structurally*...) As to how it was possible to watch the film with her once... The problem being in the many times I watch the film with her... (It is supposed to be a Christian-Judaic one-view potential of her...) Where she is similar is at the two religions, not at IQ... (Relative of the basic likeness/Germany, Jewry and France, that is my mother as Germany, Jewry and Spain...) As the two religions... And that my mother respect something like Russia... (Which differentiated/I-can-like-Dostoyevsky-and-Tarkovsky-without-Russia...) And so on... (The basic differences between me and my mother...) (I love my mother in the place of my father because of the religion question of the total religious-question...) My father, who was the greatest possible genius of flute-playing... The rest never matched... (A zero-IQ/musician, to go with a Serbian pure belief in Christ/something-purely-Christian...) Philosophy and IQ being so completely unrelated... And that his IQ went down to zero from mother's one-twenty-score on the IQ test...

And that that be as religion too... (I love my mother's Christian Judaism...)

What is the art of my philosophy? *The post-structurally-appearing...* Which never had art to go with the appearance... (My un-talent (language, writing, learning a new language or understanding the nature of language) ...) Which will always be relative... (Hermeneutics/metaphysics-of-language is natural of my philosophy...) That my philosophy always be a philosophy of language... Which was never possible to begin with, possible as the postmodernism of my philosophy... *It is not like my structural philosophy believes in language...* That I am bad at language and writing will always be the hermeneutical-philosophy: my aesthetics, as one of the major philosophical branches of my philosophy, always included hermeneutics... (Structural-philosophy...) As my Derrida/how-I-would-think-the-absurd-of-deconstruction... And that anything hermeneutical (to my philosophy) always be structural... That Derrida can be structural as the hermeneutical philosophy... (Not that I ever read Derrida...) Which is natural/*thought...* That the French-left of my philosophy always be irony/idea... Which correlated my philosophy in general... (IQ over intellect, as idea...) (The potential...) A philosophy of language *metaphysics, aesthetics* and *logic...* Which is never *potential...* It is what solves the contradiction... Meaning, I usually don't try the irrational... Something to rationalize the problem, as the rational philosophy, as to how the structural and hermeneutical correlated... (The excessive is subjective...) Or, the structural rationalized instead... (The skeptical irony of my philosophy...) The irrational... Which is Nietzsche... Which, again, never goes with the sixteen bibliographies/an included-Nietzsche... (I film the language...) Something always too theoretical to be Nietzsche... (Which, again, is never an issue...) That Nietzsche is the best great philosopher will always be an inclusion: three best great philosophers, sixteen bibliographies and philosophy, art and science... Something theoretical, as the Einstein-IQ, was okay/never-impeded-on Nietzsche... (I am the best great philosopher...) That the IQ-part be in the way of philosophy in my philosophy *generally*... (I am not solving the problem of Nietzsche in my philosophy...) The problem being all three great philosophers...

(Wittgenstein is always great-help...) Why Wittgenstein did become the third-best great philosopher... Doesn't he intend as the last-best great philosophy/Russell? (There is a vicious-contradiction to go with the way I categorize great philosophy...) Wittgenstein is the first-best genius of IQ/Einstein... (Meaning, that Wittgenstein be a two-genius as question/theoretically...) (My philosophy being an "even-Wittgenstein"/a-first-best-genius-of-philosophy-and-a-first-bestgenius-of-IQ...) To me... (As to what the aim of my philosophy is/what-is-so-original-about-my-philosophy...)

I love the challenge... (Making a literal-science out of hermeneutics...) Which was never literal... Which is great... (The science is mathematics and logic...) *I love science's IQ...* That I be bad at science... (Derrida is one of the French-left philosophers of my philosophy...) Something *Sartre*... (As the limited potential of French-left of my philosophy...) That I read *The Imaginary*... (Which is the only French-left philosophy for me to read...) Kind of like posing the interesting problem of the French-left in my philosophy/the-idea-and-idea... The literal-idea of something like the French-left philosophy, in my philosophy, and the IQ/anti-intellectual/idea-in-my-philosophy as the intellectual/German philosophy... (The idea and idea...) And that the French-left-philosophy-part have the specific purpose... I mean to be a French-left philosopher *only*/an-Einstein-IQ-and-a-German-philosophy-won't-be-compatible-any-time-soon... (*Not a literal idea/French-left-philosophy...*) I *did* read a French-left-philosophy... *Is it a literal-idea/French-left-philosophy?* (Sartre's lesser-work...) However, that that solve in the fact of all those philosophies I read that have nothing to do with me... (Sartre, Descartes and Kirkegaard...) Sartre is not one of the great philosophers of my philosophy! Relative of Notes from Underground/that-literature-can-be-philosophy-to-my-philosophy... (*Can fiction be philosophy?*) And so on... That the theory of fiction being philosophy be theory in my philosophy... (And so on...) *Does a mathematical science of logic allow for art to be possible?* (On the total problem/proposition of idea in my philosophy...) Something essential to directly write on in an idea-word essay... (*Do the idea-essays become essential of my philosophy?*) Which is an absurd question... Nothing becomes essential of my philosophy... (The one-philosophy, that will always be the very first thing I wrote in philosophy, that is the one-philosophy...) (An interesting essay to write, like the many essays I wrote...) Absurdly prioritizing idea in my philosophy/the-subject-of-idea-of-my-philosophy... (An-illusion...) Which is the usual... (A dream...) Or, that an illusion relate to metaphysics to my philosophy/*is-incomplete*... (On illusion-in-my-philosophy...) Relative of the vicious-question of art in my philosophy... (A dream being a film...) That the best film ever made to my philosophy can't be my philosophy/is-art, and what the exact percentage-inclusion-potential of art in my philosophy can be... (I write a philosophy that is five-percent-art...) And so on...

I would aspire to writing a "fact" ... Which is always the composite-argument... (A science, that is mathematically rational relative of philosophy/the-above-opinion...) And so on... (The absurd-essay...) As long as it be the idea-word essay... (Something minimalist/Webern would be art...)

Or, that I can't write something-Webern/art... (As the problem of art in my philosophy...) (What is a mathematical science of logic?) Especially in the context of mathematics/the-unknown profession/discipline... (As to what the exact relation of art to my philosophy is...) The unknown... (Mathematics is philosophy as definition...) (Relative of the IQ-question/philosophy's-relatively-primitive-IQ-as-compared-to-somethinglike-mathematics...) Is the three-IQ relation (mathematics, science and logic) art? Possibly... Which is impossible... (The three-relation being Einstein-smart...) Which is possible as Bergman... (So as to take into consideration that logic being what kind/an-interdisciplinary-field...) Something makes-known as IQ... (The complicating will always be Bergman...) I do every kind of logic, as the philosophical branch... And so on...

The-exact... (Why do I compare art to philosophy?) *It is a work of art that has to be brief, exact, cold, etc., to my philosophy...* Philosophy to me always being the half-art of half-everything... And that I mean of the three-IQ... Bergman being the only work of art to reference in the context of an Einstein-IQ... (Art to me got to the average-limit IQ-score...) (Shrinking language is to augment logic...) The-irrational... I never aspire in logic without the other two branches... And metaphysics being philosophy without the philosophical branch... (Must be something on the general problem of the general logic of my philosophy/all-logic...) That the science, that is my philosophy, always be *representation...* (Taking into consideration that the all-logic philosophical logic could be all logic...) Realism...

Always the augmented-man... *How Egocentric does my philosophy have to get to be?* A philosophy that fulfills me in every way... (I am in the century I am in/thank-God...) That there is never a Ph.D. or actual success to relate to my philosophy, apart from the professional philosopher that my philosophy is written for, never had any meaning/is indifferent... That the philosophy be two professional philosophers! (Everything always-combined beautifully...) The usual... (Never-ending-happiness instead of a clinical-depression...) Something always a *clinical-depression-potential,* in the extreme difference of infinite-happiness... (The consideration being that I intend as the very clinical-depression itself...) One of the infinite-extremes of my philosophy/something-infinite-regress... (My philosophy/optimism-and Einstein-IQ/optimism...) That too... (The infinitely-optimistic philosophy has to be infinitely-optimistic...) As to how I always had to shrink the infinite Einstein-IQ down to a usual Einstein-IQ... (The problem of my philosophy always being in the infinite-optimism...) It is never my intention to write something infinitely smarter than Einstein... (The impossible IQ is Einstein, not an infinite Einstein-IQ...) As by shrinking that optimism, of my philosophy, to a normal-limit *optimism...* The usual-problem of my philosophy: the IQ can't be infinite-Einstein or Einstein... Isn't the Einstein IQ-limit already so impossible of a German genius of philosophy? (And so on...) (Metaphysics of language...) The philosophy of language/my-philosophy, that is hermeneutics/a-philosophy-of-language... That I have clear branches-of-philosophy to think, always, will always be a philosophy of language... Or, the strange-contradiction... (A philosophy that will never know how to write or exceed in language...) A philosophy of language that is metaphysics, aesthetics and logic/has nothing-to-do-with-a-philosophy-of-language... (Must be that I mean *deconstruction...*) That my philosophy writes the one philosophy... (Deconstruction included...) My philosophy is a philosophy of language... Except, that always being my ideal-deconstruction... Whether a difference-deconstruction without deconstruction is a deconstruction... (It is a philosophy of language that isn't a philosophy of language/metaphysics, aesthetics and logic...)

(Is it a clarity of thought I try with the help of this essay?) An analytic-philosophy irony/contradiction? (So as to love what I absolutely hate...) (The optimism matched...) Or something... (Augmenting IQ over philosophy...) Or something... (I do believe in psychology...) When do I augment the language? Or, that I go back to my usual philosophical-routine...

(Probably never...) Meaning, I never lowered the language-potential first... (Those deconstructions of mine usually aren't language...) (What is the difference between my deconstruction and my idea-essay?) Language assumed a minimalist appearance... Which is as the illusion... (Watching *The Godfather, Coda: The Death of Corleone* last night, with my mother...) Is it intended with her or without her... (This time some really big "spoil" ...) What should have been a director's cut thing comes with a completely rethought title/name...

I would augment the deconstructive-mode... (That I am deconstructing *anyhow*...) (So as to lower my self-esteem...) Doesn't my philosophy appear a Hitler-Nietzsche... (That my Nietzsche be liberal of left-wing as apolitical too...) That one part never needed to generalize... (The polarity of my philosophy...) The fascist-appearance, of my philosophy, to go with a Hitler-interpretation of Nietzsche... (Must be something intended/a-lie-as-Nietzsche...) Or, a lying-appearance... (The Nietzsche is way too correct...) The never-ending-Egocentrism was always too-subjective... (Something had to match

Nietzsche as the "anti-Christ" ...) Meaning, my infinitely anti-Christian philosophy had to be the anti-Christ at the level of appearance... (The philosophy being half-Christian and Nietzsche...) A never-ending anti-Christ is too subjective "of" Nietzsche and can't be half-Christian! And that Hitler be unrelated to a liberal apolitical-left-wing of Judaism... (I write the

Judaic-Nietzsche-philosophy...) *It is a mental-illness...* (I need psychiatric help...) Or, as long as I do write an anti-

Christian appearance/a-lying-appearance... (I don't need psychiatric help...) It is an illusion... A contradiction-Nietzsche, to base on the lying-appearance, as the illusion/concept-of-illusion... (Something metaphysical, as potential...) Meaning, not a contradiction... (That my Nietzsche always be metaphysics/Heidegger/Heidegger's-interpretation-of-Nietzsche...) A dream... (Nietzsche is, to my philosophy, always the last metaphysician...) (Persona...) (Am I writing a dream?) A sequel to my deconstruction of Persona... (So, to speak...) Or something... (Which is always a composite-argument...) I don't know how to write and my philosophy being the "five-percent-art" ... And that a dream to me not belong in a writing... (Fiction to me always being the imagination that never finds itself in a film...) Imagination and dream, so to speak... (Fiction and film, so to speak...) The two-stay separate/can-be-together-as-the-question-of-the-superiority-of-an-artform/as-the-two-best-art-forms-of-my-philosophy... (How the dependence and independence of the two art-forms of my philosophy always functioned...) There is never clarity/*very-Continental*... (So as to utilize what I infinitely hate to shrink my infinite self-love...) I always search for a girlfriend! (An infinite-Narcissus doesn't match...) (Equilibrium...) (That too...) What is always so bad about my philosophy... (My infinite self-love...) Something I always had to control... (So as to "watch" the language of my philosophy...) *Is it a language-theory to go with a film-theory?* Perhaps... My philosophy of language, that was always the perfect Tractatus Logico-Philosophicus... (Whether film implies something within that language-*theoretical-possible* of my philosophy and whether Wittgenstein's version of the same thing implied film...) Wittgenstein was always a fan of the Western films! (A joke...) Or, something self-referential... (His theory of language is a Western film...) Whether he implied film or any visual art-form... And that always being in-the-general-sense... (He had significance in the world of art/as-any-art-form...) What was all art/*any-art-form...*

(The World as Will and Representation...) As the basic divisions... Schopenhauer has nothing to do with me, Wittgenstein being third-best, my philosophy being so fond of representation/never-minded-representation, Wittgenstein's early period being possible of Schopenhauer and that early-Wittgenstein as the hybrid/so-many-copies-as-reference-as-bibliography-ofappearance... (Etc...) Something always built on the potential of the fascinating self-hating-Wittgenstein... Whether he, *Continentally,* be a philosophy as the self-hating-Jew writing it... (Would make sense *Continentally...*) That a Jew have no thought, as the copy-thought from the copy-race... (The total "composite" ...) My Wittgenstein, that is Einstein, relative of that potential Continental-interpretation that is against me, that I am so nationally-Continental, and that my Wittgenstein be the self-loving-Jew as pure-value/absolutely... (Isn't the appearance "clear?") I mean to be that self-hating-Wittgenstein of Continental-potential, not a self-loving-Jew of Analytic-potential! *Is Wittgenstein's Continental-potential anti-Semitic?* (Is his Analytic-potential Semitic?) And that I do mean as that early-period... (I never read his *Philosophical Investigations...*) (I love Wittgenstein's IQ...) Lagging him ten years is as the imagination-prerequisite/my-philosophy'stheory-of-psychology... (As the contradiction/Wittgenstein-has-nothing-to-do-with-a-theory-of-psychology and that he is a theory of psychology/affirmation in the Continental context...) That his philosophy self-undermined as Analytic or Continental... (To my philosophy...) As to what interpretation of him I go with... (The absurd-Wittgenstein...) I am not deconstructing him ten years, I am lagging him ten years... That my Wittgenstein never did self-contradict as psychology, the absurd, etc... All those opposite values of him... The visual language, that is psychological with the theory of psychology as intact... (That my Tractatus Logico-Philosophicus always be visual-language to go with a theory of psychology/isn't-just-a-visual-language...) (Such a great imagination to have next to the laptop I write my philosophy with...) Can be anything... (It is same what is there next to the laptop...) As long as it be something potential of boosting the imagination... (I have to stay at the one-twenty IQ-score, if I am to continue writing a philosophy two-hundred-IQ score on the IQ-test...) What an idea-word-essay always had to go with the idea-word... (I am not deconstructing...) An idea-word being necessary of that object next to the laptop... (Always...) (The completing one-twenty IQ, to write the two hundred IQ philosophy...) That I wrote billions of philosophies... Which will never be why I do the idea-word as the object-next-to-the-laptop... (Has something to do with the absence of the deconstruction...) I write the one-philosophy... Billions-of-philosophies were never more than one philosophy *connecting...* (Every-next-form-of-same as the literal-fact of being-so...)

I don't mind an art-philosopher... Which is Nietzsche instead of Schopenhauer/optimism... As an unclear-difference...

Nietzche's optimism being so specific... (It is not like he goes with philosophical-optimism...) The doubly-*unclear...* (What is my actual-optimism as Nietzsche's twentieth-century/how-things-end-in-a-bright-way/start-optimistically-withor-without-optimism...) That there was never anything too great about that century that is Nietzsche/the-twenty-first century... (The political-contradiction...) (Something like Holocaust and Nietzsche...) And that Nietzsche's optimism be so specific prior to those negative-politics in the century essentially-Nietzsche...

(Nietzsche probably meant in an evolutionary-sense...) (That the two optimisms never match...) I something like a Trekkie, Nietzsche the optimism to base on history/something-ending-to-begin-what-ended-as-the-true/a-lie-coming-to-an-end... (Always the complicating...) Star Trek, as the lesser potential of me/lesser-talent and Nietzsche as the best great philosopher... I am the actual optimist, Nietzsche that theme/*history...* (So as to complicate every-next-extent...) Meaning, my optimism being very-specific too... (It is not like I present an argument/proof to optimism...) I mean my nature, not thought/something-that-will-have-thought to-go-with-the-idea... An Einstein-smart philosophy... (As the mixed-category...) An Einstein-smart German genius of philosophy... (The Einstein-part/optimism...) *Is the German-genius-of-philosophy-part pessimist?* (The problem of Schopenhauer and my philosophy...) (I watch Taken 3, last night, with my mother...) As long as it is with my mother... (I constantly want to fuck Maggie Grace in the ass, as to what the film is to someone like me...) *Wasn't she at that time still young enough?* And why did my mother watch the film with me? (Maggie already compensated...) (I love fucking women in the ass...) On how to create the last-limit-contradiction out of something like the profession and the sex... (On how think that *impossible?*) Must be that my philosophy is all three races... (Or something...) So as to think the philosophy in leftwing terms without philosophy... Which is never what it is... That I should have been left-wing without philosophy... (That my philosophy always amounted to German philosophy with or without what includes in the philosophy/Jewish-and French will always be the infinite-mystery...) Does somebody know how to think it? (I most certainly don't...) Must be an intended-contradiction, that is paranoid... (Or something...) Why do I want to fuck Maggie in the ass all the time? (Wouldn't something like her pussy maybe solve the issue of German-philosophy?) Must be something taking-into consideration that I am a Serb in the century I am in... (Philosophy past Heidegger in the twenty-first-century is something like me fucking her in the ass while writing a genius German-philosophy...) Or something... (Works out just fine...) Or something... (It is a *Serb,* not a German, writing the German genius of philosophy...) Or something... (So as to fuck her Aryan-wise...) Or something... (Doesn't have to be Hitler, if it is Aryan, if it is German...) Or something... (The idea word...) Or something... (So as to boost my dick...) (Am I writing on Wittgenstein and copy-thought?) That my Wittgenstein is a *self-loving-Jew* philosophy? (The idea-word as the copy-thought...) I don't know what the essay is on... (An idea-word or Wittgenstein and copy-thought?) Except, my Wittgenstein being the self-loving-Jew written by the self-hating-Jew...

So as to combine the idea of a great-mind with Einstein's IQ... (Which is always vicious...) On top of which always being that idea/great-thinker... (I am all three, as far as I know...) Which is kind-of-impossible/unreal... It is IQ over the other two... (Always...) Am I a great-mind and a great-thinker as the Einstein-IQ? (A vicious-question/Einstein-was-a-great mind...) (So as to complicate...) It is the Einstein-IQ German-genius of philosophy... Is the philosophy a great mind... (Therefore...) The Einstein-IQ being a great mind... Which is an inclusion... (Which is the exclusion...) That I can be a great mind in the context of the impossible... (Or something...) The great mind, attempting a philosophy Einsteinsmart and a German-genius of philosophy as the greatest possible German-genius of philosophy... (The unclear difference...) (Boosting the essay with the help of the idea-word and the object-next-to-the-laptop...) Which is more like writing the essay... (I am not deconstructing...) (As long as it is the idea of a "system" ...) Always the two boosting participants... And that the idea-word be that system-in-a-system thing... (I locate the word in the last paragraph...) Always... (The idea-words being from the prior-paragraph...) (I compensate...) Or, constructing... (A construction has nothing to do with me...) And that a deconstruction be relative... (My deconstruction, that was always so "constructive" ...) (The visual-language...) (An evolutionary-sense...) That my philosophy never stopped being Heidegger, Hegel and Spinoza, now as the next-form of a period in my philosophy as an illusion/appearance... (I can't change my one philosophy that I write...) (Nobody argues with my one-philosophy...) (The profession is German...) How is my optimism to create a German-genius of philosophy? As German philosophy without Schopenhauer... (Or something...) (Is that how my philosophy *optimistically-functions?*) Including Einstein, while excluding Schopenhauer? And would that be how I succeed in writing the impossible-philosophy? (The Einstein-smart-philosophy/optimism and the German-genius-of philosophy-philosophy/optimism in a German-genius philosophy/optimism...) (Or something...)

The problem of the Einstein-IQ of my philosophy... (That my IQ, presently, be at the eighteen-million-four-hundred IQ score, *presently...*) All that never-ending avocado, sleep and coffee, to go with my mother's overread-magnitude... How overread does my mother get to be? Finally? (It is that she used to be so well-read, as my Einstein-IQ, to the same extent she would read so much, for me to always achieve that regular Einstein-IQ that I am...) My Einstein IQ and her well-read potential... (She always read so much and I always stayed at that two-hundred IQ-score IQ...) Being eighteen-million-four hundred is the doubly-alien/absolutely-insane... (What to do with that never-ending above-Einstein IQ?) (I do it as language...) Or, that I have to invent a system... (The alien-IQ does have to lower back to Einstein every time I write a philosophy...) I mean a self-righteous-IQ/Einstein/something-for-a-few-Einsteins-to-read-one-day... (Writing an alien-IQ philosophy is never my intention/I-want-to-succeed-in-philosophy...) I don't write philosophy for the sake of doing so... (There is a clear lifegoal, that is my philosophy...) Two professional philosophers is not infinitely zero-professional philosophers... (So as to minimize language below the minimal-language of my deconstructions and omit the deconstruction from the language, as to what that system is...) Probably... (Or something...) (The-idea...) Or something... (Bergman, Webern and Nietzsche...) Or something... (The vicious...) Is it my usual vicious-circle/philosophy? Absolutely... I always affirm the philosophical-fact of philosophy... (Over what?) (That I love the optimism of my philosophy...) Which is natural... (That I, *always,* be so infinitely optimist in nature...) The IQ of my philosophy was always the natural fact/infinite... (The psychology matched...) And that the rest create the three-optimism too... (As the one-optimism...) I hate the depressed-idiot... (It is very depressing/an-idiot...) As those usual-extremes/contradictions of my philosophy... (Something like Nietzsche and Kafka will always be strange...) That Nietzsche meant as the relative-optimism... (It is Kafka that always gets to that clinical-depression-mystery...) (Nietzsche, as the regular one-fifty IQ-score of all philosophy, and Kafka, as the regular one-twenty IQ-score of all fiction/writers...) As to how that never contradicted... (Must be that those two "clinical-depressions" are a famous exclusion/never-got-to-the-fifty-IQ-score-of-all-clinical-depression...) (The evolutionary-sense...) (Or something...) (My mother's well-read magnitude...) She now read that many books... (To the extent that I reach the eighteen-million-four-hundred IQ-score on the IQ-test...) As to what the number of the books she read now is... (Impossible...) Absolutely-alien... (I love my optimism...) The great-thinker-part always being what is less in my philosophy... (So as to think it as the Einstein-IQ and the great-mind...) (I complicate...) (Where I always begin to overexpand on the concept of what I would mean...) An infinite-regress... (Porno used to be so yummy/infinite...) However, that that always meant too much of the screen-time... (I infinitely love my brain/it-is-obvious-what-I-alwayslove-above-everything-as-infinite-regress...) As IQ and talent... (It seems...) To me the most beautiful thing in history... (My-brain...) Meaning, a brain to me just as IQ as talent... (I infinitely love my ideal-brain...) A brain that is infinitely ideal-of-me... (I to me do achieve the absolute-talent to go with the absolute-IQ, as far as I know...) What am I to me? A never-ending genius and a never-ending genius of IQ... (My brain being natural of me *infinitely* or *infinitely*...) (I don't need psychological help...) Somebody needs to help me *physiologically*... (The never-ending German-brain that is the never-ending Einstein-IQ-brain...) How infinite is my infinite self-love? (That my philosophy always experienced that problem with the never-ending *anti-Christ*...) Something had to be Jewish-Christian as Jewish-Christian, to know that it is Jewish-Christian...

Yielding to the fact that I can't imagine too much... (Something has to compensate...) It is the theory of psychology of all my philosophy... (There is no Einstein-IQ without imagination...) *Imagination is IQ... That I am not deconstructing...* (All that is beautiful/IQ is never in China...) All those dumb fascist-Chinese people... (Or something...) Very-generic... (There was never the imagination prior to the Einstein-IQ...) Some really fascist never-ending-dumbo... (A never-ending-idiot...) Or something... (Something infinitely un-fucked-off...) Or something... (What is my relation to Kafka?) To affirm him as the second-best genius of fiction, that I have nothing to do with poetry, and that there is never the favorite writer of my philosophy, mystifies the mild-value of Kafka... (A one-twenty IQ-score on the IQ test relative of Dostoyevsky and Shakespeare as the best writers of my philosophy and that there never the best writer of my philosophy...) And that he was philosophically possible same-as-Dostoyevsky... (How can fiction be philosophy?) Kafka is never my IQ... And that he always be that second-best genius... Which is always mixed or same... (Dostoyevsky is never the best-writer/Shakespeareis-Dostoyevsky...) That I, finally, at some point, deconstruct The Idiot is never a monumental-wait... (Probably something potentially too great to think, that will end up being my deconstruction of *The Trial...*) (The natural-fact...) A never-ending idiot... (Have to be watching a porno/yummy-girly-fucked-in-the-ass...) The infinitely-incomprehensible... (Does somebody finally, *actually,* infinitely kill that never-ending-idiot?) I have no desire to watch that porno... Meaning, that I really love that infinite-woman, not that infinite-porno... (Some never-ending-idiot beyond never-ending-outer-space the never-ending-idiot...) (An-idiot...) Meaning, the idiot *infinitely-idiotic...* (Maybe also looking at the laptop-keyboard I utilize to write the essay...) A letter, to inspire that dull-imagination/imagination... (I am not deconstructing...) Something to go with the system of the essay... (The prior-paragraph and the object-next-to-the-laptop...)

The "psychological-philosophy" that is Einstein-smart is always the contradiction... (The philosophy exists for the sake of IQ!) Psychology always being that "add-on," that I never know what to do with... (Or, that I solved that psychology as that Einstein-IQ...) *It is a primitive-psychology, relatively...* (The self-conscious and the IQ-imagination/the-psychology of-Einstein...) (The psychology doesn't make any sense/is-irrational...) A theory of the self-conscious and a theory of Einstein's IQ: there is nothing logical between the two... (What would be a never-ending-dumbo writing an "irrational" without the rational...) Or something... (There is nothing to compensate since it is the-irrational to go with my philosophy...) And that that irrational-psychology always remind of Nietzsche and Dostoyevsky as the self-conscious man/the-irrational-man in the context of the problem of my philosophy *generally...* (Nietzsche, Dostoyevsky, the self-conscious, the left-wing, the right-wing, etc...) All that naturalizes of my philosophy... (Nietzsche and Dostoyevsky inventing the self-conscious-man...) (The twentieth-century...) Which is the century I always invent... (While Dostoyevsky and Nietzsche invent the self-conscious-man...) (Why I never kill off that "desire"/psychology that is all my philosophy I write...) It is never obsessive-compulsive... (I hate an infinite-porno...) Meaning, I hate a porno/love-the-woman... (Meaning, I love the infinite-woman...) Something like Piper Perri... (I infinitely love her...) Which is untrue... (I probably love an infinite-Sasha-Grey...) (It is okay to infinitely love an infinite-porn-star without an infinite-porno that that infinite porn-star is to be in...) (Piper Perri is infinitely yummy...) Except, she never did all the sexual positions... (Or something...)

(Something to go with my beautiful/Einsteins equations of my philosophy...) Einstein isn't the only impossible of my philosophy... (The national German-philosophy...) *Is it my sex that makes Einstein possible of my philosophy to begin with?* (Kafka is a mild-value...) Or something... (Two impossible make for one separate-possible...) (Something three racial doesn't solve the problem of my sex relative of my philosophy...) Must be that my philosophy always become infinitely-Egocentric... (I love my philosophy, not philosophy...) Or something... (Very-mystical...) (The poetry of it...) Or something... (*So what?*) (*May I always love the yummy-girly-fucked-in-the-ass...*) Or something... (May it go with Western-hypocrisy/I-love-West-and-East-and-everything...) That my philosophy was always all "three:" West, East and everything... (As to how my sex becomes true of my philosophy instead...) *Is that how the "retarded" of my philosophy annihilated by the time I wrote my first-philosophy/the-one-philosophy?* (It is Germany without West...) The sex does correlate with my philosophy... (I don't mean a homosexual-idiot/Plato/Aristotle...) Or something... (The-possible...) I'll be the *self-conscious-man*/Nietzsche in Notes from Underground... Which never matched all that well... (Nietzsche generalizes as the sixteen-bibliographies...) As is the self-conscious-man in Dostoyevsky's novella the "bad-writer"... (And so on...) Some strange-relation of my philosophy, in the context of left-wing already vicious as the rightwing/Nietzsche-and-Dostoyevsky... (Something had to generalize, and did make the general-value possible/left-wing liberal-as-apolitical...) *So as to think the whole thing as possible!* And that Nietzsche and Dostoyevsky already be that leftwing-problem too, as the twentieth-century... (Twentieth-century and left-wing...) (The-context...) (What is my favorite porn-star now/presently?) I stopped watching porno fifteen years ago... (Sasha Grey is ancient...) Any excessive screentime always being so bad for the precious-brain... That I infinitely love my brain/can't-be-watching-porno... (The addiction would be as to how bad for my never-ending-pride...) That Germany be just as great as IQ doesn't change the fact of staying-away-from-porno... (*Is the screen-time bad for the talent-part of the philosophy too?*) Which is same/I-have-to retain-the-IQ-part-of-the-philosophy-*anyhow*... (The IQ-part is essential of the philosophy...) With or without that I so love the IQ of my philosophy... (The IQ, also, serves to prove that a philosophy can be philosophy and IQ in a philosophy...) The philosophy doesn't exist philosophically without the IQ-part of the philosophy... (I watch Taken, last night, with my mother...) Which is strange... (It is the extended cut of the film...) The film probably improved/why-is-my-mother watching-it-with-me... *And the fact of Maggie Grace... And is the first Taken better than the other installments?* (As long as the desire retained/I-fuck-Maggie-Grace-in-the-ass...) My mother being highly-unnecessary... Yummy-girly... (Maybe joining a porno...) I can be in the porn-movie... (That I can never watch such a thing...) (Frying my brain being the natural clinical-depression, and a clinical-depression being just as bad as frying the brain...) (Doubly as so...) I infinitely exist for the sake of my brain... (That I don't mean putting a condom on/finding-a-prostitute-to-fuck...) And finding a girlfriend being like saying that Piper

Perri can be my girlfriend as by me fucking her in the ass/completing-all-the-sexual-positions... (*I solved the problem of the desire of it/the-double-Germany...*) As long as I comprehend why I fuck a woman in the ass...

(The rest probably never mattered...) Nobody fucks Maggie Grace in the ass... (Meaning, nobody fucks her...) (I'll be perfectly infinitely-happy with the fact of wanting to fuck Maggie Grace in the ass...) (The poetry of it...) (The second-best France/second-best-great-philosophy...) Or something... (The French-left makes my philosophy the German-genius of philosophy relative of the French-fact of my philosophy/that-my-philosophy-think-France-a-second-best-genius-ofphilosophy...) (Maggie Grace stays away...) Or something... (And that she aged in the meantime...) Is she still that good-looking? (As far as I know she is/she-is-older-than-me...) May she doubly stay away... (I love nonsense...) Or something...

(That she be my age-span, though...)

(Insofar...) *It is logic... Sixteen-bibliographies...* Is that as a generalized-Nietzsche, a cosmopolitan-desire or that philosophy be philosophy/cosmopolitan? (The fact of it...) Where do I start? (It is all so relative...) I always like Einstein's statements... (Not as much as his IQ, though...) That it is a natural proposition of my philosophy, though/*it-is-all-relative...* That I was always against Solomon as IQ and the-relative... (An extreme-difference of my philosophy that is infinite...) Which does become essential in-some-ways... (On wisdom, philosophy and intellect...) Or, that intellect always tied to wisdom in-my-philosophy... (Einstein purifies purely...) A very extreme-thing/an-absolutely-Einstein-philosophy... Ans that always being on relative and IQ... (That an Einstein-IQ be relative since an Einstein-IQ...) To my philosophy... (The absolute to my philosophy being zero-IQ as the fascist/absolute...) A Jewish-contradiction, so to speak... Especially as my favorite religion and why that religion would be favorite... (Something that never matched all that much...) The liberal, that is Einstein, that is IQ, as the inferior-religion/relative... (Something categorically always a mixed-category in my philosophy...) (Must be that something like my liberal polarity always meant an apolitical-left-wing/right-wing...) Or something... (Dostoyevsky, as the liberal-Christ, is the great mind without the Einstein-IQ...) Or something... (And that I am always ready to fuck Piper Perri in her fascist-ass...) (I base on "something" ...) (It is a liberal-ass...) (I am well...) (Does being in a porno give me a bad reputation with philosophy?) I never succeed in philosophy as by being in a porno movie... (That I expect to be in existence sixty-three years more...) There is plenty of time to wait... (I can lose my virginity in sixty-three years from now...) Maybe never lose that virginity at all... (Piper Perri is Miss-America, as far as I know...) Does somebody fuck her... (She being the eternal-virgin...) Or something... And isn't my girlfriend Piper Perri? (That my interpretation of Persona always be mixed-enough...) Or something... (I am not a hypocrite...) It is the "infinite-

Persona" and the billions of things I buy in the name of my chauvinist-philosophy... (Persona being one of those billions of things in the name of me...) (I love her asshole...) (What is my girlfriend...) An ugly Chinese-girl? Perhaps... (Makes sense/all-Chinese-girls-being-ugly-to-me...) Maybe Chantel/the-fat-Chinese-girl... (The double-negative...) Or Charlotte/the-mixed-race-appearance-Chinese-girl-that-appears-autistic/like-there-is-something-wrong-with-her-in-mypositive-sense/Asperger's-wise... Charlotte does appear racially-mixed, to go with my famous love for the mild-autism... (Why not find a girlfriend that can compete with my Einstein-IQ while at it?) Both being at my job-site... (I can't ask them out/I'll-lose-the-job...) And both being taken/have-a-boyfriend... (Nothing then...) As long as I mean Charlotte/a-genius IQ-potential-of-my-genius-IQ... (Or something...) Is Asperger's an Einstein-IQ rule? And does that genius Asperger's-IQ always get to Einstein's two-hundred IQ-score? (Or something...) (Kind of like a joke...) As for the sake of writing something... (Einstein finally gets to China/billions-of-Einsteins...) Except, not funny... (The billions of Einsteins are not billions of Einstein/are-very-generic/unimaginative...) And that being so funny... (He gets to them in the twenty-first century alongside that mild-autism to get to China too...) *Finally...* (Very-subjective...)

The naming-philosophy... (Clarity of thought, as what I hate most of all/analytic-philosophy...) An infinite-regress contradiction... That the essay base on nonsense/*the-irrational,* though... (An irrational essay, to be made rational as the reader/by-the-reader...) What is so clear about an *irrational?* (The unimaginative...) Without-the-deconstruction... Which is the unchanged-fact of my philosophy/an-illusion... (I am lowering the IQ back to the *Einstein-genius-IQ-measure...*) To break the essential-law of my philosophy, that is infinite/infinitely-absolute, would be just-as-impossible... The literal *every-next-form-of-same* being *infinite...* (An infinite-illusion...) Or something... (There is no reason to overexpand on the concept of it...) I already made the autistic/*minimalist* value... (Webern...) Or something... A strange essay, that is Webern... (Which is like excluding the one bibliography, from the total-bibliography...) And that that be the-mystery *anyhow...* (Art is five-percent...) Or something... Or, that the philosophy be science and art as the greater love for science/IQ... (It is a subjective half...) That my philosophy always had to define as everything and nothing *instead...* (Relative of a Webernessay/Webern-homage-essay...) *What is Webern as a science-art subjective/*IQ *philosophy that loves IQ/science over art as science and art?* (The reputation never changes...) It is an illusion that I break-off from the basic rule of my philosophy that is infinite-regress-absolute...

Something categorical/German... (The too-German to be Jewish...) Very-basic... (Idea is an anti-Semitic concept...) (Nietzsche subjectifies the-idea...) Or, what can be the best great philosopher/infinitely-German and Jewish at the same time... (Or something...) (The autism/*Kant* is a realism...) That my philosophy won't ever learn how to write... (Must be something "realistic" ...) In this essay to go with the unimaginative/Webern... Which is on-uninventive/Webern... (The strange...) That Webern be one of the bibliographies and that I directly reference him/*base-a-whole-essay-on...* He means as the nihilist-theme on the twentieth-century... (Or something...) (The illusion that I would ever grow fond of Webern...) Something infinitely-categorical... (Or something...) (Nietzsche and Webern...) Or, an impure-value, purifying as the total category... (Or something...) That I have nothing to do with nihilism... Which is infinitely-so... (My infinitely-optimist philosophy...) (What is so Nietzsche about my philosophy?) Or, what is so Webern about my philosophy? (I hate irrationalism and nihilism...) The best great philosopher and best classical-music composer... (It is always the sixteen bibliographies that make sense out of my philosophy...) The irrational and nihilist as the infinitely generalized values... And that Webern already be so coincidental as a coincidence... (The art-forms are film and fiction, not classical music...)

As to how that rational-philosophy of mine is rational/rational... (Rationalism is rational thought as the rational/rational...) Both "rational-categories" (the rational and the logical) always had to prioritize as the essential in my philosophy/why-my philosophy-exists... (That my philosophy hates empiricism and idealism...) Idealism being possible/includes-rationalism, if nothing else...

Wittgenstein is to solve the problem of imagination... *Why him?* I deconstructed him ten years ago... Must be something in the absurd-fact of absurd... Doesn't have to be him... Or, that it can be anything... (Matching my "absurd-Wittgenstein," absurdly, with the absurd question of *solving-the-imagination...*) Or something... (That it doesn't have to be him...) An impure-value... (That I probably hate the dull-essay...) The idea-word needs something on the side of the laptop... (Webern is always the negative-art-form and the nihilist...) A-coincidence... Prioritizing Webern always being the-unnatural... (That I have nothing to do with classical music or nihilism...) And that art being the lesser of the two/below-science-as-art... (So as to create a same out of the essay, as the deconstruction and my philosophy...) The idea-word and the object-next-to-the laptop... (As with the help of the object-next-to-the-laptop...)

For the sake of interest... (*It is interesting!*) Or something... Writing on the bibliography of my philosophy, as by revealing what that bibliography is... (Breaking the basic rule of my philosophy...) As long as that bibliography be just as relative as me changing that rule "absolutely" ... And that I didn't suddenly make that bibliography absolute... *The bibliography is relative...* Relative of the "divided-deconstruction" absolutely-fine... (The essay is a "construction" ...) Safe to assume, so to speak... (*It is not the difference of my philosophy...*) The relative-bibliography of self-evidence retained...

(*So as to sometimes do that too...*) The essay's system being a bit too tedious/*boring...* (Always the idea-word and object next-to-the-laptop...) Kind of monotonous *anyhow...* Why not associate the essay's name... (It is not like I idea-worded the name...) The system retains in-the-meantime... (Or something...) (The idea-word being anything but a name/surname...) (Something to go with the laptop-keyboard I utilize to write the essay...) Or something... (Very-ideal/*Hegel...*) Which is never an issue... (I get to be more ideal than him as the question a philosophical-*reading-difficulty* and Heidegger and Spinoza...) It is not like Hegel ever becomes an actually indirect-value of my philosophy relative of all that that I read that has nothing to do with my philosophy... (I read and saw everything my philosophy is...) And that I did, also, read and see so many things unrelated... Something like Hegel being what I read past everything that I am that I did read/see... (Wasn't he German?) Should be natural-enough to read him *anyhow* with or without the anti-intellectual-philosophy/my philosophy... (All those unrelated-things I read as skepticism and intellect...) Or something... (That I learn philosophy with the help of the Internet...) Reading everything my-philosophy and learning the rest through the Internet... (Which was always the basic rule of my philosophy and my philosophy's left-wing...) (The synthesis...) (So as to watch a bad-movie, with my mother, last night...) *I can't watch it...* (As long as I watch it with my mother...) Wolfgang Petersen's *Troy... Will it always be the yummy-model, to make me feel better, in the film?* This time something "racial," to go with the yummy looks... Always such a shame/I-am-okay-looks/kind-of-not-all-that-ugly... (Nothing sufficient...) *She was born in Germany... However, not-racially... That she have the percentage-Polish blood to go with the German-race...* (Or something...) (Why watch the film with my mother?) Didn't Diane Kruger improve on the film? (Doesn't have to be racially-matching...) (Maybe something to do with the fact that she is now eight years older than me/is-forty-five...) (Such a bad-movie/I-do-need-my-mother...) (So as to objectify the issue...) (Wittgenstein is not helping...) *What to do with that never-ending-bore of this essay?*

Nothing is helping... (So as to create the "imagination" ...) It is not taking place...

Just about... Wittgenstein is always great with imagination as Einstein/Einstein's-IQ... And that he be the object-next-to the-laptop... (I create the perfect-Wittgenstein...) Something like Wittgenstein shouldn't be a problem... *Not everything has to be the greatest genius of great philosophy...* (Nietzsche being one of those sixteen bibliographies...) That the best great philosophy of my philosophy always be my philosophy... (Is a perfect-Wittgenstein Nietzsche?) Or, that Nietzsche never be the IQ of my philosophy... (All three great philosophers being as the thirteen bibliographies...) *The sixteen bibliographies combine!* That "perfect-Wittgenstein" never being Nietzsche or Wittgenstein... (I don't need help in philosophy...) Not to me... (As the fascist-problem of my philosophy...) That my philosophy always base on that fascist appearance as the fascist limit... My philosophy nearly grows in the direction of fascism... (Every time...) By some limit very nearly-marginal as the limit itself... (The liberal apolitical-left-wing philosophy would always be fascist...) That it is a coincidence that it isn't fascist... (All those categories that make my philosophy my polarity instead of fascist...) (The twenty-first-century...) A fascist-tendency philosophy, always liberal, left-wing and apolitical instead... (The problem of polarity is at the apolitical!) There is nothing fascist about my *liberal* and *left-wing...* (On how to "take-that" ...) The fascist appearance and fascist-limit... (The Einstein-IQ makes my philosophy fascist...) And that it is two professional philosophers... (Relative of the self-taught-man...) All those fascist-appearance factors... (The Einstein-IQ being as the specific left-wing polarity, the two readers being in the fascist-century that hates philosophy, the self-taught-man being as the left-wing/right-wing difference of essential-concept/*left-wing...*) That something like the self-taught-man always have all three polarities to go with the concept... (That I am not a communist doesn't mean that I be a fascist instead of rightwing...) And so on... (What to do with the liberal century of all those races all eternity denied existence?) The catch...

Except, that being to those races... Isn't my race one of those races too? (That I be the self-hating-Serb...) The philosophy to me never changes the left-wing *apolitical-liberalism* polarity... (The the fascist century of technology, fascist-media, etc...) I have nothing to do with those races, seeing as I have nothing to do with my race... (That I be a fascist to both...) I probably mean as what is to me (subjectively) apolitical as liberal of left-wing... (And so as to take the half into account...) It is to those races a liberal-century anyhow... (Does the fact of the self-hating-Serb solve the contradiction?) Possibly... (It is not a polarity-contradiction...) The fascist-appearance is the fascist-appearance...

Picture-thought... (Everything agreed...) Apart from the philosophy... (Wittgenstein always being the third-best great philosophy...) My goal being that idea of a perfect-Wittgenstein/Wittgenstein-without-a-flaw... Which is always that mystery... (Isn't my philosophy the best great philosophy?) So as to care that Wittgenstein be the "imperfect philosophy" ... As to where I guess that I mean of an-impossible, again... (Must be something simultaneous...) *That, again...* (The word *impossible...*) I love being Kant's un-talent... (Or something...) His "untalented-writing" becomes *talent* in my philosophy... (Or, that I rarely think his philosophy as great...) Something comparing of the okay-talent/Kant's philosophy with his un-talent/untalented-art-of-writing... (Or something...) He was always possible of my philosophy as idea/all-those-things-I-haven't-read, that-are-a-possible-read... (Hegel, Kant, Leibniz, Spinoza, etc...) The things that can't relate to my philosophy, always possible as the philosophical or German read... (Spinoza was always the idea, Leibniz a rationalist as Germany/a-German-philosopher, Kant a German-philosopher, Hegel the Spinoza-idea of Heidegger/thesecond-best-great-philosopher-and-"dialectic"-potential as the art-of-writing/what-was-always-against-Kant's-untalentedwriting...) (Hegel's historical-dialectic, in my philosophy Hegel, Spinoza and Heidegger...) (Historical dialectic, monism and the vicious-circle...) The two circles always combined as the *triad*... (One of the essential problems of my philosophy...) The shape never matched *generally*... (Something to do with *perfect* and *thought*, again...) All three being so secondary/an-indirect value... (Relative of the famous-category/Einstein-IQ-and-*perfect-thought*...) As the vicious potential... (It is art that aspires to be *perfect* and *thought-out* in my philosophy...) Philosophy was always okay as the overlength, the imperfect, etc., the "epic-in-proportion" ... (I mean art...) (That I will never read Tolstoy will always be art...) (I don't mean philosophically...) (So as to delimit...) (I create the impossible-philosophy...) (So as to remind of art/creating-something...) Isn't the visual-language/*my-philosophy something naturally-the-absolutely-first-best Wittgenstein*... This time as the idea-word... (As to how my philosophy never thought the difference-of-my-philosophy as above my philosophy...) Why is it the object-next-to-the-laptop? (The object-next-to-the-laptop is the problem-of imagination...) *I am not deconstructing*... (That the theory of psychology always be same...) With or without the idea of *primitive-psychology*/anti-psychological philosophy that is my philosophy... (I wrote billions of self-conscious philosophies!) (That a fascist be the-idiot is the basic psychology of my philosophy...) Which is nothing new/*absolute*... (I never like the never-ending-idiot/I-love-Einstein...) As to how that fascist-problem of my philosophy always solves... (It was a fascist-limit...) That I, as far as I know, hate the-fascist... (The primitive-psychology of my philosophy never prevented from that fascist being that infinite-idiot/never-ending-zero-imagination...) That it be an irrational *primitive psychology*... (Nietzsche in "included" ...) It is sixteen-bibliographies... (I don't mean as what's above my philosophy...) Everything learns to be a never-ending slave of me inside a never-ending outer-space I constantly fart... (What doesn't abide I kill...) It is a whole extermination-camp... (I don't tolerate a never-ending idiot...) Which is always natural to say... (As that there be, somewhere, someplace, on the planet, the concept of a never-ending-idiot...) I was a never-ending slave in the prior century, so as to get to the century I am in, so as to be stabbed in the brain *infinite number of times*... (Somebody invents a new-number/thing-something, that will sufficiently describe the actual relation of the relation...) ("I-fear death" ...) (Wittgenstein always solves the imagination...)

What does Leibniz amount to? I can't know/I-never-read-him... The probable fact of him being rationalism and Germany... Did that ever combine well? Not really... (Germany is the best genius of great philosophy as the irrational prior to Nietzsche...) As to why Germany always got to that extreme first-best-place... (Nietzsche is the best great philosopher as the essential-fact of all German-philosophy...) That I make Leibniz the potential-read natural-of-my-philosophy will always be something rational and German-philosophy/the-best-philosophers-world-regionally-and-historically... And that my philosophy be so rational... (I wrote billions of rational German-philosophies...) Or something... (The idea of it...) That Leibniz always be that natural-choice of the potential-read unrelated to my philosophy! (The rational and German can't hurt...) That my philosophy be rational as idea, as the never-ending German-philosophy, probably helps... (Something mildly okay-to-read/Leibniz...) A rational German-philosophy usually being against my philosophy, relative of the German-philosophy that it is always-potential... I finish watching *L.A. Confidential,* with my mother, last night... Is it a mild-value/an-okay-film, reminding of something like *Chinatown?* (Perhaps/a-homage-film...) Or something... (How that would combine in my case...) That Chinatown be the great film never the best from Hollywood in my philosophy... (It was already a mildly mild-value/idea...) My favorite Polanski film/Chinatown, now in the form of a homage... That Polanski never be all that much to me and that his Chinatown compare to something like *The Pianist* to me...

It is rational language of visual language as Wittgenstein... Which was always a mixed-category... That Wittgenstein never be ideal of my philosophy... Meaning, the best great philosophy of my philosophy always being my philosophy prior to Nietzsche... That Wittgenstein's first-period be so essential of my philosophy will always be hard to think... (The third best great philosophy and that my philosophy never meant a great philosopher above a philosophy-art-science bibliography...) *The best great philosopher will always be an inclusion!* (Must be something as the contradiction Nietzsche...) Or something... *That there is no best great philosophy of my philosophy...* (Or something...) (A hurt...) It is, clearly, a never-ending-idiot... (I am a never-ending-enemy of something since I am private *non-stop...*)

That I always be the best in philosophy and IQ/two-talents... Which will always be vicious... (I am not separately writing something IQ and philosophy...) Both talents being in a philosophy... (The philosophical challenge, if nothing else...) Something relative of the ancient-philosophy as the completely new-philosophy... (Nobody attempted it before...) A Wittgenstein of first-best genius of philosophy and first-best genius of IQ *simultaneously...* (That my philosophy be so original...) Which will always be relative/that-it-is-ancient... (On-the-other-hand...) *Is my philosophy completely original/something-purely-original-as-new?* (That I always had to think about Heidegger's death relative of that goal/a completely-new-philosophy...) That the originality be so relative was always okay/never-impeded-on-my-never-ending self-love... *When did Heidegger die, to end philosophy in that same year?* (In case I don't have something to offer in philosophy a relative-potential of originality...) My philosophy is infinitely self-loving! /Heidegger died in that year... That Wittgenstein is the relative-same of my philosophy isn't in the way... (It is the fact of the never-ending self-love of my philosophy that solves the whole thing too...) (I hurt the three great philosophers as the never-ending *self-loving philosophy*/my-philosophy...) Such an *emotional-thing... Why do I watch Rashomon with my mother, last night?*

(*Kurosawa's Rashomon...*) The film always being the fourth-best film ever made to my philosophy... (I didn't need her...) (The film deconstructivity-correlating of Persona and 8 ½, to my philosophy...) That the four best films ever made always meant the two "strands," as to how they structured as the four best films ever made... (Something gradual...) The best dream ever made and the best structural-deconstruction prior to deconstruction ever made... (That I wrote so many deconstructions...) I know that they are same of my never-ending one-philosophy... However, that deconstruction can't

"ignore" as the magnitude... (Writing so many structural-deconstructions meant something like Persona, 8 ½ and Rashomon...) Kind of essential, in some ways... (That my philosophy never like the actual-deconstruction/Derrida, all that much...) And that those three films, to my philosophy, invented deconstruction prior to Derrida... (That there is never *deconstruction* (that deconstruction be self-deconstructive) is the structuralism that inspired it/Wittgenstein-and-Heidegger...) Meaning, that the basic rule of Derrida's deconstruction (that there is no deconstruction or deconstruction) be structural instead of postmodern, as to what my deconstructions (my-philosophy) are... Those structural-deconstructions I wrote... Meaning, Wittgenstein and Heidegger/what-inspires-Derrida as the three films... (The basic rule of Derrida's deconstruction with me always being absolutely-literal/annihilated...) Prior to the deconstruction as the self-deconstructive will always be that deconstruction and self-deconstruction never existed... (To-my-philosophy...) (*What about the deconstruction prior to self-deconstruction?*) And so on... Which was always natural/I-have-nothing-to-do-with-poststructuralism... And that being relative of the other-difference... (Structuralism and post-structuralism being without difference in my philosophy...) (*Often...*) (I do compensate that my philosophy often reminds of post-structuralism as the structural philosophy...)

Such an imagination/Wittgenstein... (Bases on the theory of psychology of my philosophy...) Which was always impossible/Wittgenstein-is-not-a-theory-of-psychology... Which is just-as-impossible... (Mine being the Continental and absurd/self-undermining Wittgenstein...) That I, *always,* so thought of Wittgenstein as psychology isn't a new interpretation... (Einstein/"psychology" and the visual-language theory...) That a theory and a theory of psychology usually mean the antithesis/anti-Wittgenstein... And that the self-conscious combine too, while at it, in my interpretation of Wittgenstein... (A three-psychology, of how I think Wittgenstein, to make the ideal/perfect Wittgenstein/my-philosophy possible to begin with...) I aspire to originality of the relative-kind with or without that I start writing my first-philosophy as to how many years past that end-of-philosophy/Heidegger's-death... (The absurd of my philosophy...) That it will always be what is so revolutionary about my philosophy (writing philosophy past the end of philosophy some twenty-eight-years, relatively) was that I invent an original way to think philosophy with or without that revolution... (A doubled effect of originality...) Or something... (As long as I mean something relatively-new/a-first-best-first-best-Wittgenstein...) That my philosophy be style, on the other hand... (Why double what is "doubled?") The never-ending self-love of my philosophy always being that end-of philosophy and temporal timespan/when-philosophy-does-end... (Watching a bad film, last night, with my mother...) As long as it is with my mother... (*Hotel Mumbai...*) I hate a cinema past the end of everything twenty-one years ago... (Some "vicious" ...) Or something... (I usually name everything ending in the first year of the twenty-first century...) *Why is Heidegger's death as to how I think a clear limit of philosophy's end?* (Must be something as Derrida's death instead...) The last great philosopher never had to be one of the best great philosophers... (Or, so as to mean when film comes to a close...) *Not the end of everything in that first year of the century I am in...* (Casino Royale, Spielberg from *A.I. Artificial Intelligence* to *Munich* and United 93 being that gradual way to ending film...) Maybe that being why... (Ending philosophy and film...) Is that how philosophy comes to an irrational end? (Mihajlo never knows how to think...) States naturalizes of its century/the-twenty-first-century, as by being a major antithesis of that natural States-century... (Isn't that always the hard thing to think as is?) The known/concrete/infinitely-literal-century, that is States, that is unrelated to States as is... (That I hate States is that I infinitely-dislike the century I am in...) The problem being in the same-category of that hate that is States and the twenty-first-century... (What helps with the "difference?") That States be the "Jewish-country" ... (After all...) Which never simplified the *same* to begin with... (As is the century I am in the relatively-anti-Semitic-century...) (The damned mixed-category, that will never resolve/*solve...*) On how to hate States and the century I am in to the same extent I hate both and in the same way I would hate both as an identical-hate... (The congenitally-retarded country/everything-infinitely-known-instead-of-an-infinite-*unknown* of States was always Jewish as Israel...) (I guess what *does* make the whole thing mildly possible of a mild-hate...) (Something Jewish...) Something to go with the tragedy of Jews: something like Einstein, as the greatest possible Jew, ever/in-history, to go with his anti-Einstein/all-known/concrete race that never matches what is so infinitely essential about a Jew/Einstein... (A same tragedy...) Or something... (It is not like the infinitely greatest Jew possible was ever Jewish...) (What is so Jewish about Einstein?) That he loved communism? That a Jew already be so infinitely tragic as Marx? (So as to always make a Jewish joke as Friends/the-TV-show/Ross...) (The paleontologist is Einstein instead of Jewish/a-Jew...) (Or something...) (Persona is the Jewish-film in the context of the left-wing metaphysics of the film...)

Something to go with inventing a new German system of philosophy as the new-system of philosophy I am... *Why do I "finally" reveal what the bibliography of my philosophy can be?* Must be something to do with my recent/yesterday's revelation from my uncle, as relative of my ideal/self-loving blood... The tiny Jewish-percentage blood is not the sale shared/same-German-percentage-of-my-blood... I was never that infinitely-disappointed... The self-hating-Serb, who was the infinitely self-loving-man, is now the infinitely self-hating-man as the self-hating-Serb... What am I to do? How am I expected to compensate such never-ending low self-esteem that never heals/needs-an-invention/cure? (So as to exchange the logical-fallacy of this essay with the infinite-low-self-esteem...) Or something... Or simply invent a way to up the never-ending German-philosophies I write to a new level of never-ending... The absolutely purely-German philosophy needs to be infinitely absolutely German infinitely... (Or something...) Or simply stop to write philosophy finally/*absolutely*... (Maybe never write a philosophy ever again...) Or something... It is infinitely clinically-depressing/Idon't-know-what-to-do-with-that-infinite-clinical-depression... The Jewish tiny-blood-percentage is without a same German-tiny-percentage-of-blood... (As long as I don't commit suicide...) Or something... (Like I say/I-do-have-all-thoseoptions-of-compensating-that-never-ending-clinical-depression-absolutely...) Maybe simply continue writing the logical fallacy... (Every next philosophy past this essay, that is to look like this essay absolutely...) Or something... Or maybe simply conceptualizing that it is so many/billions of German philosophies I wrote... (So as to simply stop with the writing part of my philosophy/concentrate-on-sending-my-philosophy-to-professional-philosophy-*absolutely*...) As long as I do have all those options... (I *don't* infinitely kill me...) (It's tragic...) (So as to augment what is so German about Persona...) Instead of a German-French potential of the film... (The "French-left" film is absolutely *German*...) Or something... (I'll simply create a pure in-itself/metaphysics out of philosophy, as by discarding aesthetics and logic...) The-system... (That my philosophy always be purely infinitely-metaphysical...) That should do it... (The in-itself and metaphysics...) (The psychology...) (Mildly...) Or something... (It's too never-ending for me...) *Prioritize metaphysics, as by discarding with the other two, to think the in-itself above everything...* That something like metaphysics already be so anti-Semitic as philosophy/anti-Semitism... (Will that solve it?) So as to create an anti-Semitic-Germany out of my philosophy... Possibly... (The-extent...) Or something... (Which is absurd/*untrue*...) The upped-Germany needs the prioritized metaphysics, not something anti-Semitic... (Or, that annihilating my aesthetical and logical potential be making my blood what I thought my blood was...) The blood wasn't anti-Semitic! (So as to simply up the Germany back to where it was...) I don't mean doubly-up-the-inferior-blood... (So as to annihilate the Marxist-potential *completely*...) Changing the polarity may help too... (Germany/the-right-wing-race...) Or something... (All sorts of things, that I can do, to compensate the never-ending clinical-depression...) What to do? Maybe end the whole thing, as by selecting the one compensating category *instead*... (Upped-metaphysics without the polarity-change...) The known... Or something... (Without adding an *irrational*...) The "irrational" German-philosophy/best-philosophy-world-regionally-and-historically is upped-metaphysics without upping the irrational... Or something... (I am infinitely-happy/that-was-a-close-one...) I nearly infinitely killed me... Or something...

Deconstructing German philosophy *only*... (That should solve it...) On the other hand, do I, in fact, believe in such stuff genetics and family-line? (It is not like science is ever above art...) That it is IQ will always be the logical or rational/mathematical science... Which is never a science... (Apparently...) That something like genetics absolutely be the antithesis... And doing a family-line as history is probably just as impossible... (History/the-most-antithetical-thing possible in an "anti-intellectual" philosophy that is anti-historical/a-priori-as-IQ-and-Christ/doubly-*a-priori*...) Why care? (That I, presently, read Hegel, for the first time, is that I get to the end of doing that read of *Phenomenology of Spirit*...) Which is untrue... I don't have to finish reading him, to create a new deconstructive-potential relative of the negative deconstructive values that are the best great philosophies possible in my philosophy/Nietzsche-and-Heidegger... (Both best-possible great philosopher never deconstructs...) My Nietzsche being impossible of a deconstruction, Heidegger being just as bad/a-bore-in-the-context-of-deconstruction-as-the-other-Wittgenstein... (Do I finish reading Hegel?) Good question... Finding a German-philosopher to learn without Internet, that is a potential German-philosophy of my philosophy... (Or something...) (The Austrian Jewish-blood hasn't changed...) And that I mean Austria... (The so-called clinical-depression-disappointment will always be as Austria...) The blood wasn't German as Jewish... (Austria is not philosophy/*Germany-is-philosophy*...) Not the same difference... (It is not like I mean *Wittgenstein* as the first-best genius of philosophy...) And that Wittgenstein be Jewish-philosophy... (And so on...) I probably don't have to finish doing a read of Hegel... (Nothing else to add...) Watching Roland Joffe's *The Forgiven* and Grey's Anatomy, last night, with my mother... A bad film and an okay/great show... (I like to think of it as *film* and *TV*...) Past that end, twenty-one years ago, is the true and inverse/same... (That a film to my philosophy always be the-writer/fiction is so as for TV, as the last extreme of negative-value, to assume that positive-value in the century I am in...) *Grey's Anatomy is a genius TV-show*... The Forgiven being infinitely-against-me as that end (twenty-one years ago) and my/my-mother's human rights... (I never do go with human rights...) *What are my human rights?* That I, and my mother, have the infinite right to fart *infinite-outer space,* now that we are in that century, we are... (We have nothing to do with human rights...) And that she be the religious and creative possible of me... (The Judaic Christian-woman, that is a classical music composer...) Should be close enough, relatively... (That she has nothing to do with philosophy or an Einstein-IQ was always relatively infinitely inconsequential...) On the side of philosophy will always be classical-music-composition anyhow... And that she be a similar religion of me... (And so on...) (Art and philosophy...) Or something... (The philosophy-part of my philosophy always included in my philosophy...) (Einstein IQ never impeded on our human rights, as far as I know...) That it will always be the three... (I don't relate to a bad moral-conscience, as relative of something like Africa/the-tiny-African-child...) That the never-ending idiot, to me/my-philosophy, always be that billionaire, not me... (As to how the life-ethics of my philosophy always went...) I am that tiny-African-child/a-philosopher... (My life-ethics, relative of my anti-ethical philosophy as the philosophical-branch...) (The never-ending billionaire always being that tiny-African-child...) (Or something...) To my philosophy... (To me...) (Some never-ending American-idiot/a-billionaire, as the infinite itself, always thinking it as possible that it is possible to think that I am that tiny-African-child...) *To the never-ending-idiot: I am not that tiny-African-child...* (Never-ending extreme of difference will always be the infinite itself...) The Jew and an American... (How infinite does that always become, in my philosophy, infinitely?) (I guess what being so great about the never-ending idiot and the black man always being that never-ending outer space...) Or something... That something like that never-ending-idiot/Skull-and-Bones-member always being black in the sense of the skin-dye, to my philosophy, will always be something like that never-ending outer-space... (Or something...) (The never-ending Scottish-idiot...) (It's a class system...) I love studying an infinite-regress, for the sake of doing so, maybe... (Why is George W. Bush to me the never-ending-Down-Syndrome as *concept?*) Isn't he half-Irish? (Must be something in the sense of both races/two-inferior races...) It is George H. W. Bush, not George W. Bush... Or something to do with the fact that I am stabbed in the brain, all my life, non-stop, constantly, maybe... (The worst politician to me being the best politician, as far as I know...) Must be something as that left-wing-contradiction, again... (Or something...) An apolitical-left-wing will never be apolitical... (Or something...) (The never-ending-Serb/George-W.-Bush being the infinite Down-Syndrome itself...) (It is always an irrational-value...) Why name something infinitely-retarded? It is not like I know that it is him... (*Who stabbed me in the brain, all my life, non-stop, constantly, maybe?*) (*Is* it George W. Bush?) And so on... (That the Germany up back to my former-blood as the deconstruction of a German-philosophy...)

The shame being way too great for me to handle... Especially in the context of my basic-nature/that-I-am-naturally-too proud... It is factually impossible to tolerate my new-blood... That a great change, in my life, always has to take place infinitely-naturally... (I stop to write philosophy, deconstruct all the German philosophers that are "deconstructible" or prioritize metaphysics in my philosophy...) Or something... The never-ending self-loving man is now the self-hating-man of clinical-depression-itself... Or something... (Which won't last for too long...) (Nothing else to add...) (Very-extreme...) Why care? (Isn't the never-ending-genius of philosophy from Germany?) (Philosophy has nothing to do with Austria...) (Wittgenstein was a Jew...) (Nothing to solve...) The former-blood already differentiated the two Germanies... (Austria *reminds* of Germany...) (Wittgenstein...) The Einstein-IQ... (As long as I did write billions of German philosophies...)The never-ending-story, about my philosophy... *(Kind of impossible/I-never-comprehend-a-story...)* Can't follow it... (Why film as fiction...) Or something... And that it be the left-wing/*theory* thing... (Or something...) That it be an infinitely unclear-story film... (Naturally...) I can never follow a film's story and always mock a story in a film... Which was always never-ending... (Naturally...) Something to go with my ADD... (Or something...) Which was always a bit too infinitely perfect... (Absolutely...) Something a film lasting more than two hours/I-hate-a-movie-that-takes-more-than-two-hours... (Or something...) Absolutely nothing strange/*naturally...* (That I always mocked everything traditional...) As infinite regress... (The contradiction being in the IQ of my philosophy...) It is not like I will ever be left-wing as communism... (Why do I mock everything right-wing?) Kind of irrational... (Anyhow/as-long-as-I-do-mean-film-as-fiction, and film being the best film ever made/Persona/something-primarily-against-the-narrative-in-a-film-*anyhow...*) That I read a writer will always be strange... (Isn't it an actual thing/ADD (Attention Deficit Disorder)?) How do I expect to comprehend the story of a work of fiction?/I read what I can't structure as story... (Very-strange...) Must be that that being the polarity question of the total-thing too... (The first-best fiction of my philosophy being right-wing...) Except, that there is no best writer of my philosophy... Is that how? /No writer becomes the best writer... (Or something...) Relative of the infinitely clear-list of film, as the infinitely unclear-list of fiction... (That is it...) (Mocking the epic-film lasting more than my usual film-*timespan...*) Or something... (Which is kind of irrational...) (I am shamed by communism instead...) Or something... (My human rights always being the three-polarity...) I may as well switch to right-wing... (Or something...) Except, something like a country's system to my philosophy being below man as Einstein and creativity... (When did that ever solve the question of my polarity at all?) I am communist as apolitical... Which is what? (Except, that being as the Egocentrism, in my case the *infinitely-self-loving-man...*) Nothing vicious at all... (I *am* right-wing...) Which is the fascist man... (Absolutely...) Or, that my philosophy be just as Egocentric as me... (That I am in the century I am in/liberally-leftwing-as-apolitical...) (The never-ending self-loving-man...) I have three systems to choose from... (Retaining the Austrian Jewish part of the blood...) Will I utilize one of those systems or simply realize that it was Austrian... *Why care?*/Austria has nothing to do with philosophy.../Wittgenstein made it to my best list of great philosophers *coincidentally* as the Jewish-philosophy of Austria... (I love Wittgenstein's IQ...) Wittgenstein... Isn't that Einstein? (To-my-philosophy...) I don't think my philosophy can appreciate all that much a style/French philosophy of an absurd as the absurd-philosophy... (His philosophy's argument is absurd or non-absurd...) Or something... (Not all that much...) Something French, to remind/appear as French-left... Which, in my philosophy, always being the idea and limit/reading-that-one-French-lefttext-of-philosophy-of-inconsequential... (How many French-left philosophies are in existence?) Or, that I read one/The Imaginary... (My philosophy being purely-German...) That there is, always, the French-left, as the question of my philosophy, will always be as the Jewish-IQ of my philosophy/that-I-can't-be-Einstein-smart-and-a-German-genius-ofphilosophy-at-the-same-time... (That my Einstein IQ always be in the way, seeing as I am French-left as philosophy...) Or something... (Context...) (I will handle it...) Somehow... (Factually as-so...)

So as to add an art-of-writing to the difference of the essay/*that-I-am-not-deconstructing...* However, that being as the bibliography... (I don't have to do anything...) And that the issue being my blood, not the difference of all my philosophy... (All sorts of things, that I have to be dealing in this essay...) The construction, bibliography and a sudden change in my blood... Do all three combine/*solve?* Or, that I probably work too hard... (That all three solved each other, probably...) Or something... *(So as to simply up metaphysics, from the purely-metaphysical-philosophy...)* What would, *usually,* mean an anti-Semitic-philosophy, in my case/now a compensated-blood/getting-my-blood-back-to-the-usual-standard-of-myphilosophy-matching-my-blood as the German-fact of my philosophy... (Meaning, simply retaining that Germany be the greatest genius of philosophy in history and on the planet...) (Do I work too hard?) (It was the Austrian part of the blood...) I don't care, as far as I know... (The essay being so without-imagination...)

(A difference-essay...) *Where is the deconstruction to go with the difference?* Which is already vicious... My deconstruction being the difference-without-deconstruction... (A useless question/*style...*) Or something... (Something to go with the vicious-question of the style of my philosophy/*French-left...*) Isn't my philosophy, always, purely German? (It is not a vicious question, though...) It is known why my philosophy relates to French-left... (Isn't the German of my philosophy always untalented as the Jewish-IQ?) That is why... (Or something...) The French-left Judaism and real-and measure... (An irrational-value/skepticism...) Probably as something of the kind *I-will-never-deconstruct-Nietzsche-andmy-philosophy-is-the-one-philosophy-with-or-without-the-deconstruction-period...* (Or something...) Perhaps... (Why is my philosophy all three Jewish-categories of me?) Tripling making-sure that my philosophy work out in the sense of greatest possible genius of philosophy/Germany is the irrational of my philosophy, as the tripled and what that value means to represent/the-skeptical... (An irrational, in the context of Nietzsche, and an irrational/skepticism/that-Nietzsche, as the best great philosopher, can't be skeptical/is-Nietzsche...) (The-imagination...) (The Einstein-combinatoric, of my philosophy, does work out/combines...) (Nothing else to add to what I have to say about my philosophy...) The method selected, to compensate my shame/finding-out-that-my-blood-being-without-relation-to-Austria-*absolutely,* is prioritizing metaphysics... (I'll be okay/I-have-three-methods-to-choose-from...) That was a close one... (Either commit suicide or find a way...) That was a close one... (So?) (On the irrational of my philosophy...) The always-irrational... (Does the three rational of my philosophy create a necessary-irrational?) Not that I care/Nietzsche-is-the-bibliographical-inclusion-that-heist... (It is art, science and philosophy in a philosophy...) Or something... (That I always had to be something like the greatest great mind possible, *in history,* as the Einstein-IQ...) That Einstein is the best great mind of my philosophy will always be something like Dostoyevsky as *Einstein...* (No great philosopher becomes a great mind of the greatest possible kind in my philosophy...) (How my philosophy always differentiates...) The great IQ, great mind and great thinker... (In my philosophy that three-difference being so absolute....) All three great philosophers of my philosophy being a greatthinker/Heidegger-did-nearly-mean-a-great-mind-of-the-Einstein/IQ-kind... (The entirely-untrue...) (That near-great Einstein-mind always being Wittgenstein...) Or something... (Heidegger never had the potential...) Meaning, that Heidegger's IQ be the Nietzsche-IQ... (Is Heidegger a Dostoyevsky-great-mind?) Doesn't have to be in the sense of IQ... And that sense can mean great-philosophy... (Is philosophy potential of the concept of a great-mind?) (The famous *three,* as to how I always mystified Heidegger...) IQ, philosophy and fiction/*writing...* (Or something...) After all, that Heidegger be so perfect as thought *to my philosophy...* (Nietzsche is the imperfect-great-philosopher-of-my-philosophy...) How did that always complicate? Isn't Nietzsche the best great philosopher? (Something to do with Heidegger's political participation and that Nietzsche be perfect as thought as the in-itself/*imperfect* as the fact of those sixteen-bibliographies writing my philosophy below-my-philosophy...) Nietzsche's imperfect being the same-language/representation and the irrational as the in-itself... (Do I mean viciously as the negative-concepts relative of Nietzsche/representation-and-the in itself?) (That is, it/what-always-solves-the-whole-thing-purely-as-my-perfect/*thought*-philosophy...) (As long as my philosophy look-German...) The rest being irrelevant... (I mean something reminding of Germany...) It is not like my "former-Austrian-blood" had philosophical potential... (Wasn't it the same Serbian challenge of Austria?) Both races being incapable of Germany/philosophy... (So as to, always, write a philosophy that does remind of Germany...) (*I'll be watching* Sudden Impact*...*) Suddenly... (Clint Eastwood becomes the best Hollywood film-director...) (Or something...)

(Which is very mixed...) Isn't it supposed to be one of the best Hollywood film-directors? (What used to be Stanley Kubrick, Francis Ford Coppolla and Ridley Scott...) So as to exchange Eastwood with one of those three... (That my philosophy never does conceptualize a *best-Hollywood-film-director...*) It's Hollywood/art-from-States/a-coincidence... (Sorting the categories of my philosophy...) Very-basic...

What is the combinatoric-IQ of my philosophy? Mathematics? (I take a rest from saying it...) I can't forever "circle" a minimalism I have been doing for years/*the-monotony...* (It is irrelevant/my-philosophy-already-being-so-circular-as-theargument/vicious...) As the basic-fact of my philosophy... (With or without Heidegger...) German philosophy *itself...* (Mainly as Heidegger, though...) The vicious-circle being within something-vicious/the-vicious-circle... Heidegger is never the best great philosopher... (That I am so essentially bound to his philosophy and Nietzsche always becomes the best great philosopher will always be vicious...) What solved the problem? That I am sixteen bibliographies as philosophy, art and science... (As to how it was always okay for Heidegger to move to that second-best genius-place relative of the three great philosophers...) That his Being and Time be so infinitely-natural of my philosophy/the-best-great-philosophy-of-my-philosophy... (Heidegger's political-participation being in the way...) Or, that his politics would, otherwise, mean an annihilated-potential... I would never become a philosopher to begin with/Heidegger-can't-be-the-best-great-philosopher... (That it was always a near margin-thing/me-becoming-a-philosopher-as-that-near-limit-coincidence...) And that something like Hegel and Spinoza complete a category too... (As the completely unrelated-bibliographies...) Both (Hegel and Spinoza) being outside of my bibliography... (How me being so infinitely-ideal of Heidegger's philosophy always worked out *just fine*...) (Not an irrational/*Nietzsche* value...) The-rational... (As the three-rational value of my philosophy...) I love a perfect with or without the question of art in my philosophy/that-I-mean-art-when-I-say-perfect... (*Perfect* and philosophy were never a comparison in my philosophy...) That one category never did have to generalize an irrationalvalue/Nietzsche-is-naturally-the-best-great-philosopher-with-or-without-my bibliography... (I do mind...) A question of care... (Without the question of perfect, though...) (Is Lynch's Dune now one of the best Hollywood films ever made too?) Lynch now being one of the best Hollywood-ones too... (Which is untrue/the-other-version-being-Alan-Smithee...) (That the production company now be one of the best Hollywood-ones too...) Or something... (An a priori value...) Except, that the film last so long... (I usually hate a film that takes more than two hours...) (I guess listening to the film's original score, that I like so much...) It is the film's music that is right next to Blade Runner... (Dune being the bad-film, to this day/without-much-change...) (That the longer version of the film be capable of something like the only Star Wars film I can watch/*Star Wars: Episode IV – A New Hope* without the add-one CGI visual effects and in widescreen...) Or something... (The same of that only-Star-Wars-film-I-can-watch...) (Something like *Star Wars: Episode V – The Empire Strikes Back* with the new add-on CGI visual effects as intact...) Or something... (Which is great/I-always-wanted-to-becapable-of-buying-the-only-Star-Wars-film-I-can-like-in-the-form-that-the-film-is-supposed-to-be...) George Lucas loves spiling a film as the conscious-state of bad CGI-visual-effects and pan-and-scan... (I never liked him, in that respect, at all...) That something like the only Star Wars film to watch already was the good-film... (It is not like he ever got to the best Hollywood genius directors possible...)

(My philosophy being intact...) To this day... (All those challenges I had to overcome...) As long as my never-ending selflove be that that never-ending outer-space, beyond every never-ending outer-space as is... Or something... (The never-ending-cardio...) Now as the most recent disappointment... (That I always do find a way...) It was the Austrian-part of-the-blood... And that I mean Germany, not Austria... And that the challenge of my philosophy be just as Serbian... (I never mind that self-hating-part of the blood in the context of my sex...) It is not like the self-hating-Serb meant a homosexual to go with the self-hate... (Or something...) I do love my primary-part-of-my-blood in the context of my sex... (I being the never-ending-heterosexual, as far as I know...) What is so self-hating about the self-hating-Serb? Isn't a homosexual impossible to think beyond a never-ending outer-space? (Or something...) As one of the most extreme possible *extremes* of my philosophy... That I am a never-ending-German is that I be the never-ending-heterosexual... (Doesn't match...) Or something... (The Germany being a pure-breed of Adolf Hitler...) (Or something...) Which is something of the kind... (A left-wing-German, who is Third-Reich/the-homophobic...) I either become left-wing without the philosophy-part or simply think the whole thing the way I always do/as-challenge/never-ending-challenge... (I never did say that I am the never-ending-philosopher without that basic never-ending-challenge/never-ending-*impossible*...) The whole point of my philosophy being that it be impossible beyond a never-ending-*outer-space*... (Or something...) The left-wing German philosophy, that is purely-Hitler/never-ending-heterosexual, as the Einstein-IQ-philosophy... (Does the three-*impossible challenge* of the whole thing help/generalize?) And that that left-wing be right-wing... (Or something...) What, apparently, does work out, in the long run, of the whole thing, absolutely... (The impossible being the Einstein-IQ, not the homophobia/Hitler...) (I am the Serb trying to achieve a German-genius of philosophy...) Meaning, I *am* a Serb trying to achieve that German-genius of philosophy... (That the question of what-left-wing would always complicate...) *What does becoming the liberal apolitical-left-wing-without-philosophy achieve?* That the apolitical be just as potential of fascism... (Or something...) (How does one analyze such a three-polarity that is a question of opinion with or without the fact of analysis/the-*objectivity*?) As question-of-opinion: the apolitical being fascist or liberal, liberal left-wing or right-wing, leftwing the political-polarity... (And so on...) (Am I communist in the sense of all three combining?) And that communism be fascism to my philosophy... (And so on...) (What is communism without my philosophy?) Does it become communist, to be a heterosexual-polarity? (And so on...) (Is the liberal apolitical-left-wing a heterosexual-polarity?) And so on... Liberal being liberal *anyhow*... (So as to see better...) (A-vision...) (Or something...) (Why I don't become my polarity without my philosophy...) That my polarity be the-unknown to me... (It is not like my polarity solves my sex...) (To me...) That the unknown/left-wing of my polarity always be the unknown as unknown... (Maybe I should become a fascist, simply...) So as to finally match my philosophy with my sex... (Or something...)

That my philosophy already had that fascist-potential in the prior-century... (The simultaneous question of this essay...) What does this essay deal with? The handicapped blood and whether I become a fascist by the time I start writing my next philosophy... (Except, that that Hitler-potential be bad for the Einstein-IQ...) Or something... (What am I expected to do with the IQ-part of my philosophy once I get to that fascist-polarity by the time I start writing my next essay?) So as to identify that Einstein already solves the fascist-problem of my philosophy... Isn't he just as impossible of philosophy as fascism? (That a fascist-philosophy be untalented...) All those great German-philosophers... (None of them were a fascist polarity...) (I complicate...) (Instead of growing in the fascist direction of the polarity...) Einstein already destroyed my philosophical potential... (I had to rebuild while retaining Einstein...) (The sex does match...) (The *heterosexual* and *Einstein* never matched...) (The overcoming...) As the basic challenge of my philosophy... (The heterosexual philosophy...) (In the long run...) Absolutely... (On how to better my philosophy...) Which is absurd... (My philosophy being self-loving *all the time*...) Or something... (What is the obsessive-compulsive of my philosophy?) The autism, a Kant, as the never-ending un-talent/zero-*art-of-writing*-infinitely, as Nietzsche/a-genius-of-writing... (The usual "relation" of ay philosophy...) Kant was potential as my deconstruction/how-I-title-my-total-deconstruction, as my philosophy/that-mydeconstruction-never-existed-to-begin-with/that-I-write-the-one-philosophy...

The meaning of *rebuild*... (Probably as an ideal-word...) Of my philosophy... Or something... Einstein meant a constructive-deconstruction/right-wing... (Or something...) One of my weaker-efforts/this-essay... Good question/whetherI-throw-this-essay-out-by-the-time-I-finish-writing-it...

(There is no deconstruction/imagination to go with my philosophy...) And that that essay's name be so absolutely against my philosophy/against-one-of-the-first-rules-of-my philosophy... (The essay compensates my bad blood...) Which is nothing original... (Every essay, that I am to write, past this philosophy, will be retaining my self-love while writing my philosophy...) Doesn't change anything... (I guess the deconstruction-part being someplace, "there," as the two-imagination/idea-word-and-the-object-next-to-the-laptop...) I don't throw out the philosophy by the time I reach my usual page-number count/proportion... Or something... And, as far as I know, that that deconstruction of mine be the inclusion/my-philosophy-itself as the constructive-deconstruction, again... (It is not like the construction hurts the deconstruction-part by that half...) Relative of the very opposite problem I have since-ten-years-ago... (My IQ never stopped going up since then...) Presently as the eighteen-million-seven-hundred IQ-score on the IQ-test... (All the time/presently...) That that IQ never stop with the routine of going-up regularly... (That the imagination-part was the necessity of my philosophy/a-primary-average-limit-IQ-part of all my philosophy relative of that basic-necessity/my-philosophy-scoring-two-hundred-on-the-IQ-test...) For my philosophy to score that regular IQ of my philosophy/*two-hundred...* (The theory of psychology of IQ was always same...) Something needs to get to one-twenty as imagination/creativity, to get to two-hundred as that imagination/the-imagination-of-the-two-hundred-score-IQ... (And so on...) However, that that be so infinitely-absurd... I am lowering the IQ back to two-hundred as from eighteen-million seven-hundred, not upping the IQ to two-hundred as from the average-limit as with the help of the imagination of the average-limit IQ-score on the IQ-test... (And so on...) That this essay be the potential lack-of-imagination will always be potentially-irrelevant as irrelevant... (The question of the essay being fascism, not retaining the IQ/finally, for the first time, matching my dick with my philosophy...) Or something... Whether my philosophy already does match my private-part in the context of the blacks/all-those-repressed-races-prior-to-the-century-I-am-in and whether the three-polarity of my philosophy did create a fascist-polarity anyhow... *(I can't forever be asking such questions as my fascist-dick fucking a woman in the ass as theory...)* What is in the way? That I seek to become a greatest possible genius and a greatest possible genius of IQ simultaneously... (Something like a fascist being the never-ending-untalented and never-ending-zero-IQ-score on-the-IQ-test...) Or something... Something simultaneously not-matching... *(Not to a fascist, though...)* Or something...

(Einstein saves the day...) Which is the IQ-part... (Watching Mary Lambert's *A Castle for Christmas,* with my mother...)

As long as it is with my mother... (It is not like it is a homophobia...) (I mean loving women, not hating a homosexual...) Or something... (Does that help?) Except, that I do fuck them in the ass... (Why I stay at my usual-philosophy is since I do love genius and IQ so-much...) Or something... (A fascist to me being zero-talent and zero-IQ.) And that I, to me, always be the *ideal-man*/a-never-ending-genius-and-never-ending-genius-of-IQ... (Switching to something like a fascist-polarity wouldn't match how I view me...) Absolutely... And that something like being my race, prior to my racial-self-hate, be matching of that fascist-dick... (Or something...) (It is not fascist, it is Serbian...) Or something... (The overcoming...) As the usual-challenge of me... (Nothing changes...) Absolutely... (What is necessary?) So as to fuck a Jewish-girl in the ass? (As long as I be my usual never-ending-traditional-man asking the Jewish girl out first as infinite-regress...) (Or something...) That should do it... (Maybe make my actual religion Judaism...) That I am the Christian, who always loved Judaism above Christ... (Or something...) (Become a Jew?) Or something... (As by switching to Judaism...) Then ask her out, then fuck her in the ass... (Maybe that always being what so essentially solves the problem of my fascist-private part...) Something to do with the right-wing left-wing... (Or something...) It is not like I am ever actually-left-wing/*it-is-admixed-polarity*... Or something... (Or, that the polarity of my philosophy never be homosexual/*pink*...) Why do I complicate? It is my profession that be so homosexual absolutely... (The polarity is left-wing as liberal of apolitical/heterosexual...) Or something... (I never stop theoretically fucking girls in the ass as for a reason...) The polarity *does* match... (It is a communist or my-polarity dick...) (Never-ending-happiness...)

(An overcoming...) The essay doesn't match the rest of my philosophy/isn't-the-*literal-every-next-form-of-same*... (That I have nothing to do with those twenty-first-century-races...) What is my philosophical-overcoming? That my philosophy always be Einstein-smart... (The IQ- and philosophy-part...) Or something... (So as to remind of Nietzsche/*overcoming*...) Which never matched "contextually" ... (Mine being about how to write a genius-philosophy that is a genius of IQ and philosophy...) How does Nietzsche relate? And, again, as the "double-affirmation" ... (I mean Nietzsche...) Why is he the best great philosopher? /Isn't he nothing great to begin with/a-great-philosopher-absolutely-*unrelated*? (That he never be the great philosopher or the best great philosopher...) That the strange-conundrum of my philosophy always had to solve *clearly*... (That he be a great philosopher...) Meaning, something compensates, for Nietzsche to mean the best great philosophy... (Does my philosophy switch to a never-ending Hitler-polarity?) That a Jew stabbed me in the brain, ten years, non-stop, constantly, all the time... (That that be the Hitler-question of my philosophy too...) Not just the private-part not matching the value... (I am wronged by a Jew...) Meaning, that Jew stabbed me in the brain ten years, non-stop, all the time... (I will create a never-ending Hitler-club, to become a never-ending-Hitler all-the-time...) Or something... (What s necessary/naturally...) Especially as the basic-fact... (I did something to a Jew first...) How of-a-never-ending-Hitler-would I-have-to-be, to avenge that never-ending homicide... (I kill all the Jews on the planet...) Non-stop... (Or something...) Simply as so... (As to how of a never-ending homicide that never-ending homicide gets to be as never-ending/non-stop...) Some things solve simply, with or without the question of reputation... (The never-ending being a bit too never-ending as itself...) Or something... (So as to switch my philosophy to a Hitler-polarity...) Maybe simply throw out what I wrote up to now... (Billions of philosophies in a container...) Whether there is enough room... Or something... Which is going to be very strange/a-never-ending-Hitler-polarity-philosophy... (Something completely original, if nothing else...) That way I can finally invent the elevator-button, as by pushing it infinitely *finally*... (As to how that Jewish-race gets to be inferior all-the-time...) Isn't it a never-ending inferior-race *non-stop*? (Beyond a never-ending outer-space...) Or something... (A never-ending-idiot-race *non-stop*...) (Something completely new to write...) A never-ending-Hitler-polarity-philosophy...A very strange-essay, that shifts me to the new never-ending-Hitler polarity and introduces the method to preserving my original-blood/the-Austrian-Jewish-percentage... (Doesn't match...) Or something... That I am now the bad-blood/kill-me can't be a never-ending-Hitler... (The essay chooses one of the two...) Can't be both... Or something... (That I join a group that extremely opposite of the never-ending-idiot stabbing me in the brain ten years all the time, non-stop, constantly...) Which is unreal as the compensating-method... (The never-ending homicide being never-ending-enough...) Or something... (Which is great...) Constantly compensating my blood every time I write a philosophy is too much work... (Or something...) I invent a never-ending Hitler-polarity! (Can be anything...) What will probably intend as an augmented selflove... (Or something...) Simply a never-ending-fascist polarity, to equate with a never-ending-Hitler polarity... (Or something...) Augmenting the self-righteous of my philosophy, from the left-wing-contradiction to a never-ending-Hitler polarity-limit... (A system...) (The value...) So as to non-stop kill all the Jews on the planet... (Will I finally invent that elevator button then?) All the time, non-stop, constantly, to push it non-stop-constantly, all the time? (Finally?) It seems as to what is necessary... (Some never-ending-idiot that of-a-never-ending-idiot...) Simply unlimited beyond a never-ending outer-space as the outer-space-itself... (Or something...) (I am five people, out of seven billion people, to be stabbed in the brain non-stop-constantly, all the time, as the man on the planet one second out of pity non-stop, constantly, all the time...) Why define that limit of the never-ending-idiot's never-ending-idiotism beyond a never-ending-outer-space? (I don't comprehend that...) It is simply an unlimited idiot beyond a never-ending outer-space the unlimited-idiot... (There is nothing to comprehend/I-comprehended-it...) Or something... (I invent a way to non-stop kill a man, his group or his race...) Non-stop... (Or something...) (It is a problem-solving...) Maybe... (Perhaps...) Or so... (Maybe...) Perhaps... (A double-affirmation...) Or so... (Maybe...) Perhaps... (Just about...) Maybe... (Perhaps...) Maybe... (It is time to correlate the wrong-interpretation of Nietzsche with Nietzsche himself...) Or something... And that extremely... (A never-ending-Hitler polarity Nietzsche...) Or something... (That Nietzsche being the only Nietzsche there ever was on the planet...) Infinitely/non-stop... (Or something...) (The never-ending being that never-ending...) A Jew goes from being a superior race to a never-ending-idiot beyond that never-ending-outer-space... (Non-stop...) I didn't know that a Jew being a never-ending idiot... (It is how never-ending?) Simply without any end at all/*never-ending...*

As the probability-theory of my philosophy... (All those theories, of my philosophy, as the theory...) I go with the usual definitions... (IQ and theory/*IQ...*) That combining so many would mean annihilating the contradiction/Nietzsche-as-the best-great-philosopher... That Nietzsche be against all three: theory, IQ, or that theory mean IQ/*theory...* (I solved it as the many-bibliographies *instead...*) It is theoretical/*Does-combining-many-kinds-of-theories-create-Nietzsche-?* Something like a left-wing theory as Einstein... Which was always vicious... (The polarity being the right-wing-*left-wing...*) Which is linear/an-Einstein-left-wing-theory... (I am attempting to kill off the other two philosophical branches...) That it is working out just fine... (The method I chose, out of three of them...) Or something... (How does that affect the language philosophy-part...) That a philosophy of language never be a branch of philosophy... (Not in a Continental philosophy...) However, that that language-philosophy be what it is in a Continental-philosophy... (Do I mean hermeneutics?) On solving the extension of my philosophy of language, that is hermeneutics, deconstruction and structuralist semiotics... (As long as it be known...) (Philosophy of language is not a branch of philosophy...) As to how that system will probably simplify *simply...* (That the three branches of philosophy were always the philosophy of language...) And so on... (That I shift my philosophy to a new plane...) Which is indifferent as different... (I don't mean changing my philosophy...) The difference being my blood, not my philosophy... (However, that my philosophy do assume that difference relative of my new blood...) Does that change my *literal/never-ending-every-next-form-of-same-philosophy?* The problem being in the other essence of my philosophy... (I suddenly break off a whole philosophical essay I write...) Which is infinitely against my philosophy... (It is two methods I have to choose from...) Switching the philosophy to a right-wing-polarity or stopping to write philosophy for the rest of my life... However, that something like the Austrian-sense help with the difference... (Assuming metaphysics without ethics and logic will be the absence of Austria...) Germany and Austria being the two separate *Germanies...* (Good question...) (On how to preserve my philosophy, while assuming a purely metaphysical approach without introducing a general-difference and whether Austria retain that difference...) And so on... I complicate...

(I don't have to change anything...) The missing part of the blood being Austrian... (I wasn't a tiny-percentage German Jew...) (What is the obsessive-compulsive disorder for...) To my philosophy/philosophy being German, not Austrian... (To my philosophy...) Everything is going to be okay... (It is fake-fear...) Or something... (Wittgenstein is the third-best great philosophy, that is Jewish, that is third-best coincidentally...) (And that I generalize/include all three great philosophers in a sixteen-bibliography *bibliography...*) *Maybe prioritize all three branches... Why not augment my philosophy?* (Which is unnecessary...) (The Austrian missing blood will never be German...) It is to my philosophy a clear-difference... (As to what I would in all likeliness do...) Prioritize all three branches... (Emphasizing metaphysics over the other two is impossible...) (The never-ending-happiness...) I don't have to deal with an impossible/no-exit... (Which is untrue/that-I-would-probably-simply-absolutely-stop-to-write-philosophy...) Now that I am not a tiny-Austrian I am a tiny-German... (Even-better...) The difference in the blood in fact being positive... (Never-ending-happiness...) (Stabbing a lacking-category, all the time, as by writing philosophy...) (It is a homicide...) Or so... (Maybe...) (An unreal-event, as I try to invent a method to compensate my new-blood...) Extremely-unreal... (Inventing a method being unreal as is...) (I retain the never-ending-constants of my philosophy and my blood prior to my uncle...) Or something...

So as to infuse my blood with German blood... (Find a new one-infusion method...) Which is too much work... (I simply stop to write philosophy...) Or something... (Much simpler that way...) Prioritizing metaphysics or introducing a right-wing polarity being a difference/*impossible...* That it always rest on the question of Austria and Germany... (Or something...) Whether a reminding-blood is good enough... (I mean Germany, not Austria...) Why care? /I do, aways, write a philosophy, for the rest of my life too... (And that I never believed in the genetic tests or history...) That science and history be against my philosophy... Isn't that the precise-irony... (That my uncle trace my family like all he wants...) Neither, science nor history, relates to my art-science philosophy that is *everything nothing...* (No difference being introduced in my blood at all...) An obsessive-compulsive disorder... (Or something...) I guess I will go with the cognitive sciences... (Or something...) So as to add science to the art and philosophy of the primitive-psychology of my philosophy... (Or something...) (What is the question of the essay?) Most certainly not equilibrating metaphysics and difference as idea... (Is it on how to become a never-ending Hitler polarity?) Which is theoretical... (I find out who wronged me/stabbed-me-in-the-brain-infinitely...) Whether I do, one day, find out who the never-ending-idiot, non-stop-, constantly, all the time, in fact is... As the question of my bibliography/whether-my-philosophy-can-reveal-its-bibliography-without-destroying-my-philosophy-as-thedifference-of-doing-so-and-breaking-the-first-rule... (The composite-problem of this essay...) Kind of infinitely simultaneous... (That I was already so harder to read than Hegel...) What is *Ingmar Bergman, Werner Herzog, Stanley Kubrick, Francis Ford Coppola, Ridley Scott, Andrei Tarkovsky, Federico Fellini, Akira Kurosawa, William*

Shakespeare, Fyodor Dostoyevsky, Franz Kafka, Heinrich Boll, Hermann Hesse, Albert Einstein, Friedrich Nietzsche, Martin Heidegger, Ludwig Wittgenstein, Anton Webern and Mihajlo Bugarinovic? Harder to read than that philosophy of mine harder to comprehend than Hegel?

Possibly/absolutely... (An augmenting absurd, that was never-ending-absurd, as the absurd of-an-absurd...) Or something... (Isn't my philosophy an Einstein-challenge as the genius German-philosophy?) To add-on a level of impossible reading difficulty more-extent than Hegel is irrational... *Why is my philosophy usually harder than Hegel?* And that Nietzsche, Heidegger and Wittgenstein be the best great philosophers... (That the philosophy never needed to be Hegel/a-reading-difficulty-level or the harder to-comprehend-than-Hegel...) (The two-extent...) Which was always just as irrational as the one-extent... (Or something...) Now as the three-extent... (An insane-essay/this-essay, that was insane...) Or something... (A strange need for insanity...) Must be something as my art-philosophy primitive-psychology, maybe... (Possibly...) Or, simply, that question of Nietzsche and my philosophy and that Nietzsche be the best great philosopher usually nothing to do with my philosophy... (Writing an *irrational* that is to make the best great philosopher the best great philosopher and a great philosopher...) Or something... And that being that I will never deconstruct him... (That too...) The total deconstructive-problem of Nietzsche in my philosophy and that I write the one-/constructive-philosophy... (The Austrian missing-blood is Austrian...)

That is a very extensive clinical-depression... (No Austrian-percentage...) Which is bad for my Einstein-IQ... Which is just as bad for my philosophy... (The whole point being that I achieve a German genius of philosophy that is Einstein-smart and a German genius of philosophy in a German-genius-of-philosophy...) Without the Einstein-IQ part my philosophy never exists to begin with... (That too...) The never-ending-happiness meant that Einstein-IQ... (What am I expected to do now?) Now that I go from never-ending-happiness to clinical-depression... (Do stop to write philosophy for the rest of my life?) The two-negative-effect, that is so never-ending, being doubly-infinite... (Or something...) On how to retain my philosophy while prioritizing metaphysics... (So as to prioritize all three branches of my philosophy...) Is that the system? (Or simply omit the philosophy-of-language and the other two branches...) That should do it... (A metaphysical philosophy against philosophy of language and without aesthetics and logic...) Or something... (A philosophy of language isn't a branch of philosophy...) (Why do I create an obsessive-compulsive disorder out of my philosophy?) (So as to concentrate on the fact that I haven't deconstructed past my deconstruction of Wittgenstein...) Or something... (So as to finish reading The Idiot...) What was always the next deconstruction... (That Wittgenstein was to lead into a Dostoyevsky-potential of my deconstruction/meanDostoyevsky-as-the-next-deconstruction-within-my-*total-deconstruction*...) Which is now insignificant... (The theme of my philosophy now being on-how-to-retain-my-philosophy-itself/my-former-blood...) Absolutely... (A third-period...) Or something... (Which is already when I enter that next-period...) The ten-years-ago... (I already entered it...) That I never stop with the idea-word and the object-next-to-the-laptop... (I take a rest from writing philosophy...) That I can always prioritize sending my philosophy... (That I write and send my philosophy to professional philosophy, as the two basic functions, of my philosophy, is now simply omitting writing philosophy...) So as to concentrate on the sending-part, for the rest of my philosophy... (So as to simply stop to write philosophy past this essay...) Or something... (Which isn't necessary...) I invent a third-period... (That something like a second period already be so absurd of the idea of a period in my philosophy/*divide*...) Or something... (The problem being with this essay's name...) Why do I relatively-reveal-what-the-bibliography-of-my-philosophy-is? Why else/I-wroteso-many-essays-on-the-bibliography-of-my-philosophy-prior-to-this-essay/as-the-third-period... (Why is the third period filled with essays on the bibliography of my philosophy?) Is it since I mean as the philosophies on limit/*unlimited?*

That my bibliography be unlimited, on the other hand... (That is why...) It is not like my bibliography existed to begin with... (The bibliography is relative...)

So as to disorder this essay... (Towards a post-structural...) The reader-freedom being structural... Which was never a pure value as the reader arranging the essay's paragraphs according to his own wishes... (Why?) What is the reader-freedom of my philosophy? Structuralism... (What is a post-structural potential?) That my philosophy orders as a first-order-logic... *How is that possible?* A structural first-order-logic-philosophy Continentally-fanatic... (That is how...) Disordering the-paragraphs achieves annihilating the idea-word basic-idea... *Is that all that terrible?* I am left with the object-next-to-the-laptop... (Which is probably way too great instead...) That it is relatively-chaotic to equilibrate all-the-time two-ideas/the-idea-word-and-the-object-next-to-the-laptop... *Or, why do I invent two simultaneous-ideas?* (*Kind of brain-damaged...*) Is it because of the construction of the essay/that-I-stop deconstructing-ten-years-ago... (Or, that something must make my constructive-deconstruction out of a construction...) Or something... (That something like a construction would be way too bad for me...) (I naturally mock a construction...) Is it that I want a clear essay on the problem of my total-mockery/that-I-mock-everything-in the-century-I-am-in and that something like right-wing will never be an actually negative-value/is-half-potential... (Or something...) Me mocking a right-wing-polarity was always mixed/unclear... A constructive-deconstruction goes with my right-wing left-wing polarity... (That I always wrote an Einstein-smart left-wing...) The mockery being a self-mockery/I-am-"right-wing" ... (Is it possible to make a mockery of something like *right* as the simultaneous problem of Einstein in my philosophy/that-I-am-an-Einstein-smart-philosophy?) That I would have to be mocking philosophy and a right-wing since I mock neither... (Whether I mock the right-wing...) That Einstein's IQ be impossible of left-wing and philosophy... (Which is relative/"Einstein" ...) Meaning, that a left-wing mean what-leftwing and philosophy be what-philosophical-polarity/polarity... (Where I am to complicate as is *left-wing...*) Is all left-wing? (Is left-wing a political polarity regardless of the question of what the left-wing's extreme is?) (That my philosophy always naturalizes Ingmar Bergman as my philosophy...) Had I been a philosophy *art*/art... The rest being so similar/absolutely-same of his Persona-period/best-film-ever-made... (Left-wing, Einstein-IQ, an apolitically liberal-left-wing polarity, that art can't Einstein's IQ, etc...) The four-correlate (me, Einstein, Bergman and Wittgenstein) was always, infinitely, *natural...* (Four Einstein-IQs...) (That all four be Einstein or Einstein be himself being the only mystery of the correlate...) Einstein's IQ being impossible of philosophy and art... (However, that that did famously solve as thought and IQ...) Meaning, my-Einstein/the-religious/art-context-of-science-in-myphilosophy... (There was never a problem at all...) Isn't Einstein, like the rest of science, in my philosophy, art and religion? That I never believed in science... (That my philosophy always be science's IQ without the science of science...) Or something... (The relation will, always, be same...) Art and science, then a greater emphasis on science's IQ/science, then everything and nothing... (As to what the mechanism of my philosophy always was...) The *everything/nothing* definition of the profession that is philosophy was always art and science as Einstein's IQ/the-subjective-of-my-philosophy... As to what the subjective, of *my* philosophy, is... (My-former-blood...) (I simply stop to write philosophy...) Except, prioritizing metaphysics being as the philosophy-of-language/my philosophy... What does that achieve, in effect? Or, maybe stay at the raised/eighteen-million-seven-hundred-score IQ... (That I lower my IQ back to my original/two-hundred-score every time I write philosophy can be one less routine...) Except, I being the man on the planet to score eighteen-million-seven-hundred on the IQ test... (Apparently absolutely...) Absolutely... (It is that I am a philosopher of language that will always find a way to compensate the prioritized-metaphysics/a-differentiating-essay...) That I am a philosopher of language was always the unknown of my philosophy/a-fallacy... Meaning, that I write billions of Continental-philosophies infinitely national of Continental-philosophy... That my philosophy was always a philosophy of language was always the never-ending-*impossible* too... The language-philosophy never integrated as the general problem/issue/isn't-anindirect-value/is-*Analytic-philosophy*-like... (That should solve it...) That I am, suddenly, the never-ending clinical depression instead of never-ending-happiness already compensated... (I am never-ending-happy beyond an outer space *absolutely*...) All that that such sudden clinical depression ever does is so as to solve one of the unknowns of my philosophy/that-I-am-a-philosopher-of-language... (There is no need to prioritize metaphysics...) (The-relative...) (I never begin writing a metaphysical philosophy...) I never stop writing all three branches... (A-bibliography...) (I like me...) Or, my never-ending self-love...

Very structural... (Every next paragraph, as the prior-paragraph...) Two ideas, correlating of the fact that the "first one" being the idea-word/*idea*... (Something on the idea of my philosophy/that-my-philosophy-being-*idea*...) The ideal, of my philosophy, that is idea, and that my philosophy usually hate everything ideal, in the context of leftwing/real, that my left-wing be ideal, and one of the Jewish categories of my philosophy/real-and-measure... (The ideal German-proportion of my philosophy/megalomania always meant an illusion in reality a Jewish proportion/*real*...) Naturally... (The problem of my fanatic German-philosophy that is *Jewish-proportion*...) *What is the contradiction?* (And so on...) (The-unknown...) Or something... That something always had to make that idea of perfect-thought perfect... (The irrational/Jewish-proportion meant three-Jewish-categories and that my philosophy be so French-left as Jewish/IQ...) And so on... (Idea and French-left, relative of my reading of the French-left/The Imaginary-as-the-only-thing-I-get-to-the-end-of, so-far, and the limit/Sartre-and-Derrida...) I can like two French left philosophers... I must make a perfect out of an irrational... (Why?) Meaning, that the Einstein-IQ always meant the idea of the perfectly-thought-out/*thought*... Which is the irony of my philosophy itself... (As to how my philosophy always looked...) (Beyond the basic rules of my philosophy will never be that I break them...) The physics-paper/irony, as the relative-bibliography of the absolute "logical"/"physical" rule... That my philosophy always be mathematics as the extreme of my philosophy/Continental-philosophy/my-fanatic-philosophy... (I love a contradiction...) As a never-ending... (Art is an extension, as the major-potential, as a lesser-thing...) (What mathematics do I mean?) So as to compensate the language of this essay... Which is absurd... (I wrote billions of such philosophies basing on the idea minimalism/a-minimalist-language...) And that my deconstructions, past the first/*learning* deconstruction, already reduce the language and transparency as idea... And that the problem of language of this essay be as the relative-bibliography/that-I-disclose-my-philosophy's-bibliography... (A simultaneous problem, as to how that would correlate...) Meaning, what is the minimalist-language as the bibliography? That I decompose language while I reveal the bibliography? That I relate Webern/something minimalist-in-my-philosophy as the bibliography? (Doesn't make any sense...) Or, that the minimalist-part make perfect sense... (I have to minimize the language as much as possible since disclosing my bibliography has nothing to do with my philosophy...) The problem being in what minimalism, in my philosophy, goes with... (Webern, Nietzsche and Bergman are to destroy me disclosing the bibliography while revealing it...) Kind of irrational... (Must be that I mean as Nietzsche and my philosophy, my deconstruction and Nietzsche, etc., again...) *I can't deconstruct Nietzsche!/What do I do with Nietzsche?* (A selected-irrational, to homage Nietzsche/the-irrational...) And so on... (Or something...) (Mainly as that I will never deconstruct the best great philosopher of my philosophy...) The rest was compensated as the general-bibliography versus specific-great-philosophers-of-my philosophy... (Nietzche is one of the great philosophers of my philosophy and one of the bibliographies of my philosophy...) Something mainly as the deconstruction...

A never-ending-philosophy... (Naturally...) Is this essay to change that? (Writing metaphysics without aesthetics and logic being like any impossible difference/a-difference...) I invent the one system, not three-of-them... (Prioritizing metaphysics or a right-wing polarity being impossible...) So as to simply stop with the writing-part of my philosophy/concentrate-on-sending-my-philosophy-out-to-professional-philosophy, absolutely/for-the-rest-of-my life... (Or something...) Except, that always being a question of the obsessive-compulsive disorder of the whole thing... (Either my last essay to write or simply resuming with my usual mode/my-philosophy/all-three-branches...)

Meaning, that my uncle's insult always be a same-to-him as is/already-as-is... (Something-irrational, it seems...) Science, history and tracing a family-line have nothing to do with... (That I have nothing to do with all three...) (I decompose the question of "care" of it...) Or something... *What is this essay?* Minimalist, to go with its minimalist language... (Which is ancient...) The *how* as the *what*... (Style and substance matching...) As the structural... Which is structural... (As the structural...) The problem being with the essay's construction... *Why am I constructing?* So as to compensate the essay's construction... (The structural being a constructive-deconstruction/structural deconstruction...) (Why am I writing a structural-construction?) (The irrational...) Must be as the irrational of the essay/that-the-essence-of-the-essay-be-that-I-select-an-irrational-referencing-of-Nietzsche/the-irrational... Is that what the essay's irrational is? Turning my deconstruction into my construction? (Or something...) That my Nietzsche doesn't deconstruct and that he be the best great philosophy of my philosophy? (Or something...) (An essay correlating of my deconstruction of Wittgenstein...) Except, that Nietzsche be the best great philosophy...

(Why does Nietzsche mean to go with Wittgenstein?) Why else? /Nietzsche is the first-best great philosophy... (Isn't Wittgenstein third-best?) And that all three great philosophers correlate... (And that all three include *bibliographically...*) Whether I invent a way to compensate that I will never deconstruct Heidegger... (Or, that I won't ever be expected to compensate that Nietzsche and Heidegger won't ever deconstruct...) That how I read Nietzsche will always be that he has to be comprehended generally/as-everything-he-wrote and my interpretation of Heidegger being essentially related to the structural-deconstruction/Wittgenstein... (To deconstruct Heidegger would always mean a deconstruction-without-imagination/*I-deconstructed-Wittgenstein...*) That The Idiot, always, be the next deconstructed... (Absolutely...) (I don't stop to write philosophy for the rest of my life...) The trajectory I had absolutely thought out ten years ago, of that deconstruction of Dostoyevsky, is, now, here/*now*... (I never forgot what I was to do...) That I have been lagging that plan ten-years/Isn't it time to, *finally,* begin that deconstruction?

(Absolutely...) I can't forever, for the rest of my life, delay that deconstruction all-my-life... (Or something...) The idea being absolutely *real*... (Why am I delaying the deconstruction ten-years?) (An irrational-essay...) Or something... (Perhaps...)

An autistic-philosophy... Which was always as the art-part... (Kind of like Kant...) I infinitely never learn how to write... (How is that to think Nietzsche/the-best-great-philosophy and Kant/the-completely-unrelated?) *How else?* Again as those sixteen bibliographies and three great philosophers... Except, that that bibliography meant relative... Is it that my total deconstruction references Kant in the sense of homage/Kant? (The-irrational...) Or something... So as to disorder the paragraphs... (Again...) (What else?) That it be three great philosophers... Aren't they just as relative as my bibliography... (The reader completes the bibliography, as by comprehending it *a priori...*) There is nothing different about the philosophy-part... (Or something...) Every reader being the reader-freedom of doing so... (Doesn't have to be sixteen...) Except, that the reader-freedom always be vicious as the structural-left-wing... (What does, finally, actually, solve the issue?) What else? That I mean a reader-freedom... (I never doubled on the reader freedom...) The reader's freedom being structuring the bibliography without having a way to know what that bibliography is... (Isn't the bibliography absolute as the relative *reader-freedom?*) It is where I deceive the reader in this essay/*my-bibliography-period*/the-idea-word/object-next-to-the-laptop-period... I disclose an absolute bibliography... (For the first time...) How breaking a philosophical/logical rule meant two *against...* I already did go against my philosophy/break-a-rule... That I am writing a construction! (A bibliographical-construction...) I don't mean a bibliography... (An irrational essay...) Simply... (Finding a way to write a deconstruction of Nietzsche without deconstructing him...) Or something... (That the structural mean left-wing...) I don't mean a construction... (My deconstruction being a constructive-deconstruction, not a construction...) As long as it be as the bibliography... (Neither is my philosophy...) At all/to-begin-with... Or something... (A deconstruction of Dostoyevsky always being the next-thing to do...) Which won't suddenly make the whole thing happy again... (It is an illusion that I stop to deconstruct...) That simply divided the deconstruction...

That the autism match... (Or something...) The never-ending bad-writing/lack-of-art will always be the shrinking proportion/Jewish-philosophy... I love a contradiction... (Or something...) Isn't a Jew to me English and Greek? (Or something?) *Why is my philosophy Einstein-smart, Judaic as the best religion/Judaism and real-and-measure?* That is why... (Or something...) Or, why my philosophy always is the shrinking-proportion... That my philosophy hate Jewish philosophy will always be that my philosophy be Jewish... (The-irrational...) Which is rational... (I mean Judaism, IQ and real-and-measure/measure...) That there be nothing irrational about the relation... (Since I am not Jewish-philosophy I am the other three Jewish-categories...) Or something... (Such a never-ending German philosophy...) Is that where I do mean *irrational?* (I am not an anti-Semite...) Or, why is my philosophy the never-ending German-philosophy? (The never-ending genius of philosophy is a never-ending Hitler-philosophy/anti Semitism...) Or something... (That I mean a right-wing-left-wing/Semitic...) Or something... (I never got to fascism...) Or something... (And that I can name it Jewish-identity, to compensate the irrational never-ending-anti Semitism...) Or something... *Isn't Jewish-identity one of the major categories of the Jew too?* (Something like 2001:

A Space Odyssey moves from a bad-movie/such-a-pure-antithesis to a level of genius at the same level as Blade Runner...) (Or something...) Except, that my philosophy love Judaism as the best religion/a-Jew-as-the-idea-of-one... (Or something...) What does rescue the whole thing? (That a Jew be against category and that Judaism mean the Jewish-inclusion as the digit one/as-IQ-and-measure...) Or something... What compensates this essay/the construction? (The illusion?) Or the illusion of that illusion? (So as to disorder the essay...) Or something... (The essay expects its reader a re-ordering/change with the *paragraphs...*) As to what the structural-reader-freedom this time is... (That the reader turns the essay into post-structuralism, so as for the philosophy to get to its original polarity/structuralism...) Or something... (I love my never-ending German-philosophy...) And that compensating my bad blood isn't becoming constructive/right-wing as the German-polarity of Germany means a simple/stopping to write-philosophy-for-the-rest-of-my-life... (Or something...) The philosophy bases on the concept of absolute-same... (The deconstructive-difference without deconstruction/my-deconstruction being the-inclusion/without-a difference...) That it is always the one system to invent, not three... (Not metaphysics, construction and not writing philosophy at all...) Or something... (The self-hating-Serb now being a self-hating-man as the self-hating-Serb...) Or something... (There is no "hope"/the-tiny-Austrian-part-of-the-blood to make me feel better...) Or something... (Except, that that hope was two-fold: as the German-part of the blood and the Austrian-part of the blood/reminding of-Germany/atypical-of-Germany...) (The obsessive-compulsive disorder...) Or something... (Something to go with the two-autism of my philosophy...) (Breaking-news...) Or something... (Or, Mihajlo didn't commit suicide...) Or something... (My never-ending German appearance *is* the never-ending German appearing German writing the never-ending German philosophy...) Nothing changes... (The concept of never-ending-happiness/the-never-ending self-loving-man...) It is an illusion that I cease to exist as my never-ending self-love... (Or, Wittgenstein was a Jew...) Or something... (I don't have to invent any system...) The lacking-part of the blood self-compensated... Or, that it was Austrian instead of German... (Some hypersensitive emotion that I am to base on...) (Now that that is over...) It is time to deconstruct The Idiot... (Was I done with the deconstruction of Wittgenstein ten years ago?) A sudden interruption... (That contracted a skin-disease where I nearly finished deconstructing him in On the Case of Italic...) Was that deconstruction's second/forms half any good? (And so on...) As long as the primary intention held... (That it was my intention divide the deconstruction anyhow...) The plan never changed... (A deconstruction of Wittgenstein and a "constructive" second half, as the inclusion/deconstruction and the potential "third-half"/the mystical...) Something nearly my The Two: a left- and right-wing part in a left-wing philosophy... (The only difference being the mystical third-half...) (With or without a *why...*) Or something... (Why the right-wing inclusion?) Philosophical rhetoric... (Since writing on the structuralism of my philosophy can be just as structural...) On the right-wing problem of my philosophy... (Or something...) (A cynical-mysticism and the mystical...)

The reader being the editor, this time as something literal... (He literally rewrites the essay, as by rearranging the paragraphs in a post-structural-fashion...) How he reads the essay... (He will write a post-structural-version first...) Something typical of the total period... (Billions of philosophies...) The "unfinished-creation" of them/reader freedom being what is expected from the reader in this essay... (Nothing new...) I have nothing to do with a construction, and so seeing as a post-structuralism as construction is hermeneutically-plain/simple... (A-simple...) (That my philosophy exist for the sake of imagination "prior" to IQ...) The same always had to find a way to equilibrate the concept of imagination/psychology... (That that Einstein-IQ always be in the way will always be the essential-part/one-of-the-reasons-why-my-philosophy-exists...) Without the Einstein-IQ of my philosophy my philosophy wouldn't exist! (The perfect-Wittgenstein...) And so on... (As the will of my philosophy...) Very-basic... What will always be the completely-new-way-to-think-a-philosophy... (The mild of that originality being with the outdated...) That I always retain that originality, of my philosophy, is for a reason... (I and philosophy being past philosophy...) As to where the care of it is... (The perfect-Wittgenstein has to be a perfect-Wittgenstein...) Absolutely... (Watching Nora Fingscheidts's *The Unforgivable,* last night, with my mother...) (As long as it is with my mother...) (I love writing this essay...) Or something... (Nietzsche being the best great philosopher of my philosophy...) Find a way/an-intermediary value, to writing a deconstruction of Nietzsche without deconstructing him, will always be way too great... (He is the best great philosopher!) Or something... (Kind of like selecting an irrational, to reference the best great philosopher...) That I will probably do something similar with Heidegger... (Wittgenstein being the only great philosopher of my philosophy possible of my deconstruction...) Inventing a way... (Or something...) (Never-ending-happiness...) The incredible-digit... Billions of philosophy, all written by me... (As long as it always be a "same-philosophy" ...) With or without the psychological-necessity of my philosophy... (That Wittgenstein always be one of the four Einstein-IQs of my philosophy...) Which is the basic-tradition of my philosophy prior to a created outer-space that I am to be in...

As to how my philosophy thinks an outer-space... (I preserve my mother *non-stop...*) Always the never-ending selfish-me... (The never-ending self-loving-man...) Or something... (Which is never-ending-*ancient...*) Or something... (One of the possibilities, of my fame/succeeding, will always be that posthumous-possible, as one of the major possible...) Or something... (So as to preserve my mother non-stop...) Or something... (She preserves me nonstop...) Or something... (It is not like it is ever know how or when I do get to that stage/find-the-two-friends-I-seek all-my-life...) Or something... (What does the editor/*reader* do with the essay?) Simply/only rearrange the paragraphs to achieve a post-structural look? (Is it a total reader-freedom towards post-structuralism/doing-anythingin-the-name-of-post-structuralism?) And how does the actual editor relate? (Prior to the reader...) (I invent a way to compensate my bad blood...) Such a question of shame... What to do with the never-ending self-hating-man? (Except, that it was the Austrian-percentage...) My autistic-philosophy, to go with the obsessive-compulsive disorder as my ADD... (Or something...) Why am I so non-stop-hypersensitive to the question of my blood? (That the reminder-part of the blood was Austrian/didn't-remind...) Or something... (Suddenly a never-ending obsessive-compulsive thing as the autism of my philosophy and my ADD, now as a *never-ending...*) Very irrational... (Is it the irrationalintention/something-to-go-with-the-irrational-of-this-essay/why-this-essay-exists...) That I do know that something like my ADD always gets to be that infinite-regress-itself/never-ending... However, that that now be never-ending as never-ending/doubly-never-ending-*all-the-time...* (Writing billions of philosophies now *doubles...*) I love an absurd... (Or, the never-ending-strange...) An absurd, to relate to my philosophy, for the first time/ever... Or something... (How never-ending does that never-ending ADD get to be now, now that it is a doubled *never-ending-ADD?*) (A doubly never-ending EMD (Einstein *Mozart-Dostoyevsky*), as to how I always represented the term *ADD...*) Since I don't know how that psychology of the actual scientific-kind defines ADD... (Is ADD being a blank-state as that poor concentration that is ADD?) In any case... My never-ending *EMD,* now doubly as so... (As long as it be an absurd thing...) It is not like doubly writing billions of philosophies makes any difference as the billions of philosophies I wrote... (It is billions of them...) Or something... (That I always prioritize IQ over intellect...) What appears very retarded as absolute-fact? (I don't know what ADD is and I always categorize me as never-ending in terms of ADD...) Very retarded as-appearance... (That there is nothing retarded about me thinking me as so ADD-itself...) It is the primary-intention... (How can philosophy be Einstein-smart without the intellectual-part of philosophy that is philosophy-itself/intellect and Einstein-smart?) (Or something...) It is the will of the philosophy... (Primarily absolutely-as-so...) (Absolutely...) That the impossible-philosophy always be simultaneous... (As the Einstein-IQ and zero-intellect...) Is that how I solve the Einstein-IQ? (The simultaneous-impossible being that one impossible/Einstein-IQ...) A doubled *child/Einstein...* (So as to undo that Einstein was misrepresented to some extent...) It wasn't a complete-child *literally...* (That he does address such stuff as Dostoyevsky and the idea of a best-great-mind as by reading Dostoyevsky...) He had to read Dostoyevsky first... (Or something...) All those combined psychological-deformities (ADD, Asperger's, dyslexia, etc.) are a theory/as-the-Asperger's... (Or something...) (Einstein as the genius-IQ, Mozart and Dostoyevsky writing something as the first-draft as the last draft/that-I-don't-do-drafts...) Or something...

So as to invent a completely new way to think philosophy... Which was always as the idea of *invention...* (Imagination being the prerequisite, as something relative of philosophy...) Philosophy and art... What is the never-ending dull-essay/this-essay? How to achieve a two-hundred-score-IQ without the basic-psychology or on how to lower an eighteen-million-seven-hundred-IQ-score back to two-hundred... (Or something...) (Why the essay always bases on the idea of "dumb" ...) A zero-imagination-essay... (Or something...) Something to do with the present state of my IQ... (The idea, of the essay, always being okay, though...) The two ideas, as the idea of idea and that one idea being the in-itself of the idea of an idea... (And so on...) Something great as idea... (Very-German/the infinitely-German...) Or something... (That compensated the essay's "dumbness" too...) It is an idea-essay as the idea-period... (Or something...) Germany being why my philosophy exists *non-stop...* That the never-ending-dumb period always elevate to my usual standard/be-my-one-philosophy as the idea-period/never-ending-Germany... (Or something...) And that it be the irrational-period... Which is great as Germany too... (The irrational-philosophies of Germany...) A simultaneous effect of that period... (Nietzsche being the best great philosopher for a reason...) As the great philosopher German-philosophy-itself as itself... (Solving that I can't deconstruct him, while proposing German philosophy itself, while realizing Nietzsche and German philosophy/German-philosophy...) I never stopped to deconstruct... (I stop to write philosophy...) For the rest of my life... (Which is unreal...) I am not shamed since I am the never-ending self-loving-man... (Why did I become so obsessive-compulsive?) As infinite-regress itself some-obsession with my blood, suddenly, non-stop, that is factually-unreal, the moment I find out that I am not Austrian right next to the Jewish... (Very-strange...) *It was an Austrian tiny-percentage-blood...* Wittgenstein was a Jew... And that he is third-best... (Way too much cardio...) Must be some scare... Or, the fear that I will become a never-ending self-hating-man as the never-ending self-loving-man-used-to-be... (I don't like being infinitely shamed and that I don't like it *infinitely...*) Or something... That I am the never-ending-self-loving man is that I love being the never-ending-self-loving-man/love-never-ending-Egocentric-people/people-self-loving-non-stop... Or something... (One of the basic irrationals of my philosophy, within an ultra-rational philosophy...) Or something... (That that Nietzsche be the best great philosophy always be so *irrational* was always as the irrational...) It is a never-ending Nietzsche-philosophy *purely,* as the never-ending Egocentric-philosophy a never-ending-Nietzsche... (How narcissistic is my philosophy *actually?*) The irrational... (A Jewish-Christian philosophy basing on the idea of never-ending-self-love...) Or something...

I try to lower my never-ending-standard... (A never-ending self-loving-man can't be half-Christian...) With or without the inferior-religion part... It is absolutely impossible to compare Christ, as one of the two religions of my philosophy, with something like a never-ending

Egocentrism, with or without the question of success/Ego... That Christ be the inferior religion relative of Judaism/the-superior-religion never helped... (The measure never matched...) Or something... So as to spoil my philosophy *consciously*... Which isn't happening... (It is an illusion...) Or, the constructive-period, that is a construction in terms of appearance... (It is an illusion that I stop deconstructing...) (I watch Damian Harris's *The Wilde Wedding,* last night, with my mother...) As long as it is with my mother... Which was okay... (Patrick Stewart disappeared for so long/is-now-experiencing-a-comeback...) That his film-presence vanished... (Completely...) Which was never too-tragic... (That he would always be exploited by what he is in...) The most genius-actor possible/ever... (In-history...) (At the same level as Ingmar-Bergman's troupe...) Some actors simply transcend acting-itself... (Or something...) Except, everything that Stewart does at in always being what will never survive... (Was there anything timeless that he acted in?) Such an exploited-one... (Which is a never-ending-exploitation...) Or something... (As long as he was in *Star Trek: First Contact*...) A Star Trek that was an instant-classic... Or something... And is, to this day, a classic... (Relative of *where*...) Does that film survive internationally? (In any case...) Watching a bad-cinema, as the never-ending genius-actor... (My mother was necessary...) All that absurd-care... (That I have nothing to do with an acting/any-acting, and am the never-ending film-director...) (A bit too much about a realism/ascertaining-talent-*realistically*...) An actor, to me, always being the never-ending-idiot and never-ending-zero-talent/a-never-ending-untalented-profession... (A never-ending zero-IQ would be going with a never-ending-zero-talent...) (Why do I expand on the question of Stewart's talent?) Must be that necessity/why-the-essay-exists... (That the basic concept of the essay/period always be nonsense, as to how I get to an irrational, to introduce that intermediary-potential/deconstructing-Nietzsche-without-deconstructing-him...) Mentioning what I watch last night and spending time with artificial-praise *all the time*... (Double-nonsense...) Or something... (I hate performing arts...) Usually absolutely... Which is the never-ending-hate... (An extra double nonsense *as itself*...) Or something... (As politics and law...) Or something... (Non-stop...) The never-ending idiot is a never-ending idiot... (Is that like a never-ending-idiot?) Maybe... Perhaps... (Potentially...) So, to speak... (On how to double the *never-ending-idiot*...) Makes perfect sense... (May a never-ending-idiot always stab me in the brain nonstop, all the time, constantly, since he is a never-ending idiot...) Except, doesn't make any sense... (How can a never-ending idiot be a never-ending idiot *doubly*...) Is that like a double never-ending-idiot? (Maybe?) (Perhaps?) (Possibly?) It is *not* a never-ending idiot... (Or something...) (Very irrational...) The doubly never-ending-idiotic is a never-ending idiot... (Perhaps...)

Is this essay to "vanish?" Completely-new: I never wrote a philosophy without Mozart and Dostoyevsky and I never wrote something I didn't like *non-stop*... A philosophy expected to choose from three endings/ways-offending-my-philosophy... (Whether I stop to write philosophy for the rest of my life, whether this essay be the last one and whether I throw the essay out...) Or something... So as to combine a right-wing polarity with non-ethical and non-logical metaphysics... (Except, that something like metaphysics mean the natural right-wing choice/rightwing...) (It was to be such a deconstruction of Dostoyevsky, *finally*...) Which is my fifth/sixth/seventh attempt... (How many times do have to begin a deconstruction of him?) So as to maybe simply give up trying/never-start-a deconstruction-of-him... (Or something...) That being so completely new too... (My original-trajectory never changes...) This time, if nothing else, as the progress-essay a *progress*/without-Mozart-and-Dostoyevsky... (If nothing else...) The becoming, this time to be that becoming, literally... (That I will probably make a second/third draft...) Which never happened to me before... Watching Toa Fraser's *6 Days,* last night, with my mother... (As long as it is with my mother...) It is great that I watch Grey's Anatomy, with her, so many times/right-after... (Which is bad...) Absolutely... (What is watching a TV-show with her...) Isn't something like following a TV-series made in the century I am in like watching Persona... (Or something...) It is the best film ever made... (So as to structure nonsense without doubling it...) What happened there/in-the-prior-paragraph? (Why do I double on the basic concept of this essay...) Nonsense isn't literally nonsense... (An irrational essay suddenly *doubly-irrational...*) (I love my ideal-brain...) Non-stop... (That the real-blood doesn't require doing-something/*fixing...*) That it be an illusion that I cease to love my dead grandmother so much... (I never loved her while she was alive...) Austria is not Germany, and Wittgenstein was Jewish... (And so on...) The reminder-part of the blood, that was never sufficient in the sense of that memory that it was reference... (Such a tiny percentage and a *reminder...*) Why was I suddenly infinitely clinically-depressed... (An-illusion...) Or something... (Non-stop...) That my blood never was ideal of my brain... And that it was never ideal of me... (Absolutely...) (A never-ending fake-clinical-depression...) My German-Jewish never-ending-brain was to match my Serbian, Austrian and Jewish blood... (I never stop to cry as that never-ending happiness/the-never-ending-tears-don't suddenly-assume-the-very-opposite-meaning...) Or something... (Such a never-ending illusion...) Going from that never-ending-happy/ecstatic man to a never-ending-clinical-depression... (It is great to experience such never-ending-happiness/that-it-was-an-illusion...) Never-ending-happiness... (Or something...) (The search-for-success doesn't suddenly assume the role of "provincial-success" ...) Or something... (I love Wittgenstein's IQ, not his philosophy...)

Does the essay go back to my first period? (Something like *The Allegorical Manifold?*) The irrational and art? (Which is absurd...) None of my philosophy, past that "ideal-appearance," relates to an irrational or art... Science is mathematics of logic... (Something triply annihilates both...) All three essays are a "sequel" ... Which is always absurd to write to begin with... (The two prior-periods being a "sequel" ...) I love my science-mathematics-logic brain as the Jewish-sense... (The German-Jewish- brain...) Or something... (The ideal-brain...) Meaning, some two antitheses ideally combine... (Philosophy and Einstein-IQ...) As the ideal the very wrong thing to think... (The German philosophy is always real/Jewish...) Meaning, as to why something like Nietzsche always meant the best great philosopher without the whole-thing/compensation... (That the Jewish mystery of my philosophy always be Judaism...) The rest being what works out as itself/on-its-own... (Measure is real as that Einstein-IQ...) Or that the total-*Jewish* of my philosophy structure the contradiction/as-a-contradiction... (A Jew as the best genius-IQ and best religion...) To my philosophy... (Or, that something like religion, to my philosophy, always mean art/what-goes with-art?) Why is Einstein a major Jewish-category of my philosophy? (That art be religion and that art never get to the IQ of science/Einstein-IQ...) To my philosophy... (Doubly...) As one of the irrational-values of my philosophy... That my philosophy always had to think something like the-irrational as possible in my philosophy ultra-rational philosophy... (Something to do with skepticism...) Whether a three-great-philosophy and sixteen-bibliography do compensate the irrational-value/Nietzsche-as-the-best-great-philosopher-of-my-philosophy... (I fill my philosophy with these tiny *irrational-values* as the skepticism...) May they irrationally/skeptically combine... (Or the one irrational of my philosophy/skepticism...) Meaning, Nietzsche and skepticism... (Art, to my philosophy, being the Christian/anti-Semitic profession...) (Austrian...) What is to fix the irrational-value of my philosophy? What else? /This essay... (The two-fold intention of this essay...) Deconstructing Nietzsche without deconstructing him and fixing the only fault I ever find with my never-ending perfect-philosophy/the-irrational... (On the other hand, that the irrational of my philosophy goes with the *three* and *sixteen* and the *three-inclusion*/all-three...) Three things compensate that Nietzsche be the best great philosopher... (What is so bad about four things making Nietzsche possible as the best great philosophy of my philosophy...) What is the difference? (I select things to fix the potentially-bad of my philosophy/the-potential-un-talent-of-my-never-ending-genius-philosophy...) As to how many things I think-up... (Which is same...) (That my memory would have to be as to how bad...) Now as the eighteen million-seven-hundred-IQ-score... (Presently, non-stop, constantly, maybe...) The present-state of my memory... (Or something...) On how to think that... (A never-ending Alzheimer's...) Or something...

So as to simply deconstruct Wittgenstein again... (Some ambivalence, in the two/three parts, in <u>On the Case of</u> *Italic,* that simply never annihilates ten years...) That I am not past one of the four Einsteins of my philosophy ten years... Which never happened before... (What is so significant about Wittgenstein?) So as to throw him out of my room, to deconstruct Dostoyevsky *finally...* Or something... (The deconstructed this time turns into an obsessive-compulsive disorder...) Or something... (The un-fucked-off...) And that being non-stop since Wittgenstein being the third-best great philosopher... (So as to simply throw him out of the vicinity of my room...) Why I have to lag him ten years will always be the never-ending mystery/*non-stop...* (Finishing to watch Andrea Di Stefano's *The Informer,* last night, with my mother...) As long as it be with my mother... Or something... The-irrational... (Is it a sign/*hyphen?*) That this essay always too-sways in the direction of France/the-French-left... (As to why I probably, in all likeliness, finally, throw the essay out with Wittgenstein/in-the-direction-of-the-container...) Something too strong-on-style to me/French... (That the essay doesn't ever get to that substance to relate as style...) There is no how as what/the-style-matching-substance... (This time a purely French-left-essay...) Which, obviously, means as the generally-untalented to my philosophy/untalented... (Something okay as the second-/third-best place/French-left philosophy...) Which is never okay... (I love my never-ending-genius-standard...) That I suddenly have to deal with a substandard-essay written by me/substandard... (I wrote billions of never-ending-geniuses of philosophy philosophies...) That the essay does have one-third of its "essay" to fix the sudden substandard... (*Will* I trash the essay?) And that the essay already be so substandard... A preface, that is the essay, that is its preface... (Which is precisely what I mean...) A stylistic-exercise/French... (An introduction to my philosophy as the metaphor/beforephilosophy-after-philosophy's-end-at-Heidegger's-death-as-the-history-of-philosophy-and-first-philosophy-everwritten...) So what? /What is so great about that? (Clearly something French/style, that I fix in the last third...) Or something... (The doubly-substandard as an illusion...) The essay being singly-substandard... And that I start writing as the first-intention of the essay/deconstructing-Dostoyevsky... Which, by now, would mean infinitely substandard... (How many times do I attempt a deconstruction of him?) So as to triple/quadruple the whole thing as the essay's name as the essay... (The essay discloses my philosophy's bibliography...) The first reader-freedom of my philosophy (the in-itself/self-evident bibliography as the self-evidence/*visual*/Wittgenstein's-first-period language) is absolutely-missing... My philosophy ceases to be my philosophy... (A first-best-first-best-Wittgenstein being why my philosophy exists...) I can't write my philosophy without writing my philosophy... (We will see what happens as that potential third-half...) Or something... (Does including me in the sixteen-bibliography possibly annihilate the untalented-essay?) The fifteen-bibliographies... (What is the mystery of the *Mihajlo-Bugarinovic?*) That those fifteen bibliographies be below my philosophy... (That I tease the reader...) Or, an illusion... (I didn't disclose my philosophy's bibliography...) All fifteen being below me and me... (What *is* the bibliography?) The Mihajlo-Bugarinovic is irrational/*included*...

As long as it be an illusion-essay... (On illusion in my philosophy...) Whether something like an illusion be strong enough and the inclusion/dream... Dream is an illusion... Meaning, dream and an illusion and that a dream be an illusion... Which never matched... (The dream-measure being above an illusion as the illusion...) Something like an illusion... Meaning, dream, as the only superior illusion of my philosophy/metaphysics... (Is an illusion metaphysical?) Or, that my philosophy means as a dream... (The illusion never included...) As the vicious problem of my philosophy... (Mathematics, science and logic as the dream/superior-art-form...) That something like film always meant one of the two art-forms of my philosophy will always be impossible/possible... (And the doubly-vicious...) The half-art of my philosophy, film as one of the two art-forms, that an art-form can't include in my philosophy and an art-form/potential-within-a-half-art-half-science... The being of my philosophy... (Wasn't it always the irony/*experience?*) A byproduct of my life... (And that always being impossible...) How am I expected to think something like Dostoyevsky and Mozart/one-draft in the context of that dialectical-becoming? (As the self-conscious-man...) (In this essay...) So as to go back to the original art-term of my philosophy from my first period... (Obscenity and art, avant-garde and art, an avant-garde work of art, the avant-garde philosophy and the avant-grade work-of-art-philosophy...) Etc... (Something always dialectically combined...) As the three-/four-avant-garde of that period, prior to the pure-appearance/*philosophy* of the second-period, and that I combine both periods as by never getting to the second period... (Or something...) The avant-garde being in the fact of that first period as the absolutely-art without the other half/science of my philosophy... (How art can be philosophy literally and that such proportions relate as my deconstruction...) Nothing too avant-garde since such relation is Continental as deconstructive... (The avant-garde about that first-period always being that it is the avant-garde work of art so extremely avant-garde, not that it be a literal work of art literally-philosophy...) That proposing art as philosophy, literally, already looks like two-centuries-apart/Nietzsche-already-proposing-it... (Thus Spoke Zarathustra...) Or something... (That the revolution be in the nineteenth-century...) That one part being as homage to Nietzsche and Nietzsche as the best great philosopher... (The vicious...) I write a mathematical *science-logic* philosophy potential of art... (The-irrational...) That my philosophy, on the other hand, always included an irrational... (So as to think

Nietzsche in terms of best great philosophy of my philosophy...) That the ultra-rational philosophy never matched...

(The two-vicious...) Germany, the irrational-philosophies, and Nietzsche, the irrational... (My "French" philosophy never becomes possible...) It is a German philosophy... (Something to go with the three-*ultra-rational-value*/three rationalism/the-irrational...) The irrational of my irrational philosophy constitutionally-irrational/three-rational... (The irrational of my philosophy being the Einstein-IQ, not the French-left...) Or, that it always be great-enough... (Three Jewish-categories...) It was never irrational that it is three... (I discard with the measure-part...) Or something... (Why is it three instead of two?) Judaism contradicts the Einstein-IQ beautifully... (When do I discard with the third Jewish-category of my philosophy?) Does something like *Jewish-measure* go with the *Jewish-IQ*? (How do a genius-IQ and idea-of-measure relate to each other?) That my philosophy go with such definitions... (The ideal being fascist/zero-IQ...) To my philosophy... (Meaning, the idea of *measure,* directly related to something like an Einstein-IQ...) (The-irrational...) A swaying-essay... (Bad-structure as intention...) Has no thought/is-irrational...

(Germany/the-ideal-race can't be the race of my philosophy...) How is that possible? Isn't Germany the only race? (That France and Jewry serve so as to combine in specific way...) (First-intention...) Except, that Nietzsche score one-fifty/one-twenty IQ-score on the IQ test... (His irrational philosophies had thought...) Or something... (The art IQ and philosophy-IQ *combining...*)

So as to read Philosophical Investigations... (An obsessive-compulsive thing...) That never happened to me before... (Past a deconstruction of Wittgenstein is him never stopping to lag past that deconstruction...) Something has to annihilate the possible... (I can't forever delay Dostoyevsky as the deconstructed...) (That I do realize the basic fact of my deconstruction/that-I-write-the-total-deconstruction...)

The idea of *forever...* Must be that I really dislike, strongly, that Heidegger joined Hitler... (Or something...) That the basic idea of my philosophy, always, be that circle-philosophy that is essentially *philosophy...* The essential German-philosopher... (I base on the same idea too...) The greatest genius of philosophy/Germany, to make consciously-the-only-philosophical-race/Germany, world-regionally and historically... (How genius does Heidegger's/my philosophy *become?*) I always had to make Nietzsche the best great philosopher... Which is always the unnatural-fact... (Something always compensated as the three-great-philosophers and fifteen-bibliographies...) And so on... (That my philosophy always had to invent a great philosopher to re lace Heidegger...) Which is as to how many compensating-techniques... (What should have been Wittgenstein as the best-great-philosophy and that Wittgenstein usually means the last-best great philosophy...) (Watching Taylor Sheridan's *Wind River,* last night, with my mother...) As long as it is with my mother... (Very obsessive-compulsive...) Or something... (The basic facts of my philosophy...) Which is always a valid question... (Whether I name my philosophy a *fact* above *opinion...*) It is what the only philosophy on the planet is... (At what something like Continental-philosophy will always be...) Philosophy is not politics, philosophy is metaphysics... Meaning, fact-above-politics... (And that such a thing included in the vicious-question...) There are no unsolved problems of philosophy... (Is philosophy possible of an opinion then?) And so on... (Philosophy is an opinion...) (That Heidegger always made his philosophy concretely *abstract...*) Something I should do too... (Except, that he directly relates to existentialism and I have nothing to do with anything-existential-*infinitely...*) Where is the problem? At his structural-deconstruction/that-he-inspired Derrida? (Except, that he go with Wittgenstein, in that respect...)

So as to make this essay "valid" in some way... A simultaneous challenge... (I strongly dislike the essay...) Whether I do throw the essay out by the time I am finished writing it... (Something completely new...) Is that going to be what is so great about the essay? And that I mean as the deconstruction without deconstruction... What does become so-impressive/very-extravagant... (Simultaneous...) Deconstructing Nietzsche without deconstructing him and deconstructing without deconstructing/compensating-that-the-constructive-essay-as-the-two-idea-of-the-initself/*idea...* As the illusion/disclosing-the-bibliography and the first essay on what follows next/what-now-?, now that my blood is real/stops-to-be-ideal... (The total-challenge, of the essay, being so never-ending...) German philosophy/the-never-ending-German/me... (That composited too...) A never-ending essay... (The ideal-blood was real as Austria and a three-blood blood unrelated to Germany since not a German blood with or without the two Austrian-difference that was same instead of different...) Or something... (Kant/autism/the-obsessive-compulsive disorder is nothing new...) That too... (As one of the ironies compensating of the strange Nietzsche-fact of my philosophy...) I devise so many techniques/ways to think Nietzsche as the best great philosopher... (What Heidegger causes, as the political-sense/political-participation, will always be as to how Nietzche becomes the best great philosopher...) The irrational (Nietzsche as the best great philosopher...) ... That Heidegger always complicated my never-ending-*impossible-philosophy*, as the never-ending extreme-difference that-never-ending... (Heidegger, the philosopher, and Heidegger, the man...) The never-ending difference being that extremely *all-the-time*... (It is so great that he does combine his political-potential in a composite way that is so never-ending, however...) *What do I have to worry about?* (Doesn't he mean as that clinical-depression/the-Hitler-era-prior-to-the-war, making an apology as the *Reuter*-magazine and "making" his wife Jewish?) And so on? (That there will always be all that apology to go with the extreme-difference/*never-ending*...) So many *Being-and* French sequels... And that I be relatively absolutely apolitical... (A strange way to "care" ...) Am I not relatively first-of-all anti-Semitic as context/mildly? Or, what is my apolitical left-wing as left-wing and Jewry? (Both?) *I am left-wing, since political, since Jewish...* And so on...

(That Heidegger can't be the best great philosopher will always be mild/as-the-limit/coincidentally...) (Watching *Beverly Hills Cop*, last night, with my mother...) Was she necessary... (An okay-film...) And old/prior-to-ending everything... (A very good funny action-irony/Eighties, as far as I know...) Truly so/*essential...* (She can be necessary as my general-dislike of that Hollywood epoch/nihilism...) I never do get to like, actually, the Eighties in Hollywood... (Naturally...) Anything-nihilist... Or, I hate every form of nihilism... (Which is natural/I-am-a never-ending-optimist...) My philosophy always being non-stop-optimist... (Isn't my "included-Nietzsche" always purely-optimist?) The specific-context of his optimism in my philosophy always realized purely-optimistically...

(What will always be so bad about my philosophy...) I exchange philosophical optimism with Nietzsche's optimism... (The incorrect, so to speak...) Nietzsche was factually not a philosophical optimist... (The great about including him...) The best great philosophy, that is the inclusion and an inclusion... (How I always fixed the impossible...) That my philosophy would always be infinitely-untalented instead of non-stop-genius... (What always rested on that limit...)

So as to add the "third-idea" ... (Writing philosophy, *presently*, being the infinite-boredom of it/the-spent imagination...) On that I write billions of essays... (Or something...) Which is vicious/the-double-problem... Writing philosophy will never be excessive to begin with... (That the dull, on the other hand, be that intention/why-my philosophy-exists...) Wagner is my enemy... Or, one of the pure values of Nietzsche of me as the irrational... Searching for ideas being the substitute/writing-my-deconstruction-without-my-deconstruction... (The rule/*imagination* was always vicious of the other rule/Jewish-measure...) A minimalist-philosophy... (So as to complicate...) What is the minimalism of my philosophy? Webern? All three/Bergman, Webern and Nietzsche? And that art can't include... (Is Nietzsche's art included?) And so on... (On how philosophy includes in my philosophy...) Does philosophy include in my *philosophy-art-and-science* philosophy? (Or, philosophy and my bibliography, as included in my philosophy...) Isn't my philosophy's bibliography the inclusion of my philosophy? (Absolutely/the bibliography-always-being-below-my-philosophy...) One has to keep in mind that my philosophy does exceed transcend the limit/never-ending-self-love... Or, the never-ending Egocentric-philosophy/vicious-anti-Christ-and-antichrist... The half-inferior-religion/Christ was always vicious/in-a-never-ending-anti-Christian-philosophy... (The impossible, so to speak...) (And the vicious...) The bibliography being that location in the century I am in... (The linear...) Relative of the never-ending-slave/me-in-my-century-that-I-go-with... I wasn't always farting a never-ending outer-space as from outside/outside... (The extreme/measure matches...) The just-Mihajlo... (The same never-ending slave, that is now to the same extent the same never-ending-master...) (A-simple...) (Something like the black man, that I am left-wing and science as the mathematical-logic will always complicate my existence...) (Is my mastery over an infinite-outer-space *pure?*) The never-ending slave, now as the never-ending master... (Which always complicated, to simplify...) I have nothing to do with that master-race in the century I am in, the left-wing is apolitical, and science is my philosophy as the Einstein-IQ/without-science/logically-as-mathematics... (The overcoming of my philosophy...) That limit between the complicating and simplifying/*the-composite-and-simple*... As long as I simplify... (Something like Persona is the antithesis of the century with or without the political-question of left-wing...) (I *did* simplify/am-the-simple/natural-master-of-a-never-ending-outer-space...) What always appears vicious in my philosophy... (The black man, left-wing and science...) Which will always be the-illusion... So-great... (I take a rest...) That I wrote billions of philosophies... (Or create an Austrian-difference/write-a-philosophy-thatreminds-of-Germany/German-philosophy...) Or something... (The Jewish philosophy can't be German...) Or that a Jew be English *philosophically*... (Why is my philosophy Einstein-smart, religion and measure?) Or, the philosophy's impossible/original/natural-challenge... (A German-Jewish philosophy that is German/a-never-ending genius-of-philosophy...) Isn't it that the Jewish categories be the Einstein-IQ, best religion and measure? (A Jew is not philosophy *non-stop?*) Except, philosophy being the anti-Semitic profession... (Something like the never-ending philosophical-genius being the same Hitler-magnitude...) Or something... (That being the impossible/original/natural-challenge...) Hitler, to go with an Einstein-IQ, the best religion and measure... (On how to differentiate the three...) German philosophy has nothing to do with Hitler... (And so on...) (What is the never-ending two-anti-Semitism of German-philosophy?) Jewish? (That my philosophy be Jewish...) Which will always be impossible... (I emphasize German philosophy as the world-region and history...) The never-ending impossible-challenge of my philosophy... (Or something...) The never-ending-idiot (Hitler) and the never-ending genius (German philosophy) ... (Always the never-ending brain-damage, that has to grow in the direction of never-ending thought...) Two Hitlers that aren't two Hitlers... ()

The intention of the essay... I keep thinking a simple as potential... Outdoing Hegel is absurd... Writing something just as impossible as Hegel was just as absurd... Meaning, Hegel and the absurd... (Both being naturally-unrelated...) Hegel, as Spinoza, of Heidegger... Heidegger being one of the major great philosophers, as far as I know... (That the Hegel-Spinoza-Heidegger always be irrational...) (The infinite-boredom...) How do I exchange the fact that there is no Piper Perri to infinitely-fuck while I wait for the temporal-timespan/time to expire as infinite-regress... My life, that is my life-term, that is that infinite-time... Finding out, one day, maybe, that I did get to that stage/found-two friends-at-last, is never-ending... I have to find something to do, as infinite-regress, while I wait... How never-ending does that time always become? As to why I always buy so many Nintendo things... So as to play the infinite-regress game/a-video-game, infinitely, as the video-game/never-ending and in a never-ending-way that is the video-game itself/the-never-ending... (Or something...) (Piper Perri doesn't love me back to love me back and love me back all the-time...) The famous two-difference... (I don't think my love for her got to the finite-regress...)

She will never love me back as finite-regress... (Let alone a never-ending-fucking as idea/non-stop...) As to why something antithetical (a video-game), non-stop, is my never-ending-thesis, non-stop, instead... (Or something...) The finite and infinite fucking was never potential... (Since a video-game always being infinitely potential/actual, actually...) How ideal does something like the never-ending-antithesis of me become non-stop? Non-stop... (That is how...) (The will being to find that never-ending-girlfriend...) The never-ending-time being slightly a bit too never-ending... (Sixty-three years, non-stop...) What is the actual number characteristic of making a description of that never-ending? Simply a never-ending sixty-three-year time... (Or something...) The concept of the never-ending boredom, that is non-stop... (The never-ending boredom being the never-ending time...) Or something... (And that Piper hasn't become the best porn star...) Not yet... (I mean fucking the pornstar that does all the sexual positions and is that yummy non-stop...) (A never-ending as the never-ending of a never-ending as the never-ending that is never-ending...) (The never-ending sixty-three-years and the posthumous fame, as the two primary ways to think the success of my philosophy, both being two professional philosophers and the never-ending-time as concept...) Or something... (What to do sixty-three years, non-stop, as the never-ending-time that is sixty-three years and the concept of a never-ending-time non-stop?) That is going to be a very never-ending-boredom-existence to base on the idea of never-ending-boredom... (I will always be turning my WiiU on, non-stop...) The concept of a never-ending-video-game, that was never-ending since a video-game, doubly never-ending in-my-case... (Isn't something like a video game already such concepts as the never-ending?) How is it possible for something never-ending to achieve a never-ending-limit beyond the first never-ending-limit? Or something... (The never-ending idiot, twenty-first-century, and me...) Or something... (There is nothing strange about the whole thing...) The never-ending outer-space being that never-ending-fart that I farted as the never-ending-possible/a-never-ending-fart... (How does a man fart the concept of a never-ending-fart?) The never-ending boredom was never-ending since a never-ending boredom boring as the never-ending boredom as a never-ending boredom as the never-ending bored that is that never-ending boredom... (On how to kill the concept of a never-ending boredom as is...)

Why do I love creating an impossible task/achieving-the-impossible? How I exchange language... (The *original* and *impossible*...) So as to attempt something completely new... (It is not like the idea of a perfect-Wittgenstein looks greater than the imperfect-Wittgenstein...) *Does something like French-left mean achieving the German genius of philosophy that is Einstein-smart and a German genius of philosophy?* (Either the French-left-part or the Judaic measure-part...) Or something... (Makes sense...) Isn't a French-left philosophy second-best? (To my philosophy...) As to how... (The other two Jewries (Judaism and measure) being an irrational way to compensating the Einstein IQ...) Meaning, three Jewish categories instead of two... Which is irrational... (The third is the natural question of the first/IQ...) (The French will always be the second-best great philosophy...) To my philosophy... (German philosophy, an Einstein-IQ and a French-left philosophy are simultaneous/retain-each-other-simultaneously...) (The never-ending-boredom...) (I love Piper's asshole...) As the connective of this essay/*period*... Something made to resemble my first period of the upped-Nietzschean-revolution-in-the-twenty-first-century... (Nietzsche...) Except, now with an avant-garde-work-of-art/-obscenity-in-art-as-Thus-Spoke-Zarathustra... Am I attempting a nostalgia, as to how I name the third-period... (Or something...) What is the difference/*same*? That there be no difference at all... (The appearance, avant-garde art, avant-garde-philosophy and the essence/mathematical-logic-of-science...) Why? (As nostalgia/that-is-why...) Or something... And that I mean the first and second period combining...

(That is why...) A strange third-period... (It is an illusion-period...) That is why... (That I am not deconstructing is that I never stop deconstructing...) The third period being my deconstruction... (That is why...) (Licking Piper's asshole...) Kind of never-ending-yummy... (As the famous problem of my philosophy...) The fascist-dick... (Or, the heterosexual philosopher...) So many things to solve about my philosophy... (Simultaneously...) (On how to write a heterosexual philosophy without switching to a fascist-polarity...) (Or, a philosophy written by a heterosexual...) Isn't the philosophy just as homosexual as any philosophy? (So as to name it talent generally...) That I always had to compensate the fascist dick and the liberal left-wing philosophy of apolitical... (My religion...) Or something... A communist liberal difference of left-wing without the *pink*... (Or something...) (Since it is not a right-wing philosophy...) Or something... (The ideal...) That being the never-ending happy-man too... (I don't have to switch to something like the homosexual...) That I be the homophobic, as far as I know, absolutely/*factually*... (Licking Piper's asshole and writing a German genius of philosophy...) How I define never-ending-happiness... (Becoming a homosexual would always mean the never-ending clinical-depression...) Or something... (The challenge is the Einstein-IQ German genius of philosophy...) (The serial killer, to kill all the homosexuals on the planet, retains the liberal-stance...) Something like becoming a homosexual would always mean simply exterminating the homosexuals from the planet/killing-every-homosexual-on-the-planet... (As by signing, after, *I-am-not-a-homosexual,* every time I do kill a homosexual...) I-am-not-a-homosexual would be my serial-killer-signature... (Or something...) (The never-ending fascist homosexual hasn't fucked off...) As far as I know infinitely... (What used to be the liberal difference...) Now as what is, clearly, a never-ending-homophobia caused by the homosexual... (So as to kill the homosexual *infinitely...*) Or something... (Such a shame/I-can't-become-a-pornstar...) What is not bad for my philosophical reputation? (Simply fucking a prostitute...) Or something... Which is okay... I don't have to become a pornstar to fuck Piper in the ass... (I can pay her money so as to do so...) (Brain damage...) Or something... (Takes time realize that...) Or something... (Or something...) Why do I complicate? (It is known why...) Since I do hate using a condom... (Or something...) I am sure that being a pornstar is doing the regular HIV tests... (Or something...) How does prostitution work in the twenty-first-century? (Do all those prostitutes do the test for AIDS too?) Regularly? (The never-ending abstract-Mihajlo...) I know something and it will always be the social issue... (I love fucking her in the ass *raw...*) Mihajlo loves Piper's asshole... (Non-stop...) Or something... (Psychoanalysis is the sexual part of seeing a shrink...) Is that what is so great about this essay? (The completely-original: integrating something like a cognitive science as my *art/philosophy* psychological difference/that-I-don't-believe-in-science...) Or something... (What is cognitive science in the context of my artistic *philosophical-psychology?*) Or something... (My irrational psychology (the self-conscious man) ...) (It is psychoanalysis, not psychotherapy...) And as my psychology/against-science... (And so on...)

An essay to psychoanalyze the reader... (Or something...) (I always love being mean...) The never-ending Egocentric-man... (Or something...) Has to be that never-ending-*simultaneous*... (Without the never-ending Einstein there is no never-ending genius of German philosophy...) And so as for both to include in a never-ending genius German-philosophy... (The never-ending extreme-difference...) (The-idea...) (Is Piper's pussy just as yummy?) (I always shrink my philosophy with the help of my never-ending boring-philosophy/zero-imagination...) The contradiction being clear... (Equilibrating the rule/*imagination...*) Something has to participate in the impossible... (The never-ending-imaginative and never-ending-boring...) As the Einstein-IQ genius of German-philosophy... (Do two *impossible* contradict/solve?) And so on... (That I always generalize the main-impossible of my philosophy...) (When do I stop with the irrational-essays?) I wrote billions of *deconstruction-without-deconstructions...* It is time to go back to my deconstruction... (Or something...) I know that the difference is indifferent... (Always...) I never stopped to deconstruct... However, that writing billions of deconstructions that don't deconstruct, to deconstruct Nietzsche without deconstructing him, is an obsessive-compulsive disorder that is never-ending/a-never-ending compulsive-disorder... (Kind of never-ending anal...) Or something... (I love Piper's asshole...) That I always hate my anal-part *non-stop...* (Or something...) A never-ending fake-homosexual-potential... (Or something...) That I always hate the homosexual... (Non-stop...) (What seems to be the desire?) Billions of anal-philosophies being like torturing me billions of times *separately...* (Or something...) Very-impossible, seeing as I being the famous never-ending sadist... (I hate being tortured...) Or, that I do love so as to non-stop-torture... (Or something...) That the never-ending-masochism be so irrational *non-stop...* (My philosophy being that never-ending sadist-dick fucking Piper in the ass...) Or something... (Or, writing a never-ending-sadist philosophy, that tortures non-stop...) Or something... (I write a philosophy that her in the ass...) (Why am I torturing me *non-stop?*) Kind of against the basic principle of my philosophy... (A never-ending sadist can't be a never-ending masochist...) Must be that that part being an irrational too... (Something to go with the irrational essays...) Or something... (An-irrational...) Or something... (I already did compensate that the fascist-dick/my-philosophy doesn't/match-philosophically/never-annihilate-thenever-ending-genius-German-philosophy/my-philosophy...) (An-irrational...) That I never needed to switch to homosexual... (Why am I creating a dick, in the form of billions of essays, that are to fuck me?) (And so on...) The irrational... (That I write philosophy was solved...) I already invented a way to equilibrate my sex and my philosophy... (I matched both with both...) (That I fuck Piper in the ass never annihilated that I am German/the never-ending-genius-of-philosophy...) Or something... (I kill the man making me write an irrational-essay...) Nonstop... (As long as those irrational essays be the same-difference/*rational...*) My never-ending clear life goal... (Thank god for that...)

The reader comprehends the visual-language... I love my philosophy *non-stop...* Which is ancient... (Non-stop...) When do I start to deconstruct again? Never/I-never-stopped-deconstructing... (The third period always being the illusion...) (It would be torture to create a separate next-period that isn't an illusion...) That the first two periods be an appearance as is... My philosophy is impossible of the idea *philosophical-period... Or something...* Seeing the language is comprehending it... (A never-ending story...) Had I any relation to a story... That my philosophy be half art... As is a story not my artistic tradition with or without that half-art... (Persona...) And that I would never correlate a story in a film anyhow... (My EMD always being the film's story...) (That I can follow a novel's story...) Maybe... (Which is the limited/that-I-am-not-a-bookworm, as to why...) Or something... (My mother is always the intellectual and well-read one...) (Why do I love Piper so much?) The lesser pornstar, a far as I know... (She never films all the sexual positions...) Pussy and mouth without the ass is never of any appeal... (Not to me...) I mean a new/young Katsuni, not Piper... (Bad-language...) Or something... (A young Sascha Grey, not Piper Perri...) Must be something like my EMD... (Or something...) Can happen... The never-ending-ADD being never-ending... (As far as I know factually...) (So as to shrink the potential...) (The never-ending sadist-dick/my-philosophy fucks a woman in the ass...) The rest was always secondary... (Or something...) (Form...) (An-autism...) Which goes with one of the basic never-ending prides of me... (Einstein-IQ/Asperger's...) (A woman's back...) Or something... (I love an impossible-challenge...) A German genius of philosophy and fucking a woman in the ass... (Extreme-difference...) Or something... I guess I will fuck her in the pussy *instead...* (That I have nothing to do with the ideal or never-ending-ideal...) That I am a never-ending German will always be my never-ending Jewish-nose... (Or something...) It is an equilibrium... (Absolutely...) (Maybe fuck her in the ass in the context of the fact that that German Jewry always becomes purely-German *non-stop...*) I stick with the ideal... (Or something...) (The never-ending-German is the never-ending-German...) Or something... (The philosophy is French-left, Judaic, etc...) All those things that my philosophy that inclusion/a-German-genius-of-philosophy-to-include-the-German-geniusof-philosophy...   The Einstein-IQ, German-genius of philosophy and both included in a German genius of philosophy... Or something... (It is time to go for Piper's asshole, to stretch it...) That she does the other lesser sexual positions and makes lesbian porn is not that I can't fix the whole thing/make-her-purely-heterosexual-and-fuck-herin-the-ass-without-the-other-two-sexual-positions...   Or   something... (As long as I don't make the all-anal porno with her and me in it/of-me-constantly-fucking-her-in-the-ass...) Or something... (The never-ending sadist-Mihajlo...) Which is nothing new... (Goes with my   basic-principle   and   matches   sexually/I-fuck-a-woman-in-the-ass-all-the   time...)   Or something... (My Russia always being so limited/Dostoyevsky-and-Tarkovsky...) Naturally... Which matched as thought too... (Both Russians of me being international with me...) The context is West-and-East... (Clarity of thought...) All that never-ending-logic I write, that is my philosophy... And it does look analytic... (An impossible challenge...) Which always doubled... (One of the extremely impossible challenges of my philosophy...) *Why do I write a never-ending-continental/German-philosophy never-ending-analytic-philosophy-logic?* It is known why... (There is never anything extreme about any logic in my philosophy/it-is-a-mathematical-logic-of-science...) And that the logic of my philosophy be almost every type of logic there is/every-logic... (Philosophical, analytic philosophy, mathematical, etc...) *What kind of logic do I exclude? The computational type? Since I have nothing to do with the greatest antithesis of me/technology?* Or something... That I hate technology *non-stop...* Which is natural... Technology hates me *non-stop.*

(The small-Piper...) She is big to me! (Or something...) That she omits a whole sexual position is no problem/I-will-go-for-her... (Or something...) (It is a fact that I love American and Korean chicks most of all...) Or something... (My girlfriend won't ever match racially...) Whether a Jewish, German or French girlfriend is real to think as possible... (Or something...) As long as something like my type is unreal enough... (An American girlfriend...) (So as to find a Korean girlfriend to fuck non-stop...) Or something... (That is a very sadist-dick that I have, to go with the never-ending sadist-man with a sadist-dick...) Or something... (As long as I mean *Miss-America...*) Or something... (The never-ending two-things-missing-in-my-life (success and girlfriend) always divided...) It is the never-ending success that is not present in my existence... (The girlfriend probably never happens non-stop...) Or something... (So as to see a shrink...) *How psychoanalytic, of the reader, does this essay get?* As psychotherapy/that-is-how... (As science, psychoanalysis and psychotherapy...) What happened? That I usually mean as art and philosophy *absolutely...* (I don't believe in science or cognitive science...) The two-difference... (Must be as irony...) Or a psychological realism... (My primitive art-and-philosophy psychology, in this essay to complete the total-science of psychology as the self-conscious/primitive-psychology...) Or something... Realism... (Dostoyevsky, Bergman, Tarkosvky and Nietzsche...) (Persona and my sex...) A never-ending-difference and the illusion... (Or something...) The hypocrite (me) ... That Persona always be the never-ending ideal-film-of-me/the-best-film-ever-made-to-me *non-stop* did base on measure... (After all...) It is not like I deal with a heterosexual-chauvinism as by watching the best film ever made... (Or something...) The ideal had to compensate as the relative-feminism and

inclusion/film, the-writer, philosophy, art, that I have nothing to do with art, that I am half-art in the sense of an augmented science/liking-science-*more,* etc... Something to go with the fact that it is an ideally/extremely-best-film-ever-made...

(What works out just fine *doubly...*) (I go for Piper's asshole...) I'll be the first man to fuck her in the ass... (Or something...) That I always love her virgin-anus... (Bad-language...) Something to go with the language of my philosophy... (Which is good-language...) That my structural-philosophy always based on the post-structural potential... (Or something...) That there is no language, real or anything to my philosophy... (My philosophy always being post-structural as the unfinished-creation, on the other hand, absolutely...) Or something... (An "objective post-structuralism" ...) Which is structural... (I probably mean as the problem of structuralism and poststructuralism/difference...) Whether something structural and something post-structural differentiated to begin with... (Being and Time is an unfinished-creation too...) Persona... (That structuralism can be unfinished...) Or something...

So as to write specifically on the "dependence" in Tractatus Logico-Philosophicus... (On the absurd Einstein-IQ that is Wittgenstein's first period...) Or something... (So as to deconstruct something like Tarkovsky...) Which is after my deconstruction of Dostoyevsky... (I haven't deconstructed Dostoyevsky yet!) And that Tarkovsky go with Dostoyevsky won't achieve anything once I do finish doing that deconstruction of Dostoyevsky *finally...* (Tarkovsky, on the other hand, being film...) And that Tarkovsky is never as great as Dostoyevsky... (My never-ending limited Russia always being so uneven...) However, that my philosophy never be a fan of Dostoyevsky... (The magnitude/Dostoyevsky-and-Tarkovsky almost matches...) Isn't Dostoyevsky Shakespeare... Meaning, the second-best film ever made, that no writer becomes best/first-best and that fiction and film be the two same-art-forms/the best-art-forms-*evenly/absolutely...* (Anything is possible...) Whether the bore of deconstructing a dream again becomes my usual-imagination on the Dostoyevsky-side of the bibliography... (Or something...) Except, how is the boredom to improve with Dostoyevsky? (Tarkovsky is the relative context of Bergman and Dostoyevsky...) (Or something...)

(Improving my writing skills will never be necessary...) That I never had to take a course in writing... (Which is great...) The mathematical logical-science-philosophy, that always simplifies... (I don't need to know how to write...) Which always went with the *language-language-language-language* of my philosophy... (Learning a new language, knowing how to write, understanding the nature of language and knowing a language...) All four language-relation being unrelated: *the philosophy of language is metaphysics, aesthetics and logic...* And that I mean a Continental-philosophy-of-language... (Meaning, the language-philosophy part was already included...) That logic of my philosophy be so extensive/never-ending... (Computational logic is the only logical exclusion...) Meaning, that the analytic-philosophy-logic, as the actual/ "separate" philosophy of language, never gets in the way of the metaphysical language-philosophy of aesthetics and logic... (That I always have that same never-ending-dream...) I love finding success in philosophy non-stop... (My philosophy, as the never-ending-ideal-of-me...) (How self-loving does that self-hating-Serb get? Isn't it a *never-ending-itself?*) Or something... (May that be the "idealism" ...) Something does have to be ideal-enough... (The never-ending-German being the never-ending-German...) That I am always real/*Jewish* has very little to do with philosophy... (Or something...) That a Jew never wrote a philosophy... (Not to my philosophy...) And that German-label always being a universal/something-I-augment-relative-of-thegeneral-opinion/the-planet... (That the Jewish categories always relate in the way I think a Jew...) That I won't ever get to know a Jew will always be talent, IQ, the best religion and measure... (Something...) On how to relate to best talent, best genius-IQ, best-religion and best-measure... (Or something...) Which is the Alzheimer's of the essay... (That a Jew never writes a philosophy...) That is how... (I don't mean Jewish philosophy...) Or something... And with the help of the French-left... (Or something...) All those skeptical-measures making sure that the German philosophy be Jewish as the German genius of philosophy in a German genius of philosophy... (I am not an anti Semite...) Writing a genius German-philosophy was always the same measure/a-Hitler-anti-Semitic-magnitude... (Or something...) As the never-ending ancient-problem of me... (A Jewish German-genius of philosophy...) As the never-ending-impossible... (The philosophy always had to be French-left...) Or something... (On how to differentiate the two Hitlers, while retaining the one Hitler/German-genius-of-philosophy...) Or something... (I am not an anti Semite and Germany being the best genius of philosophy historically and world-regionally...) *What was always the never-ending-difference of my philosophy?* That I am an anti-Semite since Hitler... (Which was never possible/I-ama-Semite...) (The duplicitous-philosophy...) Which is ancient... (Which is always the basic-appearance...) As one of the visual-aspects of my "visual-philosophy" ... (Something to go with the first-simple of my philosophy/the-idea of-a-perfect-Wittgenstein...) (Or something...) The dishonest/*appearance...* (That the philosophy solves *simply,* as the French-left and the anti-Semitic categories being-combined as the irrational/combined-Semitism of my philosophy...) It is not the total Semitic-category ever matched... (Talent is talent or IQ, religion has nothing to do with IQ, that IQ be religion in the context of science in my philosophy, religion is art/Christ and measure being that question of IQ to begin with...) (Does the total-Semitism of my philosophy combine rationally or irrationally?) That my philosophy is Jewish will always be "composite" ... And seeing as my philosophy not Jewish/has-nothing-to-do-with-Jewish-philosophy...

(Solving the Jewish problem of my philosophy...) A "Jewish" German-philosophy... (Something to go with the Jewish question of me...) Appearance and language... (That my philosophy be structural as post-structural...) What is the *Jewish question* for? (What else?) And so on... (That there is no language, the Jewish question always have that Semitic-possible as the famous anti-Semitism/Jewish-question and that I write so many philosophies on the Jewish-question as the bad language-appearance *intentionally...*) I mean a Serbian-translation of Jewish-question... (Or something...) (The never-ending-metaphysics...) That the Jewish without Jewish philosophy always had to augment to that same extent... (That my philosophy be metaphysical first/above-the-rest...) Or, metaphysics is philosophy, as to how my philosophy always went... (The vicious/art-and-philosophy/the-twenty-first-century-against-philosophy-and-art-purely is never vicious...) Not actually... (How the total hybrid always combined, as the never-ending-hybrid, will always be something like metaphysics ending anything hybrid to begin with...) The Einstein-IQ, again, being that impossible/combining-with-metaphysics... (Or, the whole idea being in metaphysics as the Einstein-IQ without annihilating metaphysics or that Einstein-IQ...) Science and politics were never in the way of the primitive-proposition... (Science, as mathematics and logic, politics, as the liberal of left-wing as the apolitical...) Meaning, the twenty-first-century stays at that *pure-antithesis-level...* (Something like the black man never annihilated the thought-part of my philosophy/that-my-philosophy-be-thought-as-thought-and-theEinstein-IQ...) Or, that I have nothing to do with the blacks... And that a black man be a Serb... (Which is where I always made sure *absolutely...*) Isn't a Serb the century I am in too? (Or something...) (A problem-solving/Einstein-genius-of-IQ philosophy that is a German genius of philosophy...) So as to always create the IQ test out of philosophy... (Does that solve it too?) The German genius of philosophy being the IQ test... (On Hitler...) (Or something...) (So as to always devise a system of philosophy...) The idea and perfect-Wittgenstein, as the idea of a perfect-Wittgenstein... (All three great philosophers are the double-inclusion...) (Nietzsche, as the best great philosopher, will always be three great philosophers and the total-bibliography...) (What is so Nietzschean about my philosophy?) The creative question of creativity and IQ/Einstein-and-Nietzsche... (Or something...) The rational Einstein-IQ-philosophy is usually anti-Nietzschean... (Absolutely...) That it be a three-rationalism... And that my rationalism always meant the rational in the sense of

"rationalism" and rational in the sense of logical... Relative of the philosophy's total problem/that-the-philosophy-be never-ending-metaphysics... Meaning, philosophy... Meaning, what never naturalized as philosophy or Nietzsche... (Philosophy is metaphysics...) *Why is Nietzsche philosophy?* (And so on...) And that my interpretation of Nietzsche always be Heidegger/the-last-metaphysician... (And so on...) My never-ending metaphysical-philosophy impossible of Einstein's IQ and Nietzsche, relative of the metaphysical-Nietzsche/*my-Nietzsche* and that the never-ending-metaphysics be never-ending/measure... (And so on...) (The irrational...) As the three-rational-value... (Is my rationalism rational or irrational?)

So as to invent a new ink-color... (Writing using my polarity color's letters...) Or something... (Always the too imaginative-for-the-sake-of-being-so...) Or something... And that finding a true-imagination is just as excessive... (The "dumb" of my philosophy was never a negative value...) It is a half: Einstein (the imagination-IQ/IQ-prerequisite) and shrinking the never-ending megalomania... (I always have to write the one-philosophy...) (I write billions of philosophies out of never-ending-boredom...) Naturally... And that something like the concept of imagination does become potential... (Deconstructing Nietzsche without deconstructing him since he is the best great philosopher...) And so on... (May it be that "half: of my philosophy that solves the impossible-philosophy...) (A simple system to comprehension...) *When do I write an actual introduction to my philosophy?* (I love writing on the irrational...) (The irrational philosopher and irrational profession/philosophy...) What is so great about this essay will always be the realist comparison of the *irrationals* and deconstructing Nietzsche!

A positive never-ending-boredom... How does one rationalize the essay, though... (It is a system-philosophy/my philosophy...) Meaning, comprehending that system... Which requires a system... (How does one read this essay?) The system being so clear: every separate-idea/*paragraph,* how it relates to the paragraph right after and the idea word... (It is a game...) Something Einstein-IQ, again, as the total-irony... (A cynical/*game* philosophy absolutely Continental...) The reader is expected to spot all the idea-words paragraph-to-paragraph and associate why they are associated as meaning... (I always love outdoing Hegel...) A never-ending reading-difficulty... (The reader then being expected to comprehend his own meaning/the-limit of discovering every idea-word as potential...) The absurd of my philosophy... (Hegel never came close...) Or something... (Einstein, Hegel, a never-ending-Hegel and genius German-philosophy...) The "relative-discovery" versus the-absolute/the-actual-number-of-idea-words... Which never ended there... (What is the object-next-to-the-laptop for?) Comparing the idea-word and idea-object as the in itself-idea/idea-word... (That the relative-meaning never stopped as the idea-word...) *And what is the meaning an idea-word?* Webern and appearance... (Paying homage to Webern...) As to where that "same" meaning continues too... (Relative of the imagination-idea/object-next-to-the-laptop...) Webern and imagination then being synthesized idea of meaning... (As to what the system of the essay is to relate to...) The "dull-Webern" and imagination/IQ pre-requisite, to ponder what the meaning of Webern would be in my half-art philosophy at all... (It is a literal homage...) *You just comprehended what the philosophy's system is!* The how of my philosophy always being the what... (Comprehending the system is synthesizing all that revealed just now/in-this-paragraph...) (Style and substance were never separated in my philosophy...) (The system-like is a system/reminds-of-a-system as the system...) *It is a system... Where does it end?* That the system be irrational as the system of/on irrational... (What is the essay's system?) Finding an irrational, to deconstruct Nietzsche, to construct Nietzsche... The-irrational, that is the essay's system... (It hasn't ended anywhere...) (Must be an essay on that Nietzsche be the best great philosopher of my philosophy and that I am a system of philosophy...) The system being someplace there... (Between Nietzsche and a philosophical system...) One of the eternal problems of my philosophy... (That Nietzsche always had to be a "Double-inclusion" as the best great philosopher and that I write system-philosophy...) Which is never a delimited problem of my philosophy or eternal... (There is no problem at all...) Nietzsche *did* doubly-include... (The illusion of my philosophy...) That my philosophy be eternally-problematic... Which was always the eternal-illusion... I treat me infinitely-morally... (*Is the essay on my never-ending-megalomania/that-I-wrote-billions-of-philosophies?*) Sorry for the excessive-language/*the-excessive*... (It is known that my philosophy is the never-ending Jewish-measure...) Must be what does match Nietzsche as should be... (The subjective is excessive/*Nietzschean*...)

Combining a positive with a negative was always the absurd... (Which is absurd!) Or, technology and the absurd being the two never-ending values of my philosophy/against-my-philosophy-all-the-time... (Is it that an absurd has perspective relative of pessimism and nihilism/is-a-question-of-opinion...) There is nothing factual about an absurd... And that technology absolutely be the never-ending-dumbo to my philosophy... (I write philosophy!) That I be congenitally retarded to technology beyond a never-ending outer-space as the concept/outer-space-itself... (Or something...) My deconstructions were always strange, in that respect... (Must be that the other simultaneity of the *positive/negative* lessened the technological effect of my deconstruction...) And that the absurd be relative as my opinion on the absurd and the absurd... (Or something...) Relative of the basic concept of my deconstruction (difference-without-deconstruction) and that I never invent a completely new deconstruction/invented-a-completely new-philosophy... (It is not a contradiction or an *extreme/contradiction*...) Relative of the opinion... (What the deconstruction does remind of...) The deconstruction looks technological to me! Which was always as any resemblance... (Is a yin-yang just as bad for me?) I hate technology and yin-yang... (Which is always the same magnitude of hate...) Or something... And that the intentional-deconstruction/my-intentional-philosophy always meant the very-opposite/the-other-way-around-*factually*... (If it is a technological-deconstruction...) That it was always potential to name the deconstruction *the-next-inclusion*... (I could be "intending" as a total-negative that is a positive/negative doubling the negative "value" ...) A never-ending-realism, so to speak... (What is on the negative side of the positive/negative?) Meaning/representation... Representation, as technology, as the least favorite thing on the planet/technology... (That my deconstruction did get to a name/term...) *Ideal-deconstruction,* as what the official name always is... (Which is combining the positive with the negative...) Meaning, isn't something anything ideal already one of the impossible-values just as hate as technology... (That I am the never-ending German will always be that I hate everything ideal...) The impossible is the genius German philosophy that is Einstein-smart and a genius German-philosophy, not a genius German-philosophy... (That Nietzsche, in that respect, always be the great philosopher ideally the best great philosopher of my philosophy...) As the great philosopher ideally German/absolutely-genius-in-the-sense-of-*genius-German-philosophy* and Jewish/Judaic... (As to why I do name him the best great philosopher...) Christ is one of the two religions as the inferior religion of the two... (That so much had to mean a double-inclusion was always relative of those pure values...) Nietzsche can be the best great philosopher of my philosophy *purely,* on the other hand... (What the double-inclusion solves will always be what that double-inclusion does solve...) (The Einstein-IQ never "prevented" ...) (That Nietzsche be the regular philosophy-IQ doesn't mean that his Judaic genius-German-philosophy isn't Judaic or *genius-German-philosophy*...)

(Must be so...)

And that my philosophy be positive *only*... Is my philosophy totally-optimist? Absolutely... Or, that it be the optimist-philosophy... (The meaning of the optimism of my philosophy...) Nietzsche's "relative-optimism" and my "absolute-optimism" ... As the context... My every-optimism and Nietzsche against-philosophical-optimism optimism... (Which was always vicious...) Nietzsche is against philosophical-pessimism *just as much*... (I respect Nietzsche's optimism *absolutely* and *relatively*...) It is never-ending... (So as to always base my philosophy on the idea of potential...) The liberal... (As the liberal-problem...) How that relates to my *three-polarity*... That potential, as freedom, as left-wing, spoiled... (Which is always intentional...) Or something... (Beyond that potential being the right-wing/delimited...) Why does my philosophy base on the idea of potential/*freedom?* Why else/the-three polarity-could-be-communist-instead... (Plainly put...) That the never-ending freedom of my philosophy always be irony, on the other hand... (How my/my-philosophy's freedom always divided...) The never-ending free-man/me and my philosophy/the-potentially-communist/fascist... (That the polarity can't ever get to a pink-polarity...) My dick always being so fascist... And that the value of something like a mild political-left-wing be absolutely non-existent to me/has-nothing-to-do-with-me... (The philosophy was always all-the-time-free-never-ending-freedom and the fascist-dick/the-vicious-polarity...) I don't mean never-ending-freedom as a left-wing-polarity... (That it be same what the polarity of my philosophy, in the end, is...) The philosophy being Einstein-smart... And that the *two professional-philosophers-philosophy* be possibly-fascist... (Being against something like the blacks would be fascist...) The three-difference... (Me, the black man and the neo-fascist...) All three separated... (Which is always relatively-mild...) *Is a three?* My philosophy, that is against the black man and a neo-fascist... (I have nothing to do with both...) Whether it was ever sufficient-enough... (I have nothing to do with racism and I have nothing to do with a black man...) (Without the neo-fascist always being that black man on-both-sides/*split*...) That I am free non-stop will always be vicious of a neo-fascist... (Or something...) (The philosophical Jewish, German and French left-wing freedom...) I am left-wing/can't-be-a-neo-fascist... (And that that left-wing always be potentially communist...) And that the never-ending-freedom be my three-polarity or communist... (And so on...) (My deconstruction was always my philosophy...) I have nothing to do with a black man or a neo-fascist... (Whether all left-wing be all left-wing and science be IQ as mathematics and logic without science...) Or something... (Maybe...) (The impossible-values...) As my vicious philosophy... (Which was always way too great...) That the vicious of my philosophy probably correlate philosophy and the generally-vicious in my philosophy... (As the three-vicious/the-basic-rule-of-philosophy-*existing*...) Or, as the basic rule of philosophy... (Relative of my philosophy's vicious and the generally-vicious of my philosophy...) That the basic rule of philosophy always was the basic rule of my philosophy... (My philosophy made philosophy's basic rule conscious in my philosophy...) The never-ending-idiot will always be Bertrand Russell... (Or, that I do explain why my philosophy gets to be so analytic-philosophy-like...) That something like analytic philosophy be the never-ending-idiot to my philosophy while writing my potentially analytic-philosophy-like philosophy... (How that always solved...) I excluded the computational logic *only...* As the only logical-exclusion of my philosophy... (It is not a contradiction...) That I write the never-ending Continental *philosophy analytic-philosophy-like* mocking analytic philosophy all the time/infinitely will never be one of the first-contradictions of my philosophy... (The never-ending idiot is the never-ending idiot...) A never-ending idiot doesn't suddenly assume the role of a major/essential "participant" ... (Russell's IQ is lowered to a zero IQ-score on the IQ test as from a two-hundred IQ-score on the IQ test with the help of the talent-part of his philosophy...) Which is ancient... (An absolute-idiot is not Einstein-smart since an absolute-idiot...)

I love my fascist-dick.... (More like Piper Perri would always be the best porn star...) That I should major in philosophy... (The self-taught-man was never the natural-concept...) I am never actually-left-wing... (It is why I don't enroll someplace, to get a degree in philosophy, finally...) What is the use? A philosophy intended for two/three professional philosophers... (Or something...) And that the century I am in be just as substandard as me... (The century didn't enroll...) Or something... (Wasting all that time and money for nothing...) And that I did self-teach me everything that is my philosophy... (Everything related to my philosophy, that I read, relative of everything that isn't my philosophy, that is utilizing the Internet to self-teach...) Doing all that, again, would be just as boring as the double-waste/money-and-time... (The next being to read everything that isn't my philosophy...) As philosophy, fiction and film... (Everything related from all three I, naturally, "read" ...) And something like Webern is what I heard... (What comes with skepticism, as well...) The art-form that doesn't relate to me... (As the "doubly skeptical" ...) Whether any art-form be related to my philosophy... (Webern was always the two-skepticism of my philosophy...) And so on... (Entering a university always failed at the level of idea/doing-so...) Absolutely... (Reading the philosophy and fiction I haven't read and seeing the films I haven't seen...) (Where does the care direct?) At the fascist-dick... (Solving that I write the relative-left-wing philosophy, not pretending like I never read or saw all that is my philosophy...) (All that is potential of my philosophy, to read...) Presently Hegel... (I never read him...) Which is nothing strange... (The German philosophy is great as German/since-he-was-a-German...) That his philosophy always be that Spinoza of Heidegger as idea... (I have nothing to do with his philosophy...) All that is potential, then the absolute never-ending-un-talent/something-like-Russell, then the postmodern writers/postmodern fiction, then the fiction coming from the century I am in... (Relatively...) The known gradual way to approach the rest *gradually...* (Why does something like the idea of a degree in philosophy keep coming back?) The obsessive-compulsive disorder... Or something... (I mean all that that I haven't read or seen...) And gradually... And as what does un-relate/has-nothing-to-do-with-my-philosophy... (The rest of German philosophy, then French philosophy, then the absolute-un-talent, then what categorizes beyond that absolute-un-talent as is...) Or something... That my philosophy always be anti-intellectual/cynical as the Einstein-IQ... (The impossible-challenge was always double...) The anti-intellectual and what that anti-intellectual-value bases on... (The genius German-philosophy and genius German-philosophy...) Impossibly... (The cynical never makes it to the German genius of philosophy...) As one more way to think how the impossible does get to possible/becomes-possible... (The doubly-impossible...) Or something... (Which is very German...) I always love outdoing Germany... (Something to go with the skepticism...) Making sure that my philosophy always be the German genius of philosophy all-the-time... (Since that making-sure always being so German *non-stop...*) (The fascist-dick will work out in the sense of same-communism...) Or something... (I don't mean a pink-polarity...) Which is a mystery... (That measure of that heterosexual dick never match as the fascist-dick...) Is the penis heterosexual or fascist? (So as to mean as to what communism, in my philosophy, is...) Fascism is communism... (And that my dick was never heterosexual all-the-time...) The measure somehow does, in the end, equilibrate... (Between heterosexual and fascist...) Or something... (That my philosophy always has that basic problem throughout/always...) I have nothing to do with a homosexual... And that I, always, be so proud of Germany as the never-ending-German... (Which never matched...) A never-ending German/philosopher is a heterosexual... (As the polarity...) And must be the context too... (Something *European difference* without West...) I don't mean West as the Western-philosophy that is West... (Or something...) The Western philosophy was always German, not Western... (That probably always retained the between-rock-and-a hard-place too...) Without East, West an outer-space or anything beyond that outer-space *natural*/thought-itself... And as dimension too... (Historically/not-just-world/outer-space-regionally...) (As the Serb trying to match the German genius of philosophy...) It is not a German writing a German genius of philosophy! (The self-hating-Serb contextually the self-hating-Croat...) Or something... (*I am a self-hating-Croat!*) The German genius of philosophy was always without West... (Absolutely...) Except, that being so relative... I am a self-hating-Serb since without history and without West... (I am a self-hating-Croat since without East, without West and without history...) Or something...

(As the problem of Webern in my philosophy...) (The history of my philosophy...) My philosophy itself... (The a priori (Einstein-IQ and the inferior/superior religion) always extended...) Does my philosophy love everything a priori literally? (The famous danger...) Something always gets as from Einstein to Hitler in the sense of the a priori being too general/every-a-priori... (Or something...) And what am I supposed to do with the a priori Christ of my philosophy? Get him to Hitler's religion? (Was Hitler a Protestant or a Catholic?) That I always appear too Hitler instead of Einstein as my anti-intellect... (What do I know?) That the two children always had that danger... (The two anti-intellects...)

(An essay on the fascist-problem of my philosophy...) Or something... Or, why my philosophy is my polarity... (Why is the two-paragraph idea-word rule the basic rule of the essay?) (The irrational...) Or, to complete that irrational... (Writing on my philosophy and the century that I am/that-there-is-no-philosophy-in-the-century-I-am in...) The irrational includes, to create an irrational... (Or something...)

(So as to complete writing this essay...) Why? (Didn't I get to the end of the essay at that part where I specify the intention/four-endings?) I write past the unfinished-creation-ending... (Why?) Must be an irony-essay... (Relative of the basic form of my philosophy/*the-unfinished-creation...*) As irony, so to speak... (Or something...) And the finishing-creation being irrational... (Is it as the essay's irrational?) Possibly... (That there is nothing rational about this essay...) (Except, that all being so irrational...) I mean a clear-irrational-category, not the irrational constituted out of many *irrationals...* (Is the essay's irrational many irrationals of inclusion within an irrational-value/in-an irrational?) (The irrational is irrational...) Or something... (I create an irrational...) The idea of a religious-irrational... (Or something...) (Irony...) That my Nietzsche be mild-religion... (Or something...) (The essay *reads* irrationally...) (Or the relative...) Relative of the relative-problem of my philosophy... (Einstein, as the main relativity of my philosophy, relative of the inferior religion as one of the two major religions...) That Christ is a major-religion will always be vicious/*half*... (It is an inferior religion as the ideal/in-the-context-of-the-ideal...) Or something... (That m philosophy be the half-art...) Does the subjective/emphasized half-science mean the irrational this essay, or the relative, this essay... (Or something...) Relative is IQ/the-liberal/potentially-getting-to-an-average-limit-IQ-first... (Or, the prerequisite of an Einstein-IQ...) That relative be essential is that Christ be a superior religion... (Is it that my philosophy always had to be dumb/unimaginative as the bad-measure/billions-of-philosophies-I-write?) Or something... (Always-possible...) Or something... (The relatively-irrational...) Or something... (Very-basic-to comprehend...) I shrink the language and its philosophy... (Or something...) Which, probably, ties in with my dissolving-deconstruction/my-deconstruction-past-my-first-deconstruction and that I write the one-deconstruction... (As the art-irony of those deconstructions...) They dissolved from the first one I wrote and always self-dissolve... (Ink-color as the color...) The colors I use to paint them being so-impossible, the deconstruction being the emphasized-science of my philosophy... (That the black ink dissipates as the color-representation/a-color-that-the painter-utilizes and representation/that-my-philosophy-always-be-so-representational...) *That the representation of my philosophy never matched the subjective half-art...* (*Why is my philosophy* representation?) Or, the strange mathematics of logic as science a-representation... (That it is always potential to say that my philosophy is an objective-half-art, as to why...) Or something... (A philosophy equilibrium of an Einstein-IQ and art...) Or something... (Which is never unnatural/what-is-so-infinitely-thought-out-about-my-philosophy/probably-theEinstein-IQ-of-my-philosophy-too...) The half-Einstein-IQ philosophy is half-art/half-philosophy... (That my philosophy always be towards a final-solution to the basic problem/that-the-German-genius-of-philosophy-includedin-itself...) The Einstein-IQ being impossible of art and philosophy... (May it be a greatest genius of art simultaneously, that included in itself...) Or something... (The catch being the IQ-difference/one-twenty-and-onefifty/how-high-art-gets-and-what-the-basic-IQ-of-all-philosophy-is...) What rests on that *thirty-difference...* (What solves that increment?) That art be the two-IQ-score/the-performing-and-creating-arts? (Or something...) Meaning, art got to one-twenty as from zero... (And that Bergman does get to two-hundred?) I never excluded the possibility that art can get to Einstein's IQ coincidentally... (Or something...) Or simply a question of increment... (I mean two hundred, not one-twenty or one-fifty...) The *art* and *philosophy* IQ being inconsequential... (Neither gets to two hundred...) *What difference does it make?*

Why complicate my impossible philosophy? (What needed to be mathematics without physics or logic...) Or something... (Must be a philosophy on the question of philosophy/*whether-philosophy-complicates-for-the-sake-ofdoing-so...*) Or something... (Possibly as a conscious two-contradiction/*realism...*) So as to realistically propose my never-ending love for Continental philosophy... (It is not like I will ever go with such question...) Philosophy (to me) can't be style without substance/impossible-to-read-without-anything-to-say... I am a Continental-nationalist, as far as I know... (I propose an extreme-realism...) Or something... (Logic, or mathematics, will always be extraneous...) Or, what is science without science? Mathematics? (That logic always be the illogical-part...) Or something...

(Except, as to how I will always rationalize the logical participation in my philosophy will always be the "caused" ...) Or something... (Logic being one of the three branches...) Which is always relative of my philosophy's analytic-philosophy-appearance... (As from philosophical logic, to analytic philosophy as appearance, to a generalized picture of a total logic to generalize the bad appearance and include the philosophical-kind without including an enemy/computational-logic...) Except, why is logic one of the three branches? And who asked me to write the wrong-appearance? (And so on...) (So as to simply name something like logic the skeptical part of my philosophy...) Must be something in the context of logic siding with aesthetics... (Or something...) Metaphysics being the only objective-branch of my philosophy... (Logic and aesthetics are the subjective fields of my philosophy!) Or, that metaphysics be philosophy itself, not a branch of philosophy... (I see a shrink...) (What is my insanity?) Asperger's? (Or simply also always thinking that mathematics go with philosophy *professionally...*) The two professions famous for the unknown without left-wing... (Or something...) That it is always potential that mathematics be a science... (Or something...) And philosophy being mathematics as the only profession without definition/the-unknown... (I am not making an extreme-realism...) It is not realistic first... (Or something...) (That mathematics always got to philosophy with the help of logic as the literally-related too...) (Not just the only two unknown "professions" ...) (The subjective...) (Or something...) Or simply the art-part of my philosophy... (I create a philosophy...) Which is very artistic... (Which means *simply...*) Philosophy has no definition... Meaning, I subjectify a philosophy as by utilizing art as the percentage-potential... (All those realist questions...) How about a first and second plain... Isn't my philosophy about the equilibrium/an-Einstein-IQ-and-German-philosophy... (Which is always the first plain...) Everything else being so secondary... (Why my philosophy would complicate science without science will always be secondary...) Meaning, as the rest of my philosophy as that "complication" ... (The question is not primary...) And that it be something like whether something like science without science be mathematics or logic? (*Is* science-without-science logic or mathematics?) Which is beautiful... (Wasn't the question already whether mathematics be logic...) So many mathematicians were logicians, and that so many great philosophers be logicians... And so on... (*Science can be Einstein-smart without science to me!*) It is a subjective question... (Whether the IQ-part of science shrinks without the science of its science...) Or something... (And that science be religion to my philosophy...) Which is vicious... (Religion being unrelated to a genius-IQ or Einstein's IQ...) Or something... (Something to go with the usual of my philosophy...) The appearance will always be a structuring-realism/*realism...* (The something being religion as idea/mild-religion since liberal...) (It is a "make" ...) Meaning, the intentionally never-ending-narcissistic philosophy... (Or something...) (The-irony...) A never-indignant-Christ as a half-Christian-Nietzsche... (Or something...) Must be possible as the inferior of the two religions/because-Christ-never-becomes-the-superior-religion-of-my-philosophy...

(Or something...) (As long as philosophy include the question of success...) It is a humble-profession *pretentiously...* (What am I expected to do with a genius of philosophy?) Philosophy can't be genius... (Billions of geniuses of philosophy always meant a vicious-profession...) Something correlating of the unknown of philosophy... (Or something...) (The mathematical science of logic is the second-plain/inconsequential...) Except, that that three-genius-IQ-relation directly relate to Einstein's IQ... (Or something...) I probably mean two-sharing-plains and the second-plain getting to the rest of the plains... (Same difference...) Or something...

Is it the visual language? (The system/idea-word, as the early-Wittgenstein-language of my philosophy...) Visually spotting that word... (Which is a strange correlate...) Wittgenstein and Webern... (That Wittgenstein relate to art...) Which never meant Webern... (As far as I know...) So as to add that irrational-value to the essay's irrational too... (I mean a work of art no-anti-Semitic...) Which was never sufficiently *Wittgenstein* or Wittgenstein... (What is Wittgenstein's aesthetics?)

(Maybe that rational-value that is rational instead...) As one of the possible ways to a generalized early-Wittgenstein... (Representation, Schopenhauer, art and pessimism...) That something Tractatus Logico-Philosophicus have that potential/*Schopenhauer...* (Schopenhauer was a great influence on art...) Which is natural of Webern as nihilism... (Art and pessimism would be art and nihilism...) In my philosophy *absolutely*... (Except, that that annihilate...) I have nothing to do with Schopenhauer or that early-Wittgenstein... (That the irony of my Tractatus Logico-Philosophicus always be something like the absurd, not a pessimism...) (I don't mean a rational-value as the Wittgensteinian-Webern...) (Or something...) Except, did that irony/irrational/absurd interpretation-of-Wittgenstein mean exchange/the-pessimist... (The absurd is pessimist and nihilist, in my philosophy...) Meaning, something like the absurd can't be included in my philosophy and something like the absurd being pessimist in my philosophy... (Or something...) (What is the Wittgenstein-Webern relation in my philosophy?) This time a rationally *irrational* value... (Or something...) Neither this essay nor the usual of my philosophy/the ultra-rational-irony... (The-unknown...) Or something... (Something to go with my polarity and the unknown polarity of my polarity...) Or something... (So as to see a shrink...) The goal, now that I deconstruct Nietzsche without deconstructing him, being to annihilate the irrational-value... (*The value is rational!*) That I never print this essay out... (Or something...) The essay will stay at the level of the file/*a-Word-file...* Or something... (I mean five endings...) The essay doesn't know how to count... (A mathematical irony...) A never-ending mathematical-essay that will never know how to count right... (Up to five...) Or something... (As the irrational/*logical* value...) I needed to be mathematics as science... (Why am I all three crowning achievements of IQ?) (Comparing the most primitive mathematics with the never-ending advanced-mathematics non-stop...) Is it an irony? Or something on my never-ending mathematical brain that is mathematically-primitive/primitive-geometry/visual-mathematics? (Absolutely...) That I am a never-ending mathematician/always-score-two-hundred-on-the-IQ-test is always as relative of my never-ending primitive knowledge of mathematics... (Except, that now being the eighteen-million eight-hundred IQ score on the IQ test, that I lower every time I write philosophy...) Or something... (My Wittgenstein...) *Combining pessimism and absurdism...* (As to how he stays at the third-best great-philosophy place...) In my philosophy... (I mean philosophically absurd...) Which is great/Schopenhauer-is-the-philosophical pessimist... Or something... (I respect Wittgenstein's early-period representation, not the representations *world-as will-and-representation...*) That my interpretation of that early-period always isolated the pessimism from the representation... (The art-part of Tractatus Logico-Philosophicus was never in the way...) That I be the subjective half-art and that a logic without art, in my philosophy, wasn't possible... (An aphorism...) Which is great... (The art becomes subjective towards a poem and an art-form...) Or something... (My half-art and his aphorism/objective-artform...) Or something... (Such a genius/*Wittgenstein...*) That I am always depressed about the mixed-genius of that genius... (What could have been what I write in philosophy...) On the other hand, that that be superfluous... (He inspired me as that mixed-genius that he is...) Or, I wouldn't become a philosopher... (Otherwise...) Why I am a philosopher at all... (Writing a perfect-early-period-Wittgenstein...) Or something... (His third-best philosophical genius always spoiled it for me...) Or something... (Non-stop...) Which is perfect... (I'll be the perfect-Wittgenstein instead...) Being Einstein-smart and the best German genius of philosophy possible, at the same time, is to me greater than a *never-ending...* (Or something...) As long as Wittgenstein was that mixed-genius... (I stole his chance from him...) Or something...

As the irrational of my philosophy... (The idea of perfect, usually something art, in the way my philosophy defines art...) That my philosophy never thought philosophy as the perfect-necessity... (Or something...) (As long as it be that completing-irrational, as to what the essay's irrational is...) An irrational... (Or something...) (How is that irrational to relate to Nietzsche's irrational?) Or, that Nietzsche be so perfect in the sense of thought with his irrational intact... (His irrational philosophy was never irrational...) The in-itself irrational, that is Nietzsche's irrational... (Meaning, I selected an irrational *logically*...) My irrational being an in-itself-irrational too... (Or something...) Which is great... (Why I write an irrational essay on the irrational will always be that deconstruction of Nietzsche without-deconstructing-him...) Or something... (The irrational is not an-irrational...) (What is next?) So as to invent a system to deconstructing Heidegger without deconstructing him... (Or something...) Wittgenstein always being the third-best great philosopher... (A bit too obsessive, though...) *Deconstructing Wittgenstein was making a deconstruction out of a philosopher for the first time!* (That <u>On the Case of Italic</u> be two-intentions (that I never deconstructed a philosopher before and that I deconstruct the third-best-one...) ...) Or something... (Whether I deconstruct Heidegger without doing so will always be inconsequential...) (Or the half-art-part getting to the other half/part...) (The subjective half-art instead of subjective half-science...) Or something... That was always next, it seems... (Making a deconstruction out of construction...) Or something... (The next period...) Which is logical... (On the nature of my constructive-deconstruction...) Except, that I was to deconstruct Dostoyevsky next... (Always...) Oh, well.../I'll be making a deconstruction out of construction instead... (Or something...) A whole period should be sufficient... (That I was going to cry...) Non-stop... (Or something...) That I didn't deconstruct him is always compensated as the following period/that-I-do-invent-a-whole-new-period... (Great!) It is like deconstructing him... (There is no difference...) I am perfectly happily-content... (Or something...) Should be close enough... (Or something...) And that this essay be so great as the deconstruction of Nietzsche *without deconstructing Nietzsche*... (Or something...) My, purely, never-ending-love... (How great does something like this essay get?) Or something... (As the third period and deconstructing Nietzsche...) Absolutely-never-ending... (Or something...) (And that it never be too late to deconstruct Dostoyevsky...) My philosophy won't ever base on the idea of a period/difference... (Not any time soon...) The deconstruction-period never existed... (*Way too perfect...*) (Crying non-stop is highly absurd/infinitely-unreal...) After all, that that deconstruction would correlate my deconstruction/that-I-write-the-one deconstructions... (That my deconstructions were never all that standard...) It was always the one-deconstruction, as the one-philosophy... (What is so great about deconstructing Dostoyevsky?) A French-left-philosophy Russian comparison? That a French-left philosopher invent the original-deconstruction? (Or something...) (That a Jew invented the deconstruction prior to my deconstruction?) Or something... (Maybe...) (Anyhow...) That my deconstruction was always flawed... (A thing one-deconstruction and one-philosophy...) (A yin-yang deconstruction of difference-without-deconstruction...) *What is so great about that?* An absurd has nothing to do with my philosophy... (And that technology (with or without the primitive technology prior to technology) be the never-ending enemy of philosophy...) And so on... (That I write the one-deconstruction will always be never-ending...) (I am not mocking technology as the *positive-negative-technology...*) (What is a French-left philosophical method and Dostoyevsky?) Except, that my deconstruction be the never-ending-German deconstruction... (I am a never-ending German-philosopher, not French...) (Maybe...) Possibly... (Just about...) *I love my never-ending-philosophy...* (Or something...) That Heidegger always usually-be-the-best-great philosopher... (The doubled-effect...) Naturally... What is, usually, a philosophy non-stop-Heidegger... (Or something...) Representing the nature of philosophy/*vicious-circle...* (And so on...) A vicious-argument philosophy as a philosophy/vicious-circle... (That it always be Heidegger's politics, as to what, infinitely, prevents from the never-ending ideal-relation/Heidegger-and-me...) Something like Nietzche had to be "added" ... (That the unknown of the total Jewish-relation of my philosophy be rational or irrational doesn't mean all those Jewish categories in an anti-Semitic sense...) IQ, talent, religion, measure, etc... (It is rational or irrational...) Which doesn't change the language... (An irrational total-Jewry...) Or something... (The irrational Jewish-potential never meant becoming an anti-Semite...) What always justifies Nietzsche in my philosophy/that-Nietzsche-be-the-best-great-philosopher-ofmy-philosophy... (Heidegger's Hitler-involvement...) Or something... (Heidegger nearly-becomes-the-best-great philosopher-of-my-philosophy...) As the Judaic-Nietzsche as-well... (Or something...) (Was the skepticism really ever-necessary?) Wittgenstein, as the third-best great philosopher, three great philosophers and fifteen bibliographies, to make sure that Nietzche can be the best great philosopher... (Or something...) A bit too excessive... (Must be the irony of my philosophy...) *As skepticism/anti-Nietzscheanism and that skepticism wasn't ever really necessary from the start/is-anti-Nietzschean...* (Isn't the Heidegger-vicinity literal?) And that it be three great philosophers instead of two... (Must be my philosophy's love for philosophy, art and science in the sense of a three same/me-loving-all-three-same...) Or something... (Which is untrue...) I am always the philosophical-fanatic... (Which is true...) I am always an Einstein-IQ-fanatic... (Why I always become the never-ending-self-loving-man as the self-hating-Serb...) Or something... (I am to me just as great as Heidegger...) And that it be an Einstein IQ Heidegger... (As the equilibrium/Heidegger-and-Einstein's-IQ-in-a-*Heidegger-great-philosophy* always becomes just as self-loving as the never-ending-infinite-regress/my-self-love-that-is-never-ending...) How self-loving does my self-love as the never-ending-self-love that is a never-ending-self-love "become?" (Or something...) The concept of a never-ending... Or something... (The difference (the self-hating-Serb and self-loving-man) meant a never-ending...) Or something... (As long as it base on the idea of a self-hating-Croat...) Or something... (The never-ending being never-ending-literally...) That I will never be West... (Germany being my-Germany/the-European-difference...) (The vicious...) That I am not East or West is kind-of-Serbian... (Is it a self-hating-Yugoslavian?) Except, that Yugoslavia include the tiny-percentage Jewish-population potential... (Or something...) Except, that a Jew can be "anywhere" ... (What is such a tiny-percentage Jewish-population for?) Or something... (I am sure Serbia or Croatia has a tiny percentage Jewish-population potential too...) Or something... (Can there exist a pure difference, as from a self-hating-Serb to a self-loving-man?) What is German philosophy and Serbia? A difference basing on an infinite regress *absolutely?* Absolutely... (Is the difference never-ending?) Serbia has nothing to do with philosophy and Germany being the only genius of philosophy world-regionally and historically... (Should be never-ending-enough...) Or something... (Does something like France make the whole thing mild instead of never-ending?) That France be a second-to-third-best great philosophy... (Absolutely...) Something like a French-left... (Not-never-ending...) Or something... (That France be the first-best genius of French-left...) (Is Jewish talent one of the major Jewish categories of my philosophy?) Potentially... (It seems Kafka included in my bibliography...) Which is the uneven measure... (Two Einstein-IQs and one second-best genius absurdly a second-best-genius...) Or something... (Whether a Jewish talent, that isn't the Einstein-IQ-kind, be related...) Or something... (There was never the-best writer-of-my-philosophy, for Kafka to be known as the difference/from-first-best-to-second-best...) I love complicating... (A never-ending genius of philosophy/German...) (Wittgenstein and Kafka, as the half-Wittgenstein and complete-Kafka...) Or something...

As a treatise on my love for Germany... (Or something...) The primitive-technology-deconstruction was irony (the two German world-fames/engineering-and-philosophy...) Or something... (The doubly-best on the planet race...) Is that the meaning behind the nonsense first-relation of my deconstruction? (On the strange/impossible Germany...) That philosophy and engineering always exceed separately non-stop... (*What is my third-period?*) Or simply that it never mattered what my philosophical-period is... (The nonsense (primitive-technological-deconstruction) always came with a sense anyhow...) How nonsense becomes sense *literally*... (Apart from the fact that the first and third period be without that technological-irony...) However, that nothing changes there too... (The second period was never a period...) (The first and third period were primitive-technology prior to blending in with the one-philosophy too...) (What is the third period?) Does this essay serve to successfully "decode?" (That the other two periods were so logical/*absolutely-clear...*) Which is never true. /What is my first period? (And so on...) A period of mine can be irrational too... (All three periods being on how to achieve a perfect-Wittgenstein...) The rational/irrational distinction was always "form" ... And that it be the one-form... (Seeing as all three periods being an illusion...) (That the period can be anything...) Which is irrational-anyhow... (The unknown (first-period), known (second period) and unknown (third period) ...) What would create a literal-dynamic as my polarity/on-the-question-of-my-polarity... (It is an illusion that I create something cynical out of my "cynical" polarity as the one-philosophy...)

Watching Dune (*2021*), last night, with my mother, to the end... (Or something...) That can happen too/she-wasn't all-that-necessary... (Or, something like Martin Campbell's Casino Royale...) That I usually hate a twenty-first century cinema... (Which is ancient/I-hate-everything-in-that-century...) *What happened?* Is it the film's length/not three-hours-in-length? *That it be an irrational-ending/half-a-story/that-I-never-respect-a-story-in-a-film?* Possibly... (That I hate the CGI-visual-effects just as much...) Or something... (To go with the question of Canada and France...)

That Canada be infinitely-unrelated to me and France never make a film... (Which is all so vicious/mixed...) Glenn

Gould was a Canadian... (*A pure genius from Canada...*) And that a French film be French-left... (Or something...) Meaning, the second-best genius of philosophy, that was always French-left in-my-philosophy... (Or something...) That a French film near becomes impossible of my philosophy... (Not actually...) What always comes with the idea of a mild-value... (Or something...) All those best great philosophers, then France as the French-left... Or something...

(How does something like Denis Villeneuve's Dune find itself next to Andrew Niccol's *Gattaca?*) An essential question... (David Lynch's Dune/a-bad-film and Denis Villeneuve's Dune/*right-next-to-Gattaca...*) On how to ascertain the irrational-value... (Or something...) Cinema prior to that century that I am in exists non-stop/is-the writer... (Something like the twenty-first-century always being untalented non-stop...) And so on... (On what an untalented film made prior to the twenty-first-century makes out of a twenty-first-century-cinema *talented-or untalented...*) Or something... (Lynch's Dune is a bad-film!) Or something... Mainly as the film's French-style as the American-literature... (Or something...) Is that why? (A strange stylistic comparison?) And that the film split the story in half... (I won 't be buying the second one *certainly...*) Or something... (And Canada can suddenly get to a genius-level/Glenn-Gould *accidentally...*) So, to speak... (That the country never got to an Einstein IQ *absolutely...*) Which was never a question of talent... (Glenn Gould always being the greatest possible genius on the piano...) Absolutely... (Is Villeneuve a French-left-cinema/*left-wing?*) Or something... (I create the possibility...) Or something... (So as to base on Casino Royale and United 93...) Or something... (The CGI visual effects can't be in the way/I-am-not-watching-Star Wars...) Or something... Or that it be the simple question of that half-story fixing godawful visual effects *non-stop...* (Or something...) (Too many things were bad about Lynch's Dune simultaneously...) The visual effects, surrealism, Star Wars as Blade Runner, etc... (Must be a simultaneity...) (First and foremost,) Or something... (I love Germany...) Non-stop... (What is the longer cut of that Lynch sad-thing/a-great-potential-way-too-great-as-the-bad-movie?) To me probably way too great... (That Lynch neer approved is that the film last longer/be-an-antithesis-of-me...) Purely... (However, that the writing credit disown too...) Does that mix well/make-the-film-ingenious-as-measure? Possibly... (A new writing credit and the irrational-length...) And that I never watched the original version of Lynch's Dune in its entirety... (I always stop watching that film half-way...) Or something... (The film being that bad to me...) Which will never be known... (It is not like I ever saw the film.../Does the second half fix the first half?) Or something... (So as to blend all the paragraphs/this-essay...) Or something... Which is system/every-two-paragraphs... (Or something...) Which was never a system... (It is an absurd-system/all-the-paragraphs-referencing-every-paragraph...) That the system of the essay retain will always be the rest of the essay that is the system-philosophy of my philosophy... (The idea-word always being the vicious-part in what otherwise means as the flawless-system/German-engineering...) The German-engineering-part of my deconstructions wasn't a problem... Or something... (Meaning...) Or something... (The absurd paragraphs being bad the absurd and an *against-a-philosophical-system...*) Or something... (As the illusion part of the essay's system...) Or something... (That an illusion was never a problem in my philosophy?) That something like the concept of illusion, in my philosophy, was always a dream/*film*/the-basic-concept-of-film-in-my-philosophy never deterred... (Or something...) The strange illusion-comparison... (I can't be writing a best film ever made and that I can write an illusion...) Or something... (Probably as what always has something to do with the three-philosophy of my philosophy/philosophy, science and art...) That my philosophy isn't art... (Or something...) Or, the subjective work of half-art that isn't an objective work of art... (Or something...) As to how illusion and a dream, in my philosophy, always subsisted peacefully side-by-side... (Or something...) *As long as writing be incapable of a dream...* Or something... And that being able to write a Persona would be impossible anyhow... (I can't be writing a work of art...) And so on... (As to why the illusion of my philosophy always stayed at illusion/never-augmented-to-the-level-of-a-dream/metaphysical-illusion...) There is no absurd that I can create (between my philosophy and art) ... My philosophy already being an absurd-problem as art and science and the anti-absurd-philosophy/my-philosophy... Or something... (I ascertain the potential...) What is the subjective of my philosophy? The subjective half-science? (Something must get to the idea of subjectivity, Nietzsche being the best great philosopher...) Which will always be vicious... (*The subjective of my philosophy is science!*) One more two-inclusion of Nietzsche in my philosophy... (Or something...) Surrealism and a dream to my philosophy always create the difference... (Or something...) (Something like Persona will never be surreal...) Or something... (That my philosophy always conceptualized the movement for the concept of unreal...) (As to why I always think the best film ever made and surrealism "separately" and why my philosophy be against surrealism...) *Surrealism was never a dream!*

Is the idea of a perfect-Wittgenstein a German genius of philosophy *Einstein-smart* and a German genius of philosophy? (That being all three periods too...) Not the three periods... (As the simultaneity of my one philosophy...) The perfect-Wittgenstein and the question/*Is-the-idea-of-a-perfect-Wittgenstein-a-German-genius-ofphilosophy-Einstein-smart-and-a-German-genius-of-philosophy-?* ...

A mine of ideas... (Or something...) I created the mine... (Or, the dangerous profession of mining...) Or something... (In the twenty-first-century probably just as safe as anything...) *It is a* Walk of Ideas... Or something... (Except, that always being so mixed...) Science, the-writer and philosophy... (Except that being kind of okay/general...) What doesn't include? (The rest being "outside" ...) Or something... (And that something like Matrin Luther included...) Which is okay... (Religion is science to-my-philosophy...) Relative of Luther... (Any form of liberal-Christianity already included in my philosophy, as far as I know...) I am *for* Luther... (And so on...) That the total Christianity of my philosophy creates the Catholicism as the inferior religion never changed the Christian-revolution of positive value/*Luther*... (What always became Protestant as Catholic, in my philosophy...) Or, the inferior-religion... (It is same what the superior form of Christianity, in my philosophy, is...) It is an inferior religion... (Like creating the Catholics out of the Protestants...) Or something... (Karl Marx never reaches an annihilated-possible...) Not actually... (My fascist-dick...) Or something... (I can be the apolitical left-wing as the Einstein-IQ all I want...) The extreme being what will always be missing in my philosophy, as relative of my fascist-penis... (Or something...) (That the Einstein-IQ contradiction always shifted in the direction of philosophy...) Which is great... (I always had to be that fascist-penis and something never-ending-*un-matching*...) On how to compensate that fascism of my penis... (It never matched my philosophy...) The hypocrite, so to speak... (Which is relative...) I am a Western-philosopher/a hypocrite... (Which never matched/the-Western-philosophy-is-the-idea-of-a-never-ending-outer-space...) Or something... (What to do with medicine, music the automobile and the-sport?) Or something... (Perfect Wittgenstein...) The imperfect-idea... (Or something...) (The very being of my philosophy...) *Being and the Never-ending...* (Or something...) Which is like mocking Being and Time/*impossible*... (Wasn't Being and Time already so never-ending?) Or something... (Absolutely...) (It is the idea of a perfect-Tractatus-Logico-Philosophicus, as to what I mean, not a perfect-Wittgenstein...) And that idea being so imperfect/absolutely-perfected-as-thesimultaneity-of-its-imperfect-idea... Or something... (Which will never change...) A perfect-Tractatus-Logico Philoophicus and a *Is the idea of a perfect-Tractatus-Logico-Philosophicus a German genius of philosophy Einstein smart and a German genius of philosophy?* ... (Or something...) (What is the problem...) That Christ be one of the two religions of my philosophy... (That religion meant science and art to-my-philosophy...) Or that Christ be the art religion... Or something... (The mine is the idea...) (And as the half-imagination of my philosophy/the-IQ pre requisite...) What is so great about an idea that is dumb beyond anything/*absolutely*? That it bases on the idea of imagination just as beyond anything/absolutely? (Or something...) Maybe... (As to how genius my philosophy always becomes as the question of genius...) Always, non-stop, constantly equilibrating the concept of imagination and concept of banality... Or something... (To go with the main-impossible of my philosophy and the impossible included in that main-impossible...) One more impossible... (Or something...) That it be how I solve the between rock-and-a-hard-place/the-main-impossible... (I introduced so many subcategories of impossible...) For, that it be an emotion that something like French-left would solve that between-rock-and-a-hard-place... (Why does the French left of my philosophy make the main-impossible so possible?) Wasn't it always an emotion/subjective/the supposition?

www.ingramcontent.com/pod-product-compliance
Lightning Source LLC
LaVergne TN
LVHW070531070526
838199LV00075B/6756